Han Heroes and Yamato Warriors

Transnational Asian Masculinities

Series Editors: Derek Hird (Lancaster University) and Geng Song (University of Hong Kong)

The first book series in the world on this topic, Transnational Asian Masculinities, explores the representations and lived realities of Asian masculinities in their transnational dimensions. Books in this series use interdisciplinary perspectives and interrogate diverse textual, visual, and ethnographic materials. They illuminate the specificities of Asian masculinities in global contexts and question some of the assumptions of Euro-American theorizing on masculinities. By approaching Asianness through ethnicity, nationality, and location—encompassing men's, women's, queer, and trans masculinities—this series unpacks the tangled assemblages of local and transnational circulations of people, ideas, and objects that have shaped Asian masculinities in all eras.

Books in the series:

Changing Chinese Masculinities: From Imperial Pillars of State to Global Real Men
Edited by Kam Louie

The Cosmopolitan Dream: Transnational Chinese Masculinities in a Global Age
Edited by Derek Hird and Geng Song

Everyday Masculinities in 21st-Century China: The Making of Able-Responsible Men
Magdalena Wong

Han Heroes and Yamato Warriors: Competing Masculinities in Chinese and Japanese War Cinema
Amanda Weiss

Mastery of Words and Swords: Negotiating Intellectual Masculinities in Modern China, 1890s–1930s
Jun Lei

Rebel Men: Masculinity and Attitude in Postsocialist Chinese Literature
Pamela Hunt

Han Heroes and Yamato Warriors

Competing Masculinities in Chinese and Japanese War Cinema

Amanda Weiss

Hong Kong University Press
The University of Hong Kong
Pok Fu Lam Road
Hong Kong
https://hkupress.hku.hk

© 2023 Amanda Weiss

ISBN 978-988-8754-27-4 (*Hardback*)

All rights reserved. No portion of this publication may be reproduced or transmitted in any form or by any means, electronic or mechanical, including photocopying, recording, or any information storage or retrieval system, without prior permission in writing from the publisher.

British Library Cataloguing-in-Publication Data
A catalogue record for this book is available from the British Library.

Digitally printed

To my parents,
Linn and Carol Weiss

Contents

List of Tables ix

Notes on Language xi

Acknowledgments xiii

1. Introduction: Remembering the War On-Screen 1
   Film as a Technology of Memory 6
   War Films as (Trans)National Memory 11
   "Manly States" 16
   The Memory Loop 20

2. The Tokyo Trial On-Screen: Establishing the Foundational Narrative 25
   MacArthur's Japan 28
   Gong'an Retribution 32
   "A Continuous Retrial" 37
   Conclusion 49

3. New Heroes in Chinese and Japanese Combat Films 51
   Masculinity and Nationalism 52
   "Marketized" Socialist Heroes 54
   "Uneasy Warriors" 62
   Conclusion 71

4. Contested Images of Wartime Rape 73
   Rape, Gender, Nation 76
   "The Rape of a Motherland" 81
   Rape and Japanese Masculinity 89
   Conclusion 96

5. Gender and Reconciliation in Sino-Japanese Melodramas 98
   Melodrama and Reconciliation 100
   The Honeymoon Period 103

Sino-Japanese Orphans   107
  Reconciliation after 2000   113
  Conclusion   118

6. Conclusion   120
  "Tears of Rage"   121
  "I Am Me, He Is Him"   125
  The Future of Remembrance   128

Table 1.1: International Box Office for World War II Films   131

Table 1.2: Pacific War Films at the Chinese Box Office (2005–2012)   132

Table 1.3: Pacific War Films at the Japanese Box Office (2005–2012)   133

Glossary   135

Bibliography   139

Index   155

Tables

Table 1.1: International box office for World War II films   131
Table 1.2: Pacific War films at the Chinese box office (2005–2012)   132
Table 1.3: Pacific War films at the Japanese box office (2005–2012)   133

Notes on Language

This book uses the pinyin system for Chinese terms unless referring to titles of books (*The Rape of Nanking* instead of *The Rape of Nanjing*) and popular names (Chiang Kaishek instead of Jiang Jieshi). For Japanese terms, it relies on the Revised Hepburn style of romanization (Shinbashi instead of Shimbashi; Hirō instead of Hiroo). Japanese, Chinese, and Korean names are typically listed with the family name first and the personal name last (Mikuni Rentarō instead of Rentarō Mikuni; Lu Chuan instead of Chuan Lu) unless discussing an established scholar or a public figure who commonly uses the reverse order. Footnotes follow the Chicago style of given name, family name for all authors.

Acknowledgments

My paternal grandfather, Lincoln Weiss, served in the Pacific during World War II as a sergeant assigned to the 775th Army Air Forces Base Unit. A radio mechanic, he was never injured or in combat, though he spent time on the Kwajalein Atoll and Guam in 1944 and 1945. While I was completing an early draft of this book, my father wrote to me, "World War II had a huge impact on him. Grandpa, a former Midwest farm boy, suddenly had his horizons hugely expanded into the Pacific Rim, into an Asian and Micronesian cultural sphere, with a riveting focus on a country and enemy (Japan) heretofore virtually unknown." When my father was serving in the army during the Vietnam War in 1970, he announced that he was going to take a trip to Japan. My grandfather apparently did not say much and simply acknowledged that "we live in a very different time."

I wonder what my grandfather would have said about my current project. My personal interest in Sino-Japanese memory began while I was living in China on and off between 2005–2009. As I attended classes at the Beijing Film Academy, Sino-Japanese relations had reached their lowest point in thirty years.[1] Japan's bid for inclusion in the United Nations Security Council coincided with a global trend of rising nationalism and the sixtieth anniversary of the end of World War II. This culminated in severe historical conflicts during the spring of 2005, as major demonstrations occurred across Asia. During that time, both China and Japan experienced an explosion of films and television shows on the Pacific War. Living in the middle of the Chinese film industry, I had the opportunity to observe and even participate in this trend as many of my Japanese classmates were recruited to play soldiers in Chinese TV programs. One of my first film jobs was translating dialogue for a film on the Flying Tigers, a group of American pilots who worked with the Chinese air force during World War II.

---

1. Mindy Kotler, Naotaka Sugawara, and Tetsuya Yamada, "Chinese and Japanese Public Opinion: Searching for Moral Security," *Asian Perspective* 3, no. 1 (2007): 93–125.

In 2015, as another ten-year anniversary loomed on the horizon, I saw TV specials and new combat films being advertised with nostalgic posters on the subways and outside video stores in Tokyo, my home since 2009. As a lecturer at Meiji Gakuin University in Yokohama from 2012 to 2014, I saw the postwar US-Japan military alliance in real life. As I passed by families of American soldiers from the Yokosuka naval base, I wondered if I was also walking by Japanese Self-Defense Forces, known to wear civilian clothes when off base due to the Japanese public's ambivalent reception of the military.[2] Having experienced the 2005 anniversary of the end of the war in one nation and the 2015 anniversary in another, I felt as if my life had in a sense been bookended by Chinese memory at one end and Japanese memory at the other. My own sense of American memory—framed by that of my family—stood in the middle. Looking back at my grandfather's comment as recalled by my father, it is remarkable to me how circumstances change as historical tides ebb and flow. Only time will tell how new generations of Chinese, Japanese, and Americans will gaze at their past and conceive of their future.

Over the years of researching and writing, I have been supported and guided by many scholars and friends. I could not have completed this book without the guidance of Yoshimi Shun'ya and Jason G. Karlin at the University of Tokyo, not to mention my doctoral committee Fujii Shōzō, Timothy Y. Tsu, and Kitada Akihiro. Other Tokyo-based scholars who offered me invaluable comments and suggestions include Nicola Liscutin, Karima Fumitoshi, Tezuka Yoshiharu, Barak Kushner, Patrick Galbraith, Tanaka Keiko, Kaminishi Yūta, Song Gukchin, Yeo Yezi, Susan Taylor, Alexandra Hambleton, Nīkura Takahito, Kondō Kazuto, Christian Dimmer, Ha Kyungjin, Ni Fengming, Jennifer Igawa, Alexander Vesey, Christopher St. Louis, and Pi Chenying. I am also grateful to Julia Bullock and Ryan Cook of the Emory University East Asian Writing Group for workshopping many of these chapters over the years, and to the Bill and Carol Fox Center for Humanistic Inquiry for supporting my research as a postdoctoral researcher from 2016 to 2017. On the other side of Atlanta, I would also like to thank Georgia Tech's School of Modern Languages, especially the Japanese Program's Kyoko Masuda, Masato Kikuchi, Aya McDaniel, Satomi Suzuki, and Aki Matsushima, as well as Dina Khapaeva and Jan Uelzmann, fellow memory studies compatriots. Thank you for allowing me to workshop much of this research at various public lectures. I also deeply appreciate Linda L. Fang and Zhai Shuhuan of Tsinghua University for their valuable assistance in collecting Chinese-language materials and filmmakers Iris Yamashita, Bill Guttentag, Jeffrey Weil, Gamal Istiyanto, and Otsuka Masanobu for agreeing to be interviewed.

Finally, I would like to thank my parents, Linn and Carol Weiss, for all their support. This book is dedicated to them.

---

2. Sabine Frühstück, *Uneasy Warriors: Gender, Memory, and Popular Culture in the Japanese Army* (Berkeley: University of California Press, 2007).

1
Introduction

Remembering the War On-Screen

> In the most extreme case, the boundaries between fact and fiction, image and the real have been blurred to the extent of leaving us only with simulation, and the postmodern subject vanishes in the imaginary world of the screen.[1]

August 15, the date that marks the end of World War II in the Pacific, has been remembered around the world in strikingly different ways. In 1945, it was enthusiastically celebrated by the Allies as Victory over Japan Day or V-J Day, perhaps most memorably in the famous *V-J Day in Times Square* photograph by Alfred Eisenstaedt. Since 1949, South Korea has referred to August 15 as Restoration of Light Day (Gwangbokjeol), a day to celebrate the end of Japanese colonial rule; in North Korea, it is remembered as Liberation of Fatherland Day (Chogukhaebangŭi nal); both of these celebrate the end of Japanese colonial rule, albeit in ways that highlight the different political systems and ideologies of the two Koreas. In contemporary Japan, August 15 is commemorated somberly as the Memorial Day for the End of the War (Shūsen-kinenbi), a subdued time wherein Japanese citizens recall the horrors of the nuclear bombs and pray for peace.[2]

August 15 has also been invoked throughout the years by associations, filmmakers, and politicians to signify a range of meanings from reconciliation to resistance. In 1951, August 15 became a date for national reconciliation, as the Japan-China Friendship Association encouraged Japanese citizens to send letters to China and Taiwan recognizing Japanese aggression in the Marco Polo Bridge Incident on that date.[3] In the 1972 Japanese film *Under the Flag of the Rising Sun* (Gunki hatameku moto ni), on August 15 of each year, a bereaved war widow

---

1. Andreas Huyssen, "Monument and Memory in a Postmodern Age," *Yale Journal of Criticism* 6 (1993): 249.
2. "Zengoku senbossha tsuitō shiki ni tsuite," Kōseirōdōshō, accessed November 4, 2014, http://www.mhlw.go.jp/houdou/2007/08/h0808-1.html.
3. Franziska Seraphim, *War Memory and Social Politics in Japan, 1945–2005* (Cambridge, MA: Harvard University Press, 2006), 121.

demands to know the truth of her husband's wartime death. In the August 15, 1982 issue of the Chinese newspaper *People's Daily* (Renmin Ribao), the following warning resounded amid the first textbook controversy between China and Japan: "Past experience, if not forgotten, is a guide to the future."[4] August 15 is also the contentious date that several Japanese prime ministers have selected to visit the controversial Yasukuni Shrine and an important date for Chinese citizens to protest Japanese historical revisionism.[5] Such diverse remembrance reflects the ways in which memory, rather than receding into the past, remains present, urgent, and ever-changing.

Discourse on war memory has emerged forcefully over the past two decades, particularly in China and Japan, the subjects of this study. The subjugation, violence, and loss of the war left physical, psychological, economic, and social wounds on both nations, or what cultural trauma studies refers to as an "interpreted shock to the cultural tissue of a society."[6] In China, the war is considered one part of a "history of pain": a century of colonial incursion, unequal treaties, lost territory, and domestic turmoil.[7] From this historical perspective, Japanese aggression in China stretches back in time before World War II to include the First Sino-Japanese War (1894–1895), the Boxer Rebellion (1900), the Russo-Japanese War (1904–1905), and the Mukden Incident or 9.18 Incident (1931). In Japan, the war marks both uncomfortable memories of aggressive colonial expansion and tremendous personal devastation and loss. The contested nature of recalling the past in Japan is reflected by its numerous names, which include the Greater East Asia War, the Pacific War, the Fifteen-Year War, and "that war."[8]

---

4. Caroline Rose, *Interpreting History in Sino-Japanese Relations: A Case-Study in Political Decision Making* (New York: Routledge, 2005), 1.
5. Prime Minister Miki Takeo of Japan made the first unofficial visit in 1975, although the visit went largely unnoticed because Class A war criminals were not enshrined until 1978. A visit in 1985 by Prime Minister Nakasone Yasuhiro prompted strong protests among Chinese students. Later visits by Prime Minister Koizumi Jun'ichiro between 2001 and 2006 incited angry reactions in countries affected by Japanese colonialism. See Alan Taylor, "Anti-Japan Protests in China," *The Atlantic*, September 17, 2012, accessed November 5, 2014, http://www.theatlantic.com/infocus/2012/09/anti-japan-protests-in-china/100370/.
6. Cultural trauma can also be considered in terms of Claude Lévi-Strauss's term "hot moment" and Gerbner's term "critical incident." For more on cultural trauma, see Piotr Sztompka, "Cultural Trauma: The Other Face of Social Change," *European Journal of Social Theory* 3, no. 4 (2000): 449. For more on hot moments and critical incidents, see Barbie Zelizer, *Covering the Body: The Kennedy Assassination, the Media, and the Shaping of Collective Memory* (Chicago: University of Chicago Press, 1992), 4.
7. Michael Berry, *A History of Pain: Trauma in Modern Chinese Literature and Film* (New York: Columbia University Press, 2011).
8. Akiko Hashimoto, "Divided Memories, Contested Histories: The Shifting Landscape in Japan," in *Cultures and Globalization: Heritage, Memory and Identity*, ed. Helmut Anheier and Yudhishthir Raj Isar (London: SAGE, 2011), 240.

Chinese and Japanese remembrance has undergone three major historical phases since the end of the war. In the first phase of memory (1945–1972 for Japan; 1945–1978 for China), postwar relations suppressed historical discussion between the two nations, obscuring the trauma of the war with the immediate crisis of the Cold War order.[9] For China, the desire to create a new socialist nation led to the repression of victim narratives during this era. The government emphasized socialist heroism in lieu of colonial victimization, and personal accounts, artistic representation, and academic studies on victimhood were not allowed. Meanwhile, Japan was protected and, in many ways, "rehabilitated" by the United States, which needed an ally in the region to battle the "threat" of communism. The countries were thus insulated from each other's national narratives and experienced a "hibernation" period.

From the signing of the Joint Communiqué of the Government of Japan and the Government of the People's Republic of China in 1972, in which the Chinese government signed away all rights to wartime reparations "for Sino-Japanese friendship," the two countries enjoyed a brief respite of friendly relations.[10] This "honeymoon period" also marked the second wave of collective memory (1972/1978–1989). In China, the 1980s saw a veritable outpouring of collective remembrance, much of it focused on the traumatic experiences of Chinese citizens.[11] These memories included not only Japanese colonialism but also the mass suffering experienced during the Great Leap Forward and the Cultural Revolution.[12] In Japan, memory of colonialism and overseas aggression had faded for the most part until American atrocities during the Vietnam War revived discussion of Japanese atrocities. Moreover, the postwar return of Japanese orphans left in China (*Chūgoku zanryū koji*) also emerged as an emotional site of Sino-Japanese reconciliation.

The third wave of memory began in 1989 and continues to this day. In China, the 1989 protests exposed the ideology vacuum created by the open-door policy and led Deng Xiaoping to conclude that "the biggest mistake for the CCP in the 1980s was that the party did not focus enough attention on ideological education."[13] Soon after, the government began to promote patriotic education

---

9. Although China signed a normalization treaty with Japan in 1972, it was not until the open-door policy instituted in 1978 that foreign companies could invest in China. That year also marks the beginning of film coproductions with Japan.
10. Chalmers Johnson, "The Patterns of Japanese Relations with China, 1952–1982," *Pacific Affairs* 59, no. 3 (1986): 402–428.
11. Daqing Yang, "Reconciliation between Japan and China: Problems and Prospects," in *Reconciliation in the Asia-Pacific*, ed. Yōichi Funabashi (Washington, DC: United States Institute of Peace Press, 2003), 69.
12. This can be seen in the "scar cinema" of the 1980s and early 1990s.
13. Zheng Wang, "National Humiliation, History Education, and the Politics of Historical Memory: Patriotic Education Campaign in China," *International Studies Quarterly* 52, no. 4 (2008): 788.

in the "Never Forget National Humiliation/One Hundred Years of Humiliation" (*wuwang guochi/bainian guochi*) campaign, which was accompanied by the construction of numerous memorials and museums after 1991.[14] This time period also showed a notable increase in anti-Japanese films and a shift in Chinese sentiment. In Japan, the end of the Cold War and death of Hirohito also marked a new stage in US-Japan relations and a change in Japanese identity. As Yoshikuni Igarashi argues, "With the disappearance of Hirohito's body—the key element in the foundational narrative—war memories returned to the Japanese media, both as nostalgia and as critical reflection."[15] In addition to the death of the wartime emperor, the Gulf War and Japan's financial involvement further prompted reassessment of Japan's lack of military and "unnatural" political situation.[16] Compounding this period of transition, Nanjing and comfort women discourse merged with American Holocaust discourse, fundamentally changing US-China-Japan memory dynamics. This period marked what Yoshimi Shun'ya refers to as "the shift from the postwar economic growth-centered nationalism of the Cold War era to the crisis-driven neonationalism of the age of globalization."[17] In other words, the unstable economic and political state of Japanese society, mixed with uncertainty about the future and an increasingly global visibility of collective memory, further contributed to this "memory boom."

The globalization of media has also fueled this rise in memory conflicts. With the advent of the internet and digitization, many Japanese war films have become widely visible, with even obscure works like Kobayashi Masaki's 1983 documentary *Tokyo Trial* (Tōkyō saiban) now rendered widely available to Chinese audiences via streaming platforms like Youku. While war films were previously limited to a domestic or art house audience, they are now broadcast internationally and come under heightened scrutiny when they aim to conceal or ignore the trauma that Japan's military expansion wreaked on invaded nations. In China, the focus on "One Hundred Years of Humiliation" has intensified Chinese nationalism and resulted in public outcries over Japanese revisionism both real and perceived, the violence of which is also broadcast internationally. When mixed with Western and

---

14. According to Wang, "The patriotic education campaign was made official by two documents issued in August 1991: 'Notice about Conducting Education of Patriotism and Revolutionary Tradition by Exploiting Extensively Cultural Relics' and 'General Outline on Strengthening Education on Chinese Modern and Contemporary History and National Conditions.'" Wang, "National Humiliation," 789.
15. Yoshikuni Igarashi, *Bodies of Memory: Narratives of War in Postwar Japanese Culture, 1945–1970* (Princeton, NJ: Princeton University Press, 2000), 204.
16. Francis Fukuyama and Kongdan Oh, *The US-Japan Security Relationship after the Cold War* (Santa Monica: National Defense Research Institute, 1993).
17. Shun'ya Yoshimi, "Television and Nationalism: Historical Change in the National Domestic TV Formation of Postwar Japan," *European Journal of Cultural Studies* 6, no. 4 (2003): 483.

regional anxiety over an economically ascendant China, this has undermined sympathy abroad.[18] Increasingly negative media depictions on both sides have contributed to shocking shifts in public sentiment, with the vast majority of Japanese citizens switching from a positive view of China in the 1970s to an overwhelmingly negative image by the early aughts (2000–2005) and continuing to today.[19]

Taking the apparent "tidal wave" of Chinese and Japanese memory in the late twentieth and early twenty-first centuries as its subject, this book explores remembering in a specific context, World War II in Asia (1937–1945), and through a specific mode, film.[20] Viewing memory as the collective narrating of the past, I begin with an overview of film-as-memory. I argue that film is a significant mode of popular memory that constructs the past in a unique way through its reproducibility, affective impact, appeals to authenticity, and manifestation of time and space. I maintain that war films are both national and transnational in ways that can dramatically limit or expand their reception. While many war films articulate a narrative centered on the national self for primarily domestic audiences, they can also travel easily due to our increasingly connected global societies and to the increased scrutiny of how other nations frame history. I elaborate on how the narratives within these films use images of race and gender to symbolize national identity, positing that by analyzing Chinese and Japanese war films, we can examine current narratives of national identity. I conclude with an overview of my central argument, which speculates that Chinese and Japanese war films from the 1980s onward demonstrate a change in prosthetic memory, which is generated by a transnational memory network I term the "memory loop." This is both fueled by and fueling a seismic shift of identity and power in the Pacific region.

---

18. For more on "One Hundred Years of Humiliation," see William A. Callahan, "National Insecurities: Humiliation, Salvation, and Chinese Nationalism," *Alternatives* 29, no. 2 (2004): 199–218, and Peter Hays Gries, "Tears of Rage: Chinese Nationalist Reactions to the Belgrade Embassy Bombing," *China Journal* 46 (2001): 25–43.
19. An overview of several public opinion polls conducted by agencies in China, Japan, Korea, and the United States concludes: "Whereas over 60 percent of Japanese surveyed in the late 1970s felt positively toward China, an equally negative view was presented by 2006. This reversal of goodwill is the same for the Chinese toward Japan." Mindy Kotler, Naotaka Sugawara, and Tetsuya Yamada, "Chinese and Japanese Public Opinion: Searching for Moral Security," *Asian Perspective* 3, no. 1 (2007): 93–125.
20. For "tidal wave," see Pierre Nora, "Reasons for the Current Upsurge in Memory," *Eurozine*, April 19, 2002, accessed April 13, 2014, http://www.eurozine.com/articles/2002-04-19-nora-en.html. America's involvement in World War II (1941–1945) is typically described as the Pacific theater of World War II, the Asia-Pacific War, or the Pacific War, with the conflict beginning with the bombing of Pearl Harbor. Chinese and Japanese involvement is usually referred to as the Second Sino-Japanese War. I use World War II throughout this book to include both Sino-Japanese events of the 1930s such as the Nanjing Massacre of 1937 (wherein American witnesses were such an integral part) and the battles between Japan and the United States.

Film as a Technology of Memory

Although there are numerous "sites of memory," including museums, archives, installations, and more, this book focuses on filmic narratives like TV dramas and feature films.[21] Like Robert Rosenstone, I maintain that film is "the chief carrier of historical messages in our culture."[22] It is a technology of memory that has transformed collective remembrance from the more localized traditions of commemorative rituals and oral histories into an immersive mass visual and auditory narrative. In addition, films not only reveal what kinds of narratives are prominent in a given culture but also allow for the diachronic comparison of how memory has changed over time. As my analysis of Chinese and Japanese war films will reveal, "memory is a process, not a thing."[23] Remembering World War II is a perpetual practice of framing, reframing, and communicating the past.[24] Notably, film-as-memory largely developed after World War II as films about the Holocaust generated fierce debates over the limits, possibilities, and stakes of representing the past.[25] Similar debates have emerged in different ways in studies on China's "scar cinema" of the 1980s, the films of Jia Zhangke, and Hiroshima-related film studies.[26] In the following section, I will explore

---

21. Whereas memory in the past was based on oral traditions, religious rituals, and spirit possession, remembrance became increasingly institutionalized in the museum and the archive. This is a trend Pierre Nora describes as our transition from *milieux* (backgrounds) of memory to *lieux* (sites, also referred to as realms) of memory. Pierre Nora, "Between Memory and History: Les Lieux de Mémoire," *Representations*, no. 26 (1989): 7–24. These sites signify "fixed points" or important events of the communal past. Jan Assmann and John Czaplicka, "Collective Memory and Cultural Identity," *New German Critique* 65 (1995): 129.
22. Robert A. Rosenstone, ed., *Revisioning History: Film and the Construction of a New Past* (Princeton, NJ: Princeton University Press, 1995), 3.
23. Jeffrey K. Olick and Joyce Robbins, "Social Memory Studies: From 'Collective Memory' to the Historical Sociology of Mnemonic Practices," *Annual Review of Sociology* 24, no. 1 (1998): 122.
24. James Wertsch and Doc Billingsley, quoting Frederic Bartlett (1932), also emphasize the "doing" of memory by highlighting the "-ing" of remembering. James Wertsch and Doc M. Billingsley, "The Roles of Narratives in Commemoration," in *Cultures and Globalization: Heritage, Memory and Identity*, ed. Helmut Anheier and Yudhishthir Raj Isar (London: SAGE, 2011), 25.
25. Shoshana Felman, "The Return of the Voice: Claude Lanzmann's *Shoah*," in *Testimony: Crises of Witnessing in Literature, Psychoanalysis, and History*, by Shoshana Felman and Dori Laub (New York: Routledge, 1992), 204–283, and Dominick LaCapra, "Lanzmann's *Shoah*: Here There Is No Why," *Critical Inquiry* 23, no. 2 (1997): 231–269.
26. In film studies, see Jin Liu, "The Rhetoric of Local Languages as the Marginal: Chinese Underground and Independent Films by Jia Zhangke and Others," *Modern Chinese Literature and Culture* 18, no. 2 (2006): 163–205, and Shuqin Cui, "Negotiating In-Between: On New-Generation Filmmaking and Jia Zhangke's Films," *Modern Chinese Literature and Culture* 18, no. 2 (2006): 98–130.

the four central ways that I see film as a unique and significant technology of remembrance.

First, films are highly immersive technologies of identification. As Tessa Morris-Suzuki argues, "Our relationship with the past is not simply forged through factual knowledge or an intellectual understanding of cause and effect. It also involves imagination and empathy."[27] Morris-Suzuki divides the representation of the past into two levels. The first, "history as interpretation," is historiography that focuses on defining the institutions, ideologies, and conditions that cause changes in societies. The second is "history as identification," a process that connotes empathizing with people in the past "to imagine their experiences and feelings, mourn their suffering and deaths and celebrate their triumphs."[28] Such "histories" tend to enforce affective identification as opposed to critical interpretation. Unlike more open-ended media forms, films do not give alternative answers to what happened in the past.[29] Even documentaries present testimonies as "fact" rather than questioning whether or not those statements are accurate.[30]

Alison Landsberg suggests that mass media like film, graphic novels, and museums have created "transferential spaces" that impart the feeling that one has accessed experiences in the past through "sensuous memories."[31] This is what she terms "prosthetic memory," that is, the feeling of having experienced something that one has not actually experienced.[32] Through the affective ties of narrative, the viewer may identify with the main character's perspective of the past.[33] More than theater, in which the tableau allows for more freedom of the gaze, or the painting, which is static and has a less collective relationship between the author/viewer/painting, film is a guided viewing experience in which the eye is "chaperoned" by way of editing, movement, and the close-up. The focus on the emotional experiences of the actor/character further highlights the ethos of the

---

27. Tessa Morris-Suzuki, *The Past within Us: Media, Memory, History* (London: Verso, 2005), 22–23.
28. Morris-Suzuki, *The Past within Us*, 22.
29. Robert Rosenstone, "The Historical Film: Looking at the Past in a Postliterate Age," in *The Historical Film: History and Memory in Media*, ed. Marcia Landy (New Brunswick, NJ: Rutgers University Press, 2001), 55–57.
30. Robert Rosenstone, "History in Images/History in Words: Reflections on the Possibility of Really Putting History onto Film," *American Historical Review* 93, no. 5 (1988): 1173–1185.
31. Alison Landsberg, "America, the Holocaust, and the Mass Culture of Memory: Toward a Radical Politics of Empathy," *New German Critique*, no. 71 (1997): 66.
32. Alison Landsberg, *Prosthetic Memory: The Transformation of American Remembrance in the Age of Mass Culture* (New York: Columbia University Press, 2004).
33. Telling a story is an important "vehicle" of transmitting individual memory to the collective. Jens Brockmeier, "Remembering and Forgetting: Narrative as Cultural Memory," *Culture and Psychology* 8, no. 1 (2002): 15–43.

past.[34] Films are "simultaneously subjective and public," framing memory in a way that is intimate but also communal and shared.[35]

Second, and perhaps most noteworthy, film is unique in terms of time. Jason G. Karlin, citing Benedict Anderson, notes that "the simultaneity of time, measured by clock and calendar, is reflected in the shared experience of reading newspapers that mark and organize events by the date at the top of the newspaper."[36] Similarly, Paul Ricoeur argues that identity is fundamentally collective and connected to time and narrative, as we create meaning in our lives by narrating it through time and via relation with others.[37] A film also creates a shared experience of the past and thus of identity, manipulating the relationship of the viewer to the past. Film and television mix the past with the present: "They have no grammatical analogues for the past and future tenses of written language and, thus, amplify the present sense of immediacy out of proportion."[38] While the viewer can choose to stop the film or leave, they can make no edits, nor can they stop the flow of time, change the camera angle, or ask the actor to perform different dialogue. Through the narrative, films also structure the "unstructurable," defining historical events as having a beginning, middle, and end.[39]

Audiences are a product of their time and will engage with texts in different ways depending on when they are viewing the text. Hans Robert Jauss and Elizabeth Benzinger's concept of "horizon of expectations" discusses the importance of the historically situated reader/audience in the interpretation of texts.[40] The reader will, by nature of their existence at a particular moment in time, be aware of and have their expectations shaped by previous texts they have read or seen. Genre is one major element in this horizon of expectation, as is historical period. Thus, an audience member in 1982 who has lived through the war will have a different "horizon" than that of an audience member in 2015 who has not. Outside of the film, historical or war films blur the present and past by appealing to heritage. Films are "based on a true story," "shot on location," the result of "years of research" and interviews. They create a sense of authenticity

---

34. Mark Moss, *Toward the Visualization of History: The Past as Image* (Oxford: Oxford University Press, 2008), 125.
35. Jeffrey Pence, "Postcinema/Postmemory," in *Memory and Popular Film*, ed. Paul Grainge (Manchester: Manchester University Press, 2003), 238.
36. Jason G. Karlin, *Gender and Nation in Meiji Japan: Modernity, Loss, and the Doing of History* (Honolulu: University of Hawai'i Press, 2014), 3.
37. Paul Ricoeur, *Time and Narrative* (Chicago: University of Chicago Press, 2010).
38. Gary Richard Edgerton, "Introduction," in *Television Histories: Shaping Collective Memory in the Media Age*, ed. Gary Edgerton and Peter C. Rollins (Lexington: University Press of Kentucky, 2001), 3.
39. Rosenstone, "Historical Film," 55–57.
40. Hans Robert Jauss and Elizabeth Benzinger, "Literary History as a Challenge to Literary Theory," *New Literary History* 2, no. 1 (1970): 7–37.

unhampered by their fictional nature through the guidance of consultants who are veterans, experts, scientists, and historians.[41] They are created by a survivor of the Holocaust or the son of a soldier or a member of an ethnic or religious group. Steven Spielberg, perhaps the most famous of the war film director-producers, creates this sense of lineage for *Saving Private Ryan* (1997) by invoking his identity as the son of a World War II veteran; he refers to his Jewish heritage in the making of *Schindler's List* (1993), and he cites his father's and uncle's military service in the Pacific for *Letters from Iwo Jima* (2006), *Flags of Our Fathers* (2006), and *The Pacific* (2010). *Schindler's List* further appeals to authenticity by having actual survivors approach the real Oskar Schindler's grave alongside their actor doubles. As Landsberg writes, "When the survivor touches the actor, the possibility emerges for a transmission of memory across radical temporal and geographic chasms."[42] Japanese actor Mikuni Rentarō, performing in the Sino-Japanese reconciliation melodrama *The Go Masters* (1982), apologizes on behalf of Japan not only through his performance as an actor but as a former soldier in China. Just as photographs used to transfer memory within the blood-related family, films transfer memories within the larger imagined family.[43] Films do not question this heritage. They do not suggest "the possibility that there may be a very different way of reporting what happened," nor do they indicate "where knowledge of the past comes from and our relation to it."[44] They are, however, somewhat held "in check" by the discourses outside of the film: reviewers, historians, and witnesses provide counterpoints to the histories presented on-screen.[45]

Actors complete the temporal experience of film by embodying the memories of the collective and channeling the spirits of "our" ancestors.[46] The bodies of

---

41. Hoskins discusses the issues of attaining authenticity in this technological era. Andrew Hoskins, "Signs of the Holocaust: Exhibiting Memory in a Mediated Age," *Media, Culture and Society* 25, no. 1 (2003): 7–22.
42. Landsberg, "America, the Holocaust, and the Mass Culture of Memory," 64.
43. Marianne Hirsch's concept of postmemory examines how children of Holocaust survivors experienced the traumatic pasts of their parents. This form of memory is primarily mediated through family photographs in an atmosphere permeated by memories of Holocaust trauma. Although Hirsch's concept refers specifically to the communicative level, it might be extended to the cultural level to explain the effect of films on the collective imaginary. Marianne Hirsch, *Family Frames: Photography, Narrative, and Postmemory* (Cambridge, MA: Harvard University Press, 1997).
44. Natalie Zemon Davis, "'Any Resemblance to Persons Living or Dead': Film and the Challenge of Authenticity," *Historical Journal of Film, Radio and Television* 8, no. 3 (1988): 457–482.
45. Robert Burgoyne, "Prosthetic Memory/Traumatic Memory: *Forrest Gump*," *Screening the Past* 6 (1999), accessed November 4, 2014, http://tlweb.latrobe.edu.au/humanities/screening thepast/firstrelease/fr0499/rbfr6a.htm.
46. Diana Taylor, *The Archive and the Repertoire: Performing Cultural Memory in the Americas* (Durham, NC: Duke University Press, 2003).

suffering characters embody the trials and tribulations of the past; the experience of visual, auditory, and emotional immersion reaches outside the narrative to inspire shock, fear, or sadness in the body of the viewer. This mediation of history combines the premodern ritual of memory with the modern apparatus of film. While we are aware that we are watching an actor or filmmaker in the present performing the events of the past, such reenactment is still a powerful linkage to our collective past. The contemporary actor "provide[s] a face for the faceless" historical figure, as Rosenstone notes in his description of how the film *Gandhi* represents a South African railway conductor who is undescribed in Gandhi's biography.[47]

Third, it can also be said that film is unique in terms of space. The diegetic world of the film—its enclosed space of narrative, space, time—is not constructed the same way as in any other form of media.[48] Film constructs three-dimensional worlds though manipulative music, sentimental story lines, persuasive editing, and seductive star power, all of which encourage the unconscious submission to the flow of the narrative. The camera in motion is a kind of "moving consciousness" that guides our gaze.[49] The diegetic world created via continuity editing, close-ups/medium shots, 3D sound, increasingly elaborate special effects, and naturalistic acting creates a different spatial experience than paintings, photographs, and museums. Sound is particularly important. As Noël Burch argues, it was not until synchronized sound that film achieved its "full diegetic effect."[50] Jonathan Crary has noted that it was the arrival of sound that first commanded the full attention of the viewer.[51] The spaces delineated in films become the visual reference for the actual battlefields of the past.[52]

Finally, films are unique in terms of reproducibility. They are often remediated across other contexts as "paratexts," which is how Jonathan Gray refers to

---

47. Although he was not described in Gandhi's biography, he is given a physical presence and depicted in the film. Rosenstone, "History in Images/History in Words," 36.
48. Metz defines diegesis as "the sum of a film's denotation: the narration itself, but also the fictional space and time dimensions implied in and by the narrative, and consequently the character, the landscapes, the events and other narrative elements." Christian Metz, *Film Language: A Semiotics of the Cinema* (Chicago: University of Chicago Press, 1974).
49. Frantz Fanon first used the phrase "moving consciousness" to refer to the nation. Frantz Fanon, *The Wretched of the Earth* (New York: Grove Press, 1961).
50. Noël Burch, *Life to those Shadows* (Berkeley: University of California Press, 1990): 255.
51. Crary notes that the late 1920s are possibly denoted as the beginning of the film-as-spectacle for Debord because of a variety of factors, including how the changing technology of the film changes the spectator's "awareness of the body," attention, perception, and even relationship with memory. Jonathan Crary, "Spectacle, Attention, Counter-memory," *October* 50 (1989): 102.
52. Michelle Pierson, "A Production Designer's Cinema: Historical Authenticity in Popular Films Set in the Past," in *The Spectacle of the Real: From Hollywood to "Reality" TV and Beyond*, ed. Geoff King (Bristol: Intellect, 2005), 139–149.

the ways in which the film text appears outside of the text in awards ceremonies, commercials, advertisements, interviews, and so forth.[53] The text of the film is therefore not limited to its broadcast: it extends far beyond its status as a film in the form of promotions, interviews, debates, and even memes broadcast outside of the film. Star image might be seen as one of the major paratexts that affect how audiences interpret the film. For example, Richard Dyer discusses the "polysemic star image," which elaborates on the construction of star image through promotion, publicity, film roles, and commentary—when a famous actor stars in a film, they bring with them the discourses that surround their star identity.[54] Thus, as George Custen remarks, referring to a film about Queen Elizabeth starring Bette Davis, "Perhaps one admires Queen Elizabeth I for her statecraft but also because she is Bette Davis."[55] Paratexts can also be popular archetypes that function as cultural memes, such as the "insistent fringes" in American films featuring the Romans or the bumbling Japanese soldier sporting a Hitler mustache seen in many Chinese films.[56] Since the 1990s, the internet has increased the speed, spread, and volume of such paratexts through user comments and mass access to media while also intensifying intertextuality as netizens create their own videos or memes in response to filmic texts.

In the following section, I explore how film intersects with national and transnational memory, underlining the ways in which war films articulate national perspectives both domestically and internationally. When globally visible, certain collective events generate controversy, disputes, and ever more attempts to "capture" that moment in time for audiences both local and global.

War Films as (Trans)National Memory

Chinese and Japanese war films are rooted in both the national and the transnational. War films operate as biographies of the nation's triumphs and losses, a collective mythmaking process that shapes national identity.[57] As Benedict Anderson famously said: "Because there is no Originator, the nation's biography

---

53. Jonathan Gray, *Show Sold Separately: Promos, Spoilers, and Other Media* (New York: New York University Press, 2010).
54. Richard Dyer, *Stars* (London: British Film Institute, 1979).
55. George F. Custen, "Making History," in *The Historical Film: History and Memory in Media*, ed. Marcia Landy (New Brunswick, NJ: Rutgers University Press, 2001), 68.
56. Roland Barthes, *Mythologies* (New York: Macmillan, 1972).
57. Collective memory and nationalism are different processes. Social forms of remembrance predate nationalism and have different theoretical foci. Collective forms of remembrance, on the other hand, existed long before the rise of nations in social groups such as religious groups and tribes. While cultural memory refers to a broad process of narrating the past through sites of memory, nationalism is the imagining of a cohesive political group of territorially bound people who are united by a shared past

cannot be written evangelically, 'down time,' through a long procreative chain of begettings. The only alternative is to fashion it 'up time'—towards Peking Man, Java Man, King Arthur. . . . World War II begets World War I; out of Sedan comes Austerlitz; the ancestor of the Warsaw Uprising is the state of Israel."[58]

New nations often emphasize their relationship to the past by establishing new calendars, stressing national origins, and highlighting moments of group triumph and trauma to unify the nation. War—its enemies and heroes, "us" versus "them," its emphasis on boundaries—is the ultimate expression of national identity. Indeed, "In the modern era, it has been the nation which has been the prime arena for the articulation of war memories and the mobilization of commemoration, since war has been central to its identity and symbolic continuity."[59] As the last worldwide conflict, World War II and its immediate aftermath further mark the identity shift that established current power balances, rivalries, and allies. The current Japanese Constitution, the American hegemony and the Chinese Communist Party (CCP) all emerged in the immediate aftermath of World War II. It was the last war to stretch around the world and involve every stratum of society, a factor that undoubtedly contributes to its longevity in the discourse of all three nations.

Like postmemory, wherein memories of the Holocaust are passed down through a family photograph in a way that imparts that experience to the child of a Holocaust survivor, the "prosthetic memory" of film can bind the individual to the larger family of the nation.[60] Early war films, according to Marcia Landy, often constructed "monumental history" by presenting a triumphant narrative of the nation. Both spectacle and the hero were important figures in these types of films, with the famous movie star representing a form of national identity.[61] War films can also confront the trauma of defeat, as in the case of American combat films of the 1980s, which dealt with waging a lost and pointless war in Vietnam.[62] By the 1990s, American war films "kicked the Vietnam syndrome" by emphasizing American heroism during World War II and by focusing on an

---

and whose narrative importantly includes the future. The two processes overlap and frequently inform each other but are discrete.
58. Benedict Anderson, *Imagined Communities: Reflections on the Origin and Spread of Nationalism* (London: Verso, 1991), 205.
59. Timothy G. Ashplant, Graham Dawson, and Michael Roper, eds., *Commemorating War: The Politics of Memory* (London: Routledge, 2004), 22.
60. Hirsch, *Family Frames*.
61. Marcia Landy, "Introduction," in *The Historical Film: History and Memory in Media*, ed. Marcia Landy (New Brunswick, NJ: Rutgers University Press, 2001), 8.
62. Gaylyn Studlar and David Desser, "Never Having to Say You're Sorry: *Rambo's* Rewriting of the Vietnam War," *Film Quarterly* 42, no. 1 (1988): 9–16.

insular world of Americans dying for Americans.[63] Some war films serve to normalize the military actions of the state, while others challenge viewers by confronting them directly with images of warfare.[64] As Gabriel Teshome discusses in his book on "third cinema," movies can also serve to dispute dominant national narratives.[65]

However, much as these films are "national," they are also globally visible to a certain extent due to the internet, translation, and international film distribution. They are created by actors and producers from around the world, analyzed by journalists and scholars globally, and occasionally spark international debate. Their stories are intrinsically transnational, dealing as they do with international incidents involving nations around the world. There is also a global trend toward transnational film production as studios attempt to share production costs and maximize their audiences. Still, the national remains significant. Films are produced and consumed by people who exist in a certain time and space; the Chinese and Japanese film and television industries have undergone different developments historically in ways that have impacted the kinds of war narratives that are produced.

Film is thus significant as a *global* mode of remembrance.[66] Through the cross-border flows of mediascapes, film-as-memory has also become increasingly visible to the Other, a process that is notably uneven. American remembrance of World War II continues to dominate, with Hollywood-produced films dominating the top World War II films internationally (see Table 1.1).[67] Indeed, Hollywood films have sometimes indirectly shaped how Chinese and Japanese filmmakers represent the war. For instance, when Chinese American author Iris Chang wrote *The Rape of Nanking*, she drew upon the language of Hollywood images of the Holocaust to present Chinese memory to Americans. This imagery was, as we will see in Chapter 4, imported back to China, where the "Schindler of Nanjing" archetype has become a central means of tying together Chinese and American memories.

---

63. Marilyn Blatt Young, "In the Combat Zone," *Radical History Review* 85, no. 1 (2003): 253–264, and Susan A. Owen, "Memory, War and American Identity: *Saving Private Ryan* as Cinematic Jeremiad," *Critical Studies in Media Communication* 19, no. 3 (2002): 249–282.
64. Mark J. Lacy, "War, Cinema, and Moral Anxiety," *Alternatives* 28, no. 5 (2003): 611–636.
65. Gabriel Teshome, *Third Cinema as Guardian of Popular Memory: Towards a Third Aesthetics* (London: British Film Institute, 1989), 53–64.
66. Indeed, a Chinese poll taken in 1996 found that 70 percent of students interviewed claimed they learned about Japan through films and TV produced in China. Yang, "Reconciliation between Japan and China," 79.
67. To compare to the less financially successful Chinese and Japanese films, see Tables 1.2 and 1.3. Only the Miyazaki Hayao film *The Wind Rises* (Kaze tachinu) competes with the Hollywood numbers, potentially in part because his films are distributed by Disney in the United States.

Still, as Wimal Dissanayake elaborates, globalization forms a "chiasmus" with the national: the local and the transnational are always intertwined.[68] Although films are said to "travel"—to be transnational—the national has remained pervasive. Films are produced and consumed by people who exist in a certain time and space.[69] Even in the production of a "transnational" film, "the national continues to exert the force of its presence."[70] Although there has been a rise in transnational coproductions to allow companies to share the rising costs of producing films and attempt to reach a broader audience, in many cases such texts fail to travel as the coproduction tends to favor one side or the other in appealing to audiences whose tastes are, ultimately, rooted in the local.[71] Films are also uniquely rooted in nationally framed paratexts—they are commemorated at national sites of memory such as national film awards ceremonies (the Japan Academy Prize) and national archives (Japan's National Film Center); films are even shown in schools as part of national education programs (e.g., *Little Soldier Zhang Ga*). In addition, cinema as an industry may be used transnationally to strengthen national "soft culture" ties as in the Beijing Screenwriting Competition for Americans. Even at international film festivals, the film's nation of origin continues to be important in its scheduling and marketing.

The Chinese and Japanese film and television industries have undergone different developments historically. In postwar China, film companies were highly regulated by the CCP—movies were produced by nationally operated studios and intended to focus on the ideological education of the Chinese masses. Since the 1980s, there has been a transition from state-owned enterprises to private production companies as well as a turn toward diasporic/transnational film production.[72] Yet production and distribution are still subject to stifling national

---

68. Wimal Dissanayake, "Globalization and the Experience of Culture," in *Globalization, Cultural Identities, and Media Representations*, ed. Natascha Gentz and Stefan Kramer (Albany, NY: SUNY Press, 2012), 25–44.
69. "Whether we focus on the ways in which memory might 'travel' via the cinema, or the Internet, for instance, that travel remains only hypothetical, or an unrealized potential, until a particular individual goes to a specific website, or a particular audience watches a specific film. For even when (and if) memory travels, it is only ever *instantiated* locally, in a specific place and at a particular time." Susannah Radstone, "What Place Is This? Transcultural Memory and the Locations of Memory Studies," *Parallax* 17, no. 4 (2011): 109–123, http://www.tandfonline.com/doi/full/10.1080/13534645.2011.605585.
70. Will Higbee and Song Hwee Lim, "Concepts of Transnational Cinema: Towards a Critical Transnationalism in Film Studies," *Transnational Cinemas* 1, no. 1 (2010): 10.
71. Hualing Fu, "Television in Post-reform China: Serial Dramas, Confucian Leadership and the Global Television Market," *China Quarterly* 201 (2010): 195–227.
72. Shuyu Kong, "Genre Film, Media Corporations, and the Commercialisation of the Chinese Film Industry: The Case of 'New Year Comedies,'" *Asian Studies Review* 31, no. 3 (2007): 227–242, and Sheldon Lu, ed., *Transnational Chinese Cinemas: Identity, Nationhood, Gender* (Honolulu: University of Hawai'i Press, 1997).

Introduction   15

laws.[73] If producers want to have their films released through official channels or to avoid being censored at home, they have to submit them for review by the State Administration of Radio, Film, and Television (SARFT), often referred to as "the censors" in Western media. Moreover, Chinese filmmakers who proceed to show films without passing SARFT or non-Chinese films with themes deemed negative by the government can be subject to government blacklisting, as in the case of Jiang Wen's *Devils on the Doorstep* (Guizi laile, 2000).

Japanese postwar cinema peaked in the 1950s and 1960s as film studios like Nikkatsu, Daiei, Toho, and Toei produced financially and critically successful films for both Japanese and international audiences. The arrival of television—begun in the 1950s and popularized through the 1960s and 1970s—led to audiences focusing more on television than on feature film attendance (a trend that is global in nature).[74] As Yoshimi has argued, television in Japan since the 1990s shows two tendencies—a turn toward the transnational in terms of capital and a turn toward the national in terms of narrative content.[75] In particular, there has been a shift from nationalism centered around a unified timetable to nationalism structured around national crisis.[76] We might argue that for many Japanese, the transnational historical disputes of the 1990s constitute another such national crisis. A second major difference is that Japanese cinema has, unlike Chinese cinema, been primarily shaped by capitalist forces. As a result, there is less focus on political dogma (such as "mainstream melody" films, or *zhuxuanlü*, films that are in "harmony" with the national narrative), and more emphasis on films that will appeal to audiences.[77]

Audiences in China and Japan also differ. Chinese audiences have undergone a change from the top-down imposition of limited dogmatic texts to a landslide of media. From the early 1980s, according to Michael Curtin, "As political and economic pressures combined with a technological shift towards satellite, cable, and VCR, they fueled the rising aspirations of citizens, who now had access to more information and imagery than would have seemed imaginable only a few years before."[78] Despite television being a relatively recent trend, it was adopted and disseminated into Chinese homes quickly during that period. Moreover, the

---

73. Stanley Rosen, "Foreword," in *Television in Post-reform China*, ed. Zhu Ying (London: Routledge, 2008).
74. Shun'ya Yoshimi, "'Made in Japan': The Cultural Politics of Home Electrification in Postwar Japan," *Media, Culture and Society* 21, no. 2 (1999): 149–171.
75. Yoshimi, "Television and Nationalism," 461.
76. Yoshimi, "Television and Nationalism," 484.
77. For more on mainstream melody films, see Jeffrey C. Kinkley, *Corruption and Realism in Late Socialist China: The Return of the Political Novel* (Stanford, CA: Stanford University Press, 2006), 212.
78. Michael Curtin, *Playing to the World's Biggest Audience: The Globalization of Chinese Film and TV* (Berkeley: University of California Press, 2007), 192.

wide availability of films online and on the street via pirated forms suggests, rather conversely, that many Chinese viewers may have access to more films than Japanese audiences. For instance, the 1983 NHK drama *Tokyo Trial*, relatively hard to find in Japan, has been translated and is widely available online from the Chinese search engine Baidu. In Japan, it is believed that older audiences tend to view films more than younger audiences in the theaters, though big-budget films and multiplexes may be reversing that trend. As a result of globalization and the decline of the traditional film industries, most people are watching films at home. For both national audiences, the paratexts surrounding these discourses—the internet in particular—are increasingly significant in shaping the meaning of these texts.

In sum, the war film is—perhaps more than any other film genre—based in the national. However, the pasts represented in a war film can be represented in different ways depending on the perspective of the creators, the discourses prominent at that time, and increasingly global systems of consumption and distribution.

"Manly States"

In the representation of an abstract concept like "nation," gender and race are important visual markers. Indeed, the conflicts among nations are often performed through overt appeals to collective and normative narratives of race and gender.[79] Many modern nations build their legitimacy and identity on the "ethnosymbolic" narratives of the past.[80] This is connected to concepts of collective storytelling like "mythomoteur," an ethnic group's origin myth, such as Japan's narrative of the "Yamato minzoku."[81] As for gender, the state itself is often represented as male in the public imaginary; international relations might be seen as the competition of masculinities.[82] As R. W. Connell emphatically states, "The historical processes that produced global society were, from the start,

---

79. As Rita Felski suggests in her discussion of modernity, "If our sense of the past is inevitably shaped by the explanatory logic of narrative, then the stories that we create in turn reveal the inescapable presence and power of gender symbolism." Rita Felski, *The Gender of Modernity* (Cambridge, MA: Harvard University Press, 2009), 1.
80. Anthony D. Smith, "Memory and Modernity: Reflections on Ernest Gellner's Theory of Nationalism," *Nations and Nationalism* 2, no. 3 (1996): 371–388.
81. Anthony D. Smith, *The Ethnic Origins of Nations* (Oxford: Basil Blackwell, 1988), and John Alexander Armstrong, *Nations before Nationalism* (Chapel Hill: University of North Carolina Press, 1982).
82. Marysia Zalewski and Jane L. Parpart, eds., *The "Man" Question in International Relations* (Boulder, CO: Westview Press, 1998).

gendered."[83] Colonialism produced gendered notions of conquest, labor, and social norms, all encompassed by a racial hierarchy that was itself gendered. Early cinema coincided with the height of global imperialism, and, as such, much early cinema shows racist images of colonized peoples.[84]

Such discourses of nation, race, gender, and power connect to the concept of postcolonial masculinities.[85] As Hooper notes, the West—exemplified by the Caucasian male—has shaped the terms by which non-Western nations are imagined. Western power represents a kind of hegemonic masculinity juxtaposed against the marginalized masculinities of nonwhite, non-Western powers.[86] Cinema itself has also been shaped by a "gendered Western gaze."[87] For instance, the men of dominated nations have frequently been framed in Western-produced films as weak or "feminized" figures or as hypersexual savages to justify colonial intervention in local matters. Such representations shaped expectations of men in postcolonial societies by forcing them to "measure up" to a narrow, normative colonial definition of masculinity that continues to shape perceptions of masculinity in formerly colonized nations to the present day.[88]

American discourse has, for the most part, represented Asian men as feminine outside of the perceived masculinity of martial arts. Yen Ling Shek suggests that Asian masculinity within the United States is situated within a hegemonic (dominant and ideal) white masculinity and is considered subordinate to that masculinity.[89] Similarly, Gina Marchetti argues that films featuring Asian people in America have struggled to reconcile the nation's purported democratic ideals with their insistence on the dominance of the white male.[90] This narrative

---

83. R. W. Connell, "Globalization, Imperialism, and Masculinities," in *Handbook of Studies on Men and Masculinities*, ed. Michael S. Kimmel and Jeff R. Hearn (London: SAGE, 2005), 71–89.
84. Robert Stam and Louise Spence, "Colonialism, Racism and Representation," *Screen* 24, no. 2 (1983): 6.
85. For a short overview, see Lahoucine Ouzgane and Daniel Coleman, "Postcolonial Masculinities: Introduction," *Jouvert: A Journal of Postcolonial Studies* 2, no. 1 (1998): 1–10.
86. Charlotte Hooper, *Manly States: Masculinities, International Relations, and Gender Politics* (New York: Columbia University Press, 2001).
87. Ella Shohat, "Gender and Culture of Empire: Toward a Feminist Ethnography of the Cinema," *Quarterly Review of Film and Video* 13, no. 1–3 (1991): 45–84.
88. Margrethe Silberschmidt, *"Women Forget That Men Are the Masters": Gender Antagonism and Socio-economic Change in Kisii District, Kenya* (Copenhagen: Nordic Africa Institute, 1999) and Robert Morrell and Sandra Swart, "Men in the Third World: Postcolonial Perspectives on Masculinity," in *Handbook of Studies on Men and Masculinities*, ed. Michael S. Kimmel and Jeff R. Hearn (London: SAGE, 2005), 90.
89. Yen Ling Shek, "Asian American Masculinity: A Review of the Literature," *Journal of Men's Studies* 14, no. 3 (2006): 379–391.
90. Gina Marchetti, *Romance and the "Yellow Peril": Race, Sex, and Discursive Strategies in Hollywood Fiction* (Berkeley: University of California Press, 1993), 218.

developed out of anxiety over the immigration of male Asian laborers and a desire to express economic and military power over an emasculated Asian Other.[91] The perceived "emasculation" of the Asian American male has been "a vexatious issue to the community."[92]

A "stronger" nationalism is often constructed in response to the Other's masculinity. Dibyesh Anand, in a much-cited study, reads violent Hindu nationalism in part as a response to the construction of an imagined Muslim masculinity. According to his analysis, Hindu men imagine themselves as emasculated by a "dangerously virile Muslim masculinity" and the peaceful and secular ideas of Buddha and Gandhi."[93] Such imaginings of emasculation at the hands of a (more) masculine Other sometimes prompt a reimagining of the self. China and Japan have also responded to the hegemonic masculinity of America with their own images of masculinity.

Japanese masculine nationalism has been heavily shaped by interactions with the West. Karlin argues that two forms of masculinity emerged in Meiji Japan—one "feminine" masculinity based on the European dandy, one "masculine" version based on nativism and imperialism. Both were ultimately a response to the foreign influence of modernity.[94] Meanwhile, Igarashi calls the "foundational narrative" of the US-Japan postwar narrative until the 1980s the idea that the male United States saved the female Japan.[95] This is embodied in the famous "wedding photo" of Douglas MacArthur and Hirohito, wherein the tall, relaxed general—coded as masculine—towers over the short, formal emperor—coded as feminine.[96] This relationship has been complicated by the US-Japan alliance, which remains the cornerstone of Japanese security and one of the main reasons Japanese society was able to suppress memories of war until the end of the Cold War.

Meanwhile, contemporary Chinese masculinity and nationalism have been shaped in part by both Japan and the West. The early post-Mao era prompted a "search for men" (*xunzhao nanzihan*, searching for manly men) in response to the new transnational economy. During this era, Hollywood stars and Japanese actors came to epitomize new images of masculinity, as well as a possible future

---

91. Jinqi Ling, "Identity Crisis and Gender Politics: Reappropriating Asian American Masculinity," in *An Interethnic Companion to Asian American Literature*, ed. King-Kok Cheung (Cambridge, MA: Cambridge University Press, 1997), 314.
92. Ling, "Identity Crisis and Gender Politics," 313.
93. Dibyesh Anand, "Anxious Sexualities: Masculinity, Nationalism and Violence," *British Journal of Politics and International Relations* 9, no. 2 (2007): 260.
94. Jason G. Karlin, "The Gender of Nationalism: Competing Masculinities in Meiji Japan," *Journal of Japanese Studies* 28, no. 1 (2002): 41–77.
95. Igarashi, *Bodies of Memory*, 20.
96. Igarashi, *Bodies of Memory*, 30.

path for Chinese identity.[97] In popular media, Chinese masculinity was used as a metaphor for successful Chinese globalization, with the fantasy image of the Chinese male/Caucasian female romance a popular mid-1990s trope.[98] As Sheldon Lu suggests, the "victory that Chinese men are able to score with foreign women symbolizes not only the resurrection of Chinese masculinity but also a triumph of the Chinese nation itself."[99] More recently, the "One Hundred Years of Humiliation" nationalist campaign might be seen as a narrative of Chinese emasculation at the hands of European, American, and particularly Japanese powers. A well-known phrase used to describe the politically weak China during the eighteenth and nineteenth centuries—"sick man of Asia" (*dongya bingfu*)—still resonates as a humiliating insult today. Japanese imperialism was largely based on the idealization of the racial superiority of the Japanese race over the rest of Asia, a perception many Chinese find emasculating and degrading.[100] Ironically, recent Chinese discourse jockeys for more respect internationally by reproducing such gendered narratives of racial superiority.

Women often have different symbolic roles in the construction of nation. One of the main differences in how men and women are represented in texts on nationalism is in terms of action. As Rick Wilford notes, women are often articulated in more symbolic terms, whereas men are represented as the subjects and driving force behind nation building.[101] As the "national state is essentially a masculine institution," women act as supporting players in roles designed to "reflect masculinist notions of femininity and of women's proper 'place.'"[102] Women are frequently enlisted in national struggles, only to be removed from leadership once the nation is established.[103] Thus, if men are represented as the nation's brain and brawn, women are represented as its heart and womb: the home for whom the

---

97. Zhong highlights the character of Rambo, played by Sylvester Stallone, and Takakura Ken. Xueping Zhong, *Masculinity Besieged? Issues of Modernity and Male Subjectivity in Chinese Literature of the Late Twentieth Century* (Durham, NC: Duke University Press, 2000), 41.
98. Sheldon H. Lu, "Soap Opera in China: The Transnational Politics of Visuality, Sexuality, and Masculinity," *Cinema Journal* 40, no. 1 (2000): 25–47.
99. Lu, "Soap Opera in China," **37.**
100. Even much Japanese cinema until the 1980s was made with the notion that Japan was "above" the rest of Asia. Tezuka Yoshiharu, *Japanese Cinema Goes Global: Filmworkers' Journeys* (Hong Kong: Hong Kong University Press, 2011), 171.
101. Rick Wilford, "Women, Ethnicity and Nationalism: Surveying the Ground," in *Women, Ethnicity and Nationalism: The Politics of Transition*, ed. Robert E. Miller and Rick Wilford (London: Routledge, 1998), 1.
102. Joane Nagel, "Masculinity and Nationalism: Gender and Sexuality in the Making of Nations," *Ethnic and Racial Studies* 21, no. 2 (1998): 243–251.
103. Cynthia Enloe, *Bananas, Beaches and Bases: Making Feminist Sense of International Politics* (Berkeley: University of California Press, 1989), 62.

soldier nostalgically reminisces, the mother he calls for when wounded, the girl he has left behind, and the land that he protects. As the passive motherland and as victims of war, women are often purported to be "why we fight."

As Matthew Evangelista argues, expressions such as "motherland," "mother tongue," and "the birth of the nation" further reveal the ways in which women are enlisted in the imagining of the nation.[104] Women give birth to the nation's "ethnic collectivities," they represent the "boundaries of the symbolic identity of their group," they are "cultural carriers" of their collective's symbols, and they represent difference from other collectivities.[105] This is the "vocabulary of kinship" that unites the nation through the affective language of family ties.[106] In countries that define themselves by their ethnicity, the birth rate of the dominant ethnic group becomes a question of survival. Seen in this light, Japan's "birth rate problem" is based on anxieties of reproducing the desired "Yamato race." The wartime rape of women leaves physical and psychological wounds not only on individuals but also on the nation, as can be seen in the current disputes over Nanjing and comfort women.

How men treat women from another nation is also a marker of their own national identity. The "white knights" in American films of the 1950s and 1960s were represented as democratic saviors who "rescued" Chinese and Japanese women from their oppressive, backward cultures through idealized American values.[107] Wartime sexual violence committed by the Japanese Imperial Army is highly controversial in Japan in part because it problematizes narratives of the right, which are based on myths of disciplined military masculinity and racial superiority. Thus, gender and race, as "fundamental" identities that frequently—though not always—"operate through visual markers on the body," are an important signifier of difference in these films.[108]

The Memory Loop

Over the past several decades, Chinese and Japanese war films have continuously returned to the same moment in time in an effort to "remember the past." The repeated attempt to depict the same event is part of what I envision as a "memory loop," or a transnational memory network. The memory loop is an

---

104. Matthew Evangelista, *Gender, Nationalism, and War: Conflict on the Movie Screen* (Cambridge: Cambridge University Press, 2011), 1.
105. Floya Anthias and Nira Yuval-Davis, *Woman-Nation-State* (New York: Macmillan, 1989), 8–11.
106. Anderson, *Imagined Communities*, 143.
107. Marchetti, *Romance and the "Yellow Peril."*
108. Linda Martin Alcoff, *Visible Identities: Race, Gender, and the Self* (Oxford: Oxford University Press, 2005), 3.

ongoing process characterized by repeated attempts to collectively remember a specific event that involves multiple nations such as the Nanjing Massacre or the Tokyo Trial, or a larger, less temporally specific collective experience like a world war or colonialization. The memory loop shares characteristics with Anna Reading's concept of globital memory, which imagines memory as an assemblage of embodied, local, and global memory agents who delineate memory in ways shaped by uneven hierarchies of power.[109] However, in visualizing this specific debate over memory in the Pacific as a transnational loop, I aim to highlight the importance of specific national memory discourses as "nodes" that connect and interact within this global assemblage and the particular ways in which they overlap and diverge. By using the term "loop," I aim to emphasize the cyclical nature of this process, as each national discourse returns to the same shared historical event year after year, often propelled forward by the real or imagined narrative of the other nation(s). While the memory loop is perpetually in search of a destination (e.g., the remembrance of the particular event or the establishment of a globally recognized official narrative of that event), the event can never be fully captured. Propelled onward by the momentum of mutual visibility, as well as history's continuously building layers of discourse and compounding collective pain and controversy, the cycle of memory can be infinite on a memory loop. War films are not mere static sites of memory; they are what makes up this interconnected superhighway of remembrance. Transformed by each domestic and transnational discursive contact, these films continue to circle, overlap, and intersect in search of the same ineffable moment in time.

In this book, I analyze how these films participate in a memory loop in terms of visual representation (framing, mise-en-scène, costumes, makeup, camera movement, editing), audio (music, sound effects), and narrative structure (plot, heroes, victims, conflict, resolution), drawing inspiration from the work of David Bordwell and Jacques Aumont, among others.[110] I also draw from Astrid Erll's framework, which divides the paratexts of "film as memory" into what she terms the intra, inter, and pluri layers. The inter layer refers to the narrative inside the film, or the text. The intra layer is the interaction between texts, such as premediation (genre conventions, previous literatures) and remediation (how the film is represented again and again in other contexts and through other texts). The final layer is the pluri layer, the context around the film such as academic controversies and awards ceremonies.[111] These filmic texts are further mediated

---

109. Anna Reading, "Memory and Digital Media: Six Dynamics of the Globital Memory Field," in *On Media Memory: Collective Memory in a New Media Age*, ed. Motti Neiger, Oren Meyers, and Eyal Zandberg (London: Palgrave Macmillan, 2011), 241–252.
110. David Bordwell, *Narration in the Fiction Film* (New York: Routledge, 2013) and Jacques Aumont, ed. *Aesthetics of Film* (Austin: University of Texas Press, 1992).
111. Astrid Erll, "Literature, Film, and the Mediality of Cultural Memory,' in *Media and Cultural Memory*, ed. Astrid Erll and Ansgar Nünning (Berlin: Walter de Gruyter), 389–390.

by the pluri layers of the individual and collective identities of the filmmakers and the governmental and market constraints. This book is thus a diachronic and cross-cultural comparative study in which I compare Chinese and Japanese films within their respective cultures and with each other. I approach these texts from the historical context, the context of the production, the narrative of the film, and the film's difference from past versions. The narrative of these films, as well as their production and reception, reveals the interplay of local, national, and cosmopolitan processes of memory. Through their intranational, intragenerational, and transnational dimensions, we can explore individual, communicative, and cultural intersections of memory.

My selection of films centers on the popular and contemporary, as I aim to discover the dominant trends of remembrance. I am also concerned with the specific trends that inspired transnational debates over memory, or memory loops centered on specific events and issues, like the Tokyo Trial or wartime sexual violence. I select films on the basis of their popularity or ubiquity, such as how well they performed at the box office or whether they played on a major television network or were widely advertised (see Tables 1.2 and 1.3 for Chinese and Japanese war films at their respective box offices). In addition, because the discourse is more "fractured" in Japan among right, left, and mainstream, I juxtapose popular Japanese films against less popular films from the right or left to discuss the differences in mainstream and more right- or left-wing discourses. In Chapter 4, since there are no recent mainstream Japanese films on the Nanjing Massacre, I discuss how rape is represented in right- and left-wing discourses. Although I mention prominent international art films like *Devils on the Doorstep* (Guizi lai le, 2000), *Lust, Caution* (Se, jie, 2007), and *The Emperor's Naked Army Marches On* (Yuki yukite shingun, 1987) briefly, my central focus is on the films that reached the widest audience domestically and which had the greatest impact on domestic narratives of remembrance.

In Chapter 2, I discuss what I see as the foundational event of the East Asian WWII memory loop, which is the perceived "foundational narrative" of the war as established at the postwar International Military Tribunal for the Far East or Tokyo Trial (1946–1948). The Tokyo Trial narrative positions the United States as hero, Japan as perpetrator, and China as victim. The popular Chinese film *Tokyo Trial* (2006) challenges both this narrative, portrayed as American "meddling," and the Japanese revisionist narrative, which is presented as the sole Japanese perspective on the war. Japanese films demonstrate two trends. Mainstream films focus on victimhood while concurrently retaining aspects of the foundational narrative; right-wing films appeal to heroism, ignore East Asia, and argue for a more equitable US-Japan relationship. While the victimhood narrative is still dominant, the heroic narrative, appearing at a time when heroic narratives are more prominent in Japan, is significant.

In Chapter 3, I explore the rise of new masculinities in Chinese and Japanese combat films as further evidence of Chinese and Japanese challenges to the so-called Tokyo Trial narrative of the war. These films are the most domestic and least controversial of the memory discourses, as the heroic action film is uncontroversial genre-wise and generates little energy in terms of a transnational memory loop. In combat films, the memory dispute is imagined as the competition of masculinities. The emergence of new Chinese heroes shows an increasingly aggressive challenge to Japanese revisionism through the clash of Chinese and Japanese cultural tropes (*karate* versus *wushu*; Chinese machetes and "drawing sword spirit" versus Japanese *katana*) and a changing relationship with Taiwan, as the *Hanjian* (Chinese collaborators) are subtly rehabilitated. Mainstream Japanese films show a problematic victim-hero and the softening of the upper levels of the military, whereas more "right-wing" films portray the unambiguous veneration of military sacrifice and a desire for normalization.

Chapter 4 discusses the problematic representation of the Nanjing Massacre and so-called comfort women, a euphemism for women who were forced into sexual slavery during the war. More than any other discourse, these films display the most diverse and problematic responses to war memory. They are also the most interconnected and dynamic memory loop, highlighting the uneasy overlapping of Chinese, American, and Japanese memory discourses. Chinese and Japanese films on wartime rape—often via dialogue with equally problematic narratives in America—tend to obscure the trauma of individual women in order to support broader political narratives. Many Chinese films struggle to narrate an "emasculated" past, whereas Japanese right- and left-wing films on Nanjing tend to fight over the national honor or dignity of the Japanese soldier and broader issues of national identity.

Chapter 5 examines Sino-Japanese remembrance outside of American memory discourses. This chapter discusses attempts in Chinese and Japanese popular media to build a narrative beyond the Tokyo Trial. Tracing different stages of reconciliation narratives, it argues that there has been a slow disappearance of reconciliation in China and Japan both outside the narrative (via coproductions) and inside the narrative (via the image of familial reconciliation). Recent narratives even twist the Sino-Japanese family—originally a symbol of national reconciliation—into a vehicle for nationalism.

I conclude that the promotion of nationalism in China and Japan has not been advanced as much by state nationalism as by cultural nationalism, such as debates over the issue of war remembrance in academic journals and popular media such as magazines, television, and manga. These debates are by their nature transnational, a memory loop generating ever more memory discourse through high-speed translation, migration, and communication. These expressions of popular nationalism have emerged in the post–Cold War period in part as a response to shifts in the power relations in the Pacific caused by economic and ideological uncertainty, a rising China, and an ambiguously situated United States. Structurally, the internet has globalized media, generating immediate visibility and new ways of visualizing the past. Moreover, changes in the market system, particularly in China, have changed the way that war films have been produced and sparked new kinds of narratives. As I will maintain, increasingly savvy Chinese audiences are becoming more demanding consumers; their desire for more complexity often produces new kinds of narratives. In Japan, the generational "fading" of memory, rising nationalism due to economic uncertainty, and producers' desire to capitalize on action spectacles has contributed to the rise in politically ambiguous war films.

As with the date August 15, generation after generation of filmmakers and audiences return to the same moment in time in an attempt to define the past. The emergence of the East Asian memory loop circling around the question of remembering WWII suggests an intensification of the post-1989 transformation of Chinese and Japanese domestic identity and a shift in US-China-Japan relations. It also demonstrates the tension of narrating collective pasts in a technologically and financially interconnected era. Gender is central to the representation of (trans)national memory, with male soldiers, judges, political leaders, and patriarchal father figures representing Japanese and Chinese challenges both to each other's geopolitical power and to the perceived American "foundational" narrative of the war. This process continues to intensify through the transnational memory loop, which drives this cycle of transmission, translation, and reassessment.

2
The Tokyo Trial On-Screen

Establishing the Foundational Narrative

History is a continuous retrial.[1]

The postwar trials that followed the conclusion of World War II aimed to establish the foundational narrative of the war. Perceived as an American affair due to the influence of General Douglas MacArthur, the American occupation of Japan, and the army of American lawyers and soldiers involved, the trial is in many ways "ground zero" for memory disputes in East Asia and the first major historical event around which the memory loop circles. The narrative of the International Military Tribunal for the Far East (IMTFE) has been contested since its inception by legal scholars, Japanese officials, and even the justices who presided over the trial itself. The IMTFE also featured some of the earliest testimony about the Nanjing Massacre, a highly contested event of the memory loop. As the first internationally recorded and reported narrative of the war, the ways in which the trial aimed to establish the perpetrators, victims, and heroes of the conflict can be seen as the initial narrative of the war and a starting point for a discussion of contemporary remembrance in China and Japan.

Following the 1945–1946 Nuremberg Trials, the Allied forces began legal proceedings against Japan. A large part of the prosecution at these trials rested on the then relatively new concept of war crimes, mentioned briefly in the St. James Declaration of 1942 and the Moscow Declaration of 1943 and outlined in the Nuremberg Charter (also called the London Charter) of August 1945.[2] The Nuremberg Charter defined three legal categories of wartime crimes: crimes

---

1. Chizuko Ueno, "The Politics of Memory: Nation, Individual and Self," trans. Jordan Sand, *History and Memory* 11, no. 2 (1999): 140.
2. In stark contrast to uncritical acceptance of war crimes in recent popular discourse, the 1961 film *Trial at Nuremberg* revolved around an American judge's struggle with this concept.

against peace, war crimes, and crimes against humanity.[3] In the Japanese postwar tribunals, these conformed to the A (crimes against peace), B (conventional war crimes), and C (crimes against humanity) trials, respectively, though B and C crimes were difficult to differentiate and thus referred to jointly as B/C crimes.[4] The most famous of the war crime trials in Asia was the International Military Tribunal for the Far East, also referred to as the Tokyo Trial, which was held in Tokyo from April 29, 1946, to November 12, 1948. Although another fifty war crimes tribunals were conducted in other cities across Asia, including Nanjing, Singapore, and Manila, in academic and popular discourse only the Japanese trials have remained significant.[5] In large part this is because the Tokyo and Yokohama trials established a master narrative of the war that positioned the Allies as heroes, the invaded nations as victims, and Japan as perpetrator. This historical narrative has been scrutinized and debated since its inception.

Numerous legal scholars and historians have pointed out the inadequacies of the Yokohama and Tokyo trials. At the conclusion of the Tokyo tribunal, Justices Radhabinod Pal of India, Bert Röling of the Netherlands, and Henri Bernard of France all issued dissenting opinions that contested the validity of certain legal aspects of the trials. In the early 1970s, historian Richard Minear referred to the trials as "victors' justice," citing issues such as the participation of biased judges and a lack of attention on the crimes of both the emperor and the Allies.[6] In more recent literature, John R. Pritchard notes the immense legal shortcomings of trials, including hastily drawn-up procedures, unequal distribution of power between the prosecution and the defense, denial of evidence beneficial to the defense, and incompetence among lawyers and judges.[7] Another problem was the way in which justice was doled out, with subjects of colonized nations like Korea

---

3. Crimes against peace were defined as planning or participating in a "war of aggression" or a war that violates international treaties. War crimes were defined as murdering or enslaving civilians or prisoners of war and destroying land and property. Crimes against humanity were defined as genocide, persecution, and enslavement. Theodor Meron, "Reflections on the Prosecution of War Crimes by International Tribunals," *American Journal of International Law* 100, no. 3 (2006): 556.
4. John W. Dower, *Embracing Defeat: Japan in the Wake of World War II* (New York: W. W. Norton, 2000), 443.
5. According to John Dower, "With two exceptions . . . these local trials established no precedents, attracted no great attention, and left no lasting mark on popular memory outside Japan." Dower, *Embracing Defeat*, 443–444.
6. Minear cited American mass bombing and Russian abuse of Japanese POWs. Richard Minear, "'The Trial of Mr. Hyde' and Victors' Justice by Takeyama Michio," *Japan Focus*, August 11, 2006, accessed November 4, 2014, http://www.japanfocus.org/-Takeyama-Michio/2192.
7. John R. Pritchard, "International Military Tribunal for the Far East and Its Contemporary Resonances," *Military Law Review* 149 (1995): 25.

and Taiwan also prosecuted for war crimes.[8] Even the concept of war crimes was highly unorthodox: as Theodor Meron states, "The idea of bringing perpetrators of war crimes before a tribunal was so novel, so contrary to ordinary practice, that it almost never happened."[9]

However, not all academics agree that the trials were totally flawed. Proponents of international tribunals argue that "by superseding national interests, international courts purport to establish a 'true' narrative of events and punish those found 'guilty' of atrocities. The resulting 'judgment' is seen as having the potential to heal ruptured memories, deter future aggressors and guide a restoration of 'normalcy.'"[10] According to Gary Bass, the politics of war crimes tribunals do not merely distill into the issue of "victor's justice," since enemies could just as easily be punished in more draconian ways.[11] For Yuma Totani, the trials displayed numerous successes; she further argues that claims that prosecutors withheld information or that MacArthur protected Emperor Hirohito from prosecution have been grossly exaggerated or misstated.[12] Totani notes that Awaya Kentarō takes the middle ground, suggesting that the trial was neither victor's justice nor a resounding success.[13]

The war again returned to the courts in the early 1990s as survivors and families of victims from across Asia sued the Japanese government for compensation and apology.[14] The testimonies of the "comfort women," or survivors of Japan's wartime system of sexual slavery, opened up a new wave of discussion on the war and on the significance of the legal system in establishing the truth of the past. These trials continued into the next century. In 2000, The Hague convened a meeting to present testimonies from survivors of the comfort woman system. In the early aughts, American politician Michael Honda had resolutions calling on Japan to unequivocally recognize the comfort woman recognized at both the

---

8. Barak Kushner, "Pawns of Empire: Postwar Taiwan, Japan and the Dilemma of War Crimes," *Japanese Studies* 30, no. 1 (2010): 111–133.
9. Meron, "Reflections," 551.
10. James Burnham Sedgwick, "Memory on Trial: Constructing and Contesting the 'Rape of Nanking' at the International Military Tribunal for the Far East, 1946–1948," *Modern Asian Studies* 43, no. 5 (2009): 1230.
11. Gary Bass, *Stay the Hand of Vengeance: The Politics of War Crimes Tribunals* (Princeton, NJ: Princeton University Press, 2000), 8.
12. Yuma Totani, *The Tokyo War Crimes Trial: The Pursuit of Justice in the Wake of World War II* (Cambridge, MA: Harvard University Asia Center, 2008).
13. Totani, *Tokyo War Crimes Trial*, 249.
14. Sarah C. Soh, "Japan's Responsibility toward Comfort Women Survivors," Japan Policy Research Institute Working Paper No. 77 (2001), http://www.jpri.org/publications/workingpapers/wp77.html.

state and national levels.[15] Against this background, several prominent films on the tribunals emerged around 2005, the sixtieth anniversary of the end of World War II.

In this chapter, I will explore how Chinese and Japanese films reimagine the foundational narrative established at the postwar trials. I focus on gender, arguing that trial films represent the conflict over history as a conflict between state masculinities. In these films, male Chinese, Japanese, and American judges, commanders, and soldiers debate who should be labeled a perpetrator, who should be allowed to judge, and who should decide the official narrative of the war. For both China and Japan, the American presence at the trial dominated the proceedings, so I begin with a discussion of the perceived image of America's role in the trial and how perceptions of General MacArthur's masculinity in particular shaped this discourse. I then turn to the Chinese film *Tokyo Trial* (Dongjing shenban, 2006), which was heavily promoted in the Chinese mainland, screened extensively at universities in Beijing and Shanghai, and broke opening weekend box office records at that time.[16] Finally, I discuss two high-profile films on both the Tokyo (A-class war criminals) and Yokohama (B/C-class) trials: *I Want to Be a Shellfish* (Watashi wa kai ni naritai, 2008) and *Best Wishes for Tomorrow* (Ashita e no yuigon, 2007), trial films that are part of a long history of debate over the meaning of war crimes within Japanese discourse. Produced at the height of the mid-aughts East Asia history conflict, these tribunal films deal with the question of who gets to write the official "history," or master narrative of the past, in ways that reveal how each film attempts to redefine the foundational narrative of the Pacific War.

MacArthur's Japan

The postwar Tokyo and Yokohama trials have been perceived in Japan as an American affair, and as such, the image of America is pervasive in the films to be discussed. As John Dower states: "Like Nuremberg, the Tokyo Trial was law, politics, and theater all in one. Unlike Nuremberg, it was 'very much an American performance.' . . . The lights dazzled everyone and often were described as almost blinding—not so much perhaps in the manner of a movie premiere as of a film being made."[17] Part of this perception was also due to race, as the selection

---

15. Kinue Tokudome, "The Japanese Apology on the 'Comfort Women' Cannot Be Considered Official: Interview with Congressman Michael Honda," *Japan Focus*, May 31, 2007, accessed June 10, 2014, http://japanfocus.org/-Michael-Honda/2438.
16. "Dongjing shenpan piaofang chixu zou gaodapo shichang guaiguan," *Renmin Ribao*, September 20, 2006, accessed November 25, 2013, http://culture.people.com.cn/BIG5/22219/4835448.html.
17. Dower, *Embracing Defeat*, 461.

of judges at the IMTFE suggested that it was "fundamentally a white man's tribunal." The three Asian judges (out of eleven) in fact exceeded what the Allies originally intended, as they had planned on inviting only one Chinese judge to preside although the vast majority of victims and occupied nations were Asian.[18] This perceived and real Americanization of history has continued to today as a major accelerator for the memory loop, punctuated in recent East Asia history debates in what Lisa Yoneyama terms the "Americanization of Japanese war crimes." This includes the efforts of American-based interest groups, scholars, and politicians to commemorate and demand justice for the Nanjing Massacre and comfort women in American public discourse.[19] In discussing how filmmakers in China and Japan respond to the narrative established at the postwar trials, we are also discussing how people in the two nations perceive America's larger role in war remembrance from the trials to the present day.

General Douglas MacArthur looms large within this discourse, particularly in America and Japan. After the war, MacArthur was designated the Supreme Commander for the Allied Powers (SCAP), a role that gave him tremendous power over the postwar transformation of Japanese society. For the Americans, the occupation of Japan was an opportunity to "turn the page" on the US-Japan relationship and, in the face of rising fears of communism, establish a military base and alliance in the Pacific. As SCAP, MacArthur oversaw the surrender, occupation, and demilitarization of Japan. He also had a major hand in protecting the emperor from the postwar trials, rewriting the Japanese Constitution, and overseeing postwar censorship of the Japanese media. As such, MacArthur shaped the trials by deciding who could and could not be placed on trial, who could appoint judges, and how the trials were framed in the media at the time. As soldier and commander, he further became a representation of American military and American ideology in ways informed by race and gender.

In the United States, MacArthur has been represented as an eccentric military hero, a skilled commander with a strong penchant for self-aggrandizement. While largely lauded for his performance in the postwar era, his bald desire for

---

18. Dower argues that the Tokyo Trial was essentially an American trial. For instance, "the IMTFE was based on American legal traditions, with the concept of 'conspiracy' itself (the American prosecution's main legal strategy) a strikingly Americanized dimension of the indictment." Dower, *Embracing Defeat*, 462–469.
19. Lisa Yoneyama, "Traveling Memories, Contagious Justice: Americanization of Japanese War Crimes at the End of the Post–Cold War," *Journal of Asian American Studies* 6, no. 1 (2003): 57–93. One might even claim that the United States has been formative in the construction of World War II memories on-screen. Of the top twenty-two World War II films at the box office globally, eighteen are American films. The remaining four—and in particular, the film *Life Is Beautiful* (1998)—received a boost from American distribution. See "International and US Domestic Box Office for World War II Films since 1980" in the Appendix.

political power and removal by President Truman for contradicting the administration during the Korean War led to his military and political career ending in disgrace. Due to these reasons, American films depict him as a somewhat ambiguous hero. MacArthur's approach to the occupation of Japan has been framed as largely benevolent and democratic, an image reminiscent of the "white knight" narratives described by Gina Marchetti in her studies on Hollywood fiction of the 1950s and 1960s.[20] In the film *MacArthur* (1977), for example, Gregory Peck plays the commander as a leader sympathetic to the suffering of Japanese society in the aftermath of war. The film highlights devastated Japanese streets and MacArthur's investment in bringing American ideals like women's rights to Japan. It also portrays MacArthur's measured use of power and his democratic respect for other cultures, as he expresses understanding of the status of the emperor and emphasizes the importance of avoiding overly strict measures with the Japanese in several scenes. At the same time, it critiques MacArthur's desire for fame and power through scenes of him posing for photographs and comparing himself to Julius Caesar. The film also juxtaposes MacArthur's American masculinity against Japanese masculinity in scenes reminiscent of the MacArthur "wedding photo," as Prime Minister Shidehara plaintively begs to renounce war within the constitution, his chin quivering before a stoic MacArthur. With crying/reliance often coded as feminine and stoicism/power as masculine, this scene builds on narratives of colonial masculinities that portray a female Japan reliant on a male United States.

The film *Emperor* (2012) again portrays America as a "white knight" that saves a feminized Japan from its violent hypermasculine imperial past, albeit in ways that incorporate more elements of Japanese discourse on MacArthur. The film follows a narrative similar to James Michener's postwar book, which was later adapted into the film *Sayonara*, wherein a white male American soldier (General Bonner Fellers, played by Matthew Fox) falls in love with a Japanese woman and, by extension, with Japan itself. Throughout the film, General Bonners observes General MacArthur's wily management of his role as Supreme Commander. Notably, MacArthur is played here by Tommy Lee Jones, beloved in Japan for a long-running series of coffee commercials, a comedic and likable image more connected to a grandfather than a military occupier. Jones again draws upon the American image of MacArthur as a studied self-promoter in an early scene where he dons his uniform and corncob pipe as a costume, stepping outside to greet photographers as he exclaims, "Let's show them some good old-fashioned American swagger." MacArthur's studied embodiment of "American swagger" thus frames him as a strategic military commander and savvy promoter well aware of the power of the media.

---

20. Gina Marchetti, *Romance and the "Yellow Peril": Race, Sex, and Discursive Strategies in Hollywood Fiction* (Berkeley: University of California Press, 1993).

A later scene in *Emperor* incorporates Japanese discourse as well, possibly because this was a US-Japan coproduction. In Japan, MacArthur was seen as the "gaijin shogun," a powerful figure who ruled unseen. The title of the film speaks to this perception of power and the ways that MacArthur was seen as the ultimate leader in Japan at the time. He is also well-known for protecting Emperor Hirohito from the war crimes trials, a controversial choice that did not force him to take responsibility for his actions during the war. MacArthur is lectured by his colleagues on proper etiquette before meeting the emperor, including a prohibition on looking Hirohito in the eye or touching him. While the emperor commences their meeting formally in accordance with protocol and tradition, MacArthur immediately meets his gaze and shakes his hand, posing for the famous photograph with his hands on his hips. MacArthur's purposeful embodiment of casual masculinity in both this and other scenes is meant to express both American power and American ideology: MacArthur is so powerful he can disregard rules; he is so secure in his power that he can be informal and relaxed; his casual style is an embodiment of the democratic flattening of hierarchy and class. While this can be seen as offensive posturing, he also assures the emperor of his respect, telling him that "this" (meaning the occupation) "is not about punishment." Through mutual cultural respect centering on this final meeting between the "two emperors" of postwar Japan (Hirohito and MacArthur), American multiculturalism and democracy are depicted as transforming Japanese society for the better. As the protagonist states: "We are the occupying power. But we must be seen as liberators, not conquerors."

Finally, it should also be noted that the trial film itself is essentially an American genre and this in turn affects the filmic representation of trials. Stefan Machura and Stefan Ulbrich suggest that the influence of Hollywood trial films is so pervasive that English legal experts, Spanish anthropologists, and German defendants were shocked to discover the reality that their legal systems operated differently. The authors argue that part of the popularity is because the American adversarial system is far more cinematic than the European inquisitorial system. American legal procedure "is more hospitable to scenes of intense drama, featuring classical confrontations between two antagonists and conflicts between good and evil."[21] Stephen McIntyre also notes, "Studying courtroom drama in Chinese cinema is akin to studying Peking opera in Hollywood cinema: just as Peking opera emerged from the unique milieu of nineteenth century Beijing, the archetypal courtroom drama originated in the United States' notoriously legalistic culture."[22] Indeed, Chinese audiences often compare Chinese courtroom dramas

---

21. Stefan Machura and Stefan Ulbrich, "Law in Film: Globalizing the Hollywood Courtroom Drama," *Journal of Law and Society* 28, no. 1 (2001): 117–132.
22. Stephen McIntyre, "Courtroom Drama with Chinese Characteristics: A Comparative Approach to Legal Process in Chinese Cinema," *East Asia Law Review* 8 (2013): 2.

to the numerous trial films produced in the United States, as evidenced in reviews on the film to be discussed.

Gong'an Retribution

The year 2006 saw the release of the Chinese film *Tokyo Trial* (Dongjing shenban), a blockbuster historical epic produced by mainland companies with the participation of Chinese actors and producers from the People's Republic of China, Hong Kong, and Taiwan. The film was shown at universities and schools across the nation, its frequent broadcasting and blockbuster ticket sales a testament to its widespread political and popular support. The vast majority of Chinese film critics praised the historical and commercial value of *Tokyo Trial*, celebrating its financial success and "deep" historical understanding.[23] Numerous academics also extolled the film's potential for promoting so-called patriotic education (*aiguozhuyi jiaoyu*), a term used to refer to the post-Tiananmen history campaign that focuses on "national humiliation" of the past.[24] Depicting the IMTFE from the perspective of the tribunal's sole Chinese judge, Mei Ru'ao, the film follows Judge Mei's battle to be heard over revisionist Japanese soldiers, Australian chief justice William Webb, and Indian justice Radhabinod Pal. It also features the parallel narrative of Xiao Nan, a Taiwanese reporter who studied in Japan. Through Mei's personification of Chinese justice and Xiao Nan's disappointing reunion with former Japanese "friends," the film resolutely rejects American and Japanese narratives and establishes the Chinese historical perspective.

Tokyo Trial establishes the Chinese position between Japanese and American narratives in an early scene. Upon Judge Mei's arrival in Tokyo, two drunken Japanese soldiers attack his car. The camera isolates Mei, the Japanese soldiers, and Mei's American bodyguard in three separate close-ups, emphasizing the juxtaposition of China, Japan, and the United States. The soldiers belittle Mei, downplay his role at the trial, and demand that he leave the country: "We were beaten by America. Everyone else should get out of Japan!" This Japanese challenge to "get out of Japan" is an order to "get out of the historical debate," an insulting

---

23. Ziju Yang, "Shenshi lishi shijian de hongda xushi: Qian yi dianying *Dongjing Shenpan*," *Dianying Pingjie* 23 (2006): 33–34. Notably, *Tokyo Trial* departs from accepted histories in several ways. For example, Cheng notes that a scene that inspired a huge response among Chinese audiences—the damning testimony of a traumatized character named Wang Defu—was not historically accurate. Daoyi Zong and Lu Chan also argue that that the fraternization of Judge Mei and reporter Xiao Nan would have been considered inappropriate during the trial. See Zhaoqi Cheng, "Cong *Dongjing Shenpan* dao dongjing shenpan," *Shi Lin* 5 (2007): 19–33; Daoyi Zong and Lu Chan, "Dianying *Dongjing Shenpan* de buzu he ying shang," *Xinwen Aihao zhe: Xia banyue* 3 (2007): 4–7.
24. Guibo Zhao and Qian Tan, "*Dongjing Shenpan* de aiguo zhuyi qinggan he sixiang jiaoyu," *Dianying Pingjie* 5 (2008): 42.

reminder that Japan often ignores or rejects the Chinese narrative within World War II discourse. Mei does not respond to the insult and instead cautiously analyzes the situation. Despite Mei's calm motion for the tense guard to lower his gun, the American soldier overreacts, shooting and killing both of the Japanese soldiers. Thus, early on, Mei's masculinity, which is defined by his restraint, sense of justice, and ability to assess the situation, are sharply contrasted with the emotional and aggressive Japanese and the overtly forceful Americans.

Mei's first duty is to punish the Japanese and reject the historical narrative of the Japanese right. As McIntyre suggests, *Tokyo Trial* emerges from the courtroom drama, or *gong'an* narrative, of the judge's resolute performance of justice.[25] Unlike the twists and turns of American courtroom dramas, Chinese *gong'an* narratives focus on the experience of the judge—the term *gong'an* refers to the desk of the judge from which they gaze upon the accused. These narratives assume the defendant is guilty, as "Chinese tradition reflects a highly punitive sense of justice, which is not achieved through presumptions of innocence, guarantees of due process, adversarial litigation, or jury verdicts, but through the swift punishment of criminals at the hands of authoritarian judges."[26] Following the logic of the *gong'an* narrative's assumption of guilt, there is no question of whether or not the Japanese committed war crimes—all male Japanese characters in the film are depicted as violent, belligerent, duplicitous, or mentally unbalanced. As Mei observes from the judge's seat, the defense's elderly Japanese lawyer childishly blusters and raves when confronted by irrefutable testimony from witnesses; Japanese witnesses break under questioning from American prosecutor Joseph B. Keenan; an unhinged defendant (Ōkawa Shūmei, based on a true story) strikes Tōjō Hideki on the back of the head. Mei carefully catalogs the crimes of these Japanese soldiers throughout, then forcefully but stoically delivers the final, inexorable judgment of "guilty" at the end. This is not only a judgment of actual offenses committed during the war but also a judgment of the perceived contemporary Japanese narrative of the war. Through these proceedings and the final guilty verdict, Mei declares their narrative invalid.

Trial also significantly furthers the goals of the patriotic education campaign by expanding it to include Hong Kong and Taiwan. Part of this occurs through an appeal to "Chineseness" by including Chinese actors from Hong Kong, Taiwan, and Mainland China. Fang Qingqing and Yan Jun argue that the film promotes collective national identity by appealing to a collective sense of *minzu* (national and ethnic identity—the Chinese racial majority is called the *Han minzu*, or Han ethnicity).[27] Both Chinese and central "Japanese" characters are played

---

25. McIntyre, "Courtroom Drama," 1–2.
26. McIntyre, "Courtroom Drama," 2.
27. Qingqing Fang and Jun Yan, "*Dongjing Shenpan* jiexi," *Dianying Pingjie* 17 (2007): 41–42.

by famous Chinese actors from Hong Kong (Damian Lau and Eric Tsang) and Taiwan (Ken Zhu and Kelly Lin). The trial is thus performed by a united Chinese diaspora reenacting collective past traumas together. Furthermore, the film reincorporates the Kuomintang (KMT) into the main Chinese narrative. Much of the evidence compiled at the trial was obtained through the cooperation of the American forces and the Chinese Nationalist government. As such, the trial was mostly suppressed in the CCP narrative until recently, as the KMT has been reimagined as an ally, reflecting Chinese overtures to Taiwan. In this way, the film also constructs a shared narrative of the war and a way for the Chinese mainland to strengthen ideological ties with Hong Kong and Taiwan.

In addition, Mei fights for a larger voice in the global debate on history by challenging the other judges at the trial. He disagrees with the seating arrangement suggested by the Western members of the tribunal, a setup that would place Western nations in the center. He insistently requests a middle seat from the chairman of the trial, William Webb, an Australian who is implied to be American in the film:[28] "The whole world's photographers and reporters are now out there in the courtroom. They're going to take photos and write news reports on this seating arrangement. When these photos and reports reach China, do you know what is going to happen? The entire Chinese people will reproach me for my cowardice and incompetence. If I agreed to this arrangement, I would be insulting my country. I'd be insulting all my countrymen's suffering, sacrifice, and perseverance in resisting Japanese aggression. . . . Sir William, can you understand?"

Mei's issue is the photograph itself, the moment in which "who gets to judge" is defined forever in the annals of history. Representing China at the center of that photograph is a demand to be placed centrally in the global master narrative. When calm negotiation does not work, Judge Webb threatens Mei by arguing that such a stance will irreparably harm the relationship between China and the United States. The diminutive but proud Mei stands firm to the taller Webb's "American" bullying. He rationally points out the cowardice and hypocrisy of the Allies, criticizes England's actions during the war, and powerfully concludes, "In this war against Japanese aggression, China has suffered the most, for the longest, and hardest!" His perseverance pays off. In an image that recalls official photographs of the judges at the IMTFE, Judge Mei resolutely takes a seat at the center and represents his country framed against a background of international flags, flanked on both sides by the larger Western judges. While short and outnumbered by the bullying Allies—a height difference he proudly acknowledges

---

28. Webb is played by US actor Dan Ziskie with an American accent; in the film Webb also threatens Mei by suggesting that the United States will not be happy with the seating arrangement. To those viewers unfamiliar with history, it would appear that Webb is American.

and uses to his advantage in an early meeting with the other judges—Mei stands up to American pressure and declares the Chinese position at the center of war remembrance. This image of a "small China" standing up to bullying foreign powers ties into the powerful "national humiliation" narrative so prominent today.[29]

Even as American characters are depicted as aggressive, the film also appeals to American support for the Chinese narrative. After the first major conflict between the Mei and the Americans, Judge Webb warmly congratulates Judge Mei, saying, "Dr. Mei, you win. Your country should be proud to have a fighter like you." Although this affirmation could be read as a desire to gloat over "beating America," its warmth and the happiness with which Judge Mei receives the acknowledgment suggests Chinese desire for American recognition and validation. American men are also enlisted in the emasculation of the Japanese, with the American prosecutor towering over the cowering Japanese lawyer in an image reminiscent of the MacArthur/Hirohito photograph. This is juxtaposed with the earlier stand of the proud but diminutive Mei, whose size is articulated as a sign of strength and not emasculation. Finally, Westerners importantly both establish historical truth and deliver the final judgment. Western observers give the testimony proving the Nanjing Massacre; the American lawyer gives the final impassioned closing argument. This suggests that while the film rejects American hegemonic masculinity, it also concurrently desires American confirmation of the Chinese narrative.

Part of the reason for this depiction of the United States is due to the complex US-China relationship. Although China and America were allies who worked together both during the war and at the trials, there is tension within this relationship.[30] American and Chinese concerns are somewhat aligned in the recent Nanjing debate, yet American discourse on Nanjing also concurrently feminizes China as a passive mass of faceless victims. This is in sharp contrast to how Americans are typically depicted within these same narratives, which is as heroic Western saviors of the Nanjing Safety Zone and righteous wielders of justice at the Tokyo Trial. Chinese narratives, meanwhile, tend to emphasize heroics over victimization. According to Rana Mitter, of late the name Antifacist War is beginning to replace War of Resistance against Japan, the common Chinese term for World War II, "as writers seek to portray Chinese resistance not simply as a solo act of opposition to Japan, but rather as part of an act of collective

---

29. In reality, the Chinese judge and prosecution faced numerous embarrassments and setbacks during the trial (which they felt had been monopolized by the Americans). Sheng Zhao, "Dongjing fating shang de Zhongguo faguan yu jiancha guanmen: Jian lun dongjing shenpan de yiliu wenti," *Daqing Shifan Xueyuan Xuebao* 29, no. 2 (2009): 139–143.
30. This was complicated by the Chinese civil war fought between the Kuomintang and the CCP.

resistance to the Axis powers."[31] In Mitter's reading, "The implication is clear: at an earlier time when its contribution was needed, China delivered, and it should now be trusted as it seeks, once again, to enter international society playing a wider role."[32] In films like *Tokyo Trial*, there is a demand for wider global—and particularly American—recognition of Chinese heroics during the war.

Chinese audiences had diverse reactions to the film. Although it was widely promoted by the government and played in schools, on the Chinese film review site Douban the film has an average rating of 7.3/10 with 54,613 reviews—the majority (42 percent) are four stars, followed by three stars (35.9 percent)—a somewhat mixed result. The top-voted commentary by user Jiang Shengzou criticizes the lack of historical depth and the highly political nature of the film. Jiang notes that the film has only emerged lately because of the party's changing attitude toward the KMT, and also brings up the film's lack of discussion of the Japanese emperor and of Unit 731, a covert biological and chemical warfare research unit run by the Imperial Japanese Army, questioning whether these were ignored to avoid problematizing contemporary Sino-American relations.[33] Such analysis illustrates the awareness Chinese audiences have of the US-Japan relationship, as well as a savvy critique of internal party politics that suppressed the trial from Chinese narratives until after the early aughts. The second-highest-rated review, by user Wang Xinxi, lambastes the film on both narrative and historical fronts.[34] Citing American films, they note that *Trial* lacks the tension of Hollywood courtroom dramas; they also criticize the film for its historical inaccuracies and even compare the film unfavorably to the 1983 Japanese NHK drama *Tokyo Trial* (Tokyo saiban) as being similarly emotional and superficial. In sum, Chinese audiences, while generally receptive to critiques levied at the Japanese, overall desired a more sophisticated film in terms of both historical realism and narrative tension.

Chinese trial films present a contemporary challenge of the perceived Japanese foundational narrative, which is frequently represented as a unified revisionist narrative. Meanwhile, the American narrative is represented as both allied with and allied against Chinese memory. In one sense, there is the impression that Americans/Westerners are important witnesses in establishing the truth of the war. In another sense, there is the feeling that American power within this memory discourse should be challenged. This is both a challenge to the American narrative and a challenge to the United States itself, a show of Chinese power and legitimacy that ties into the dominant humiliation narrative.

---

31. Rana Mitter, *Forgotten Ally: China's World War II, 1937–1945* (New York: Houghton Mifflin Harcourt, 2013), 375.
32. Mitter, *Forgotten Ally*, 375.
33. Shenzou Jiang, September 15, 2009 (12:07 p.m.), review of *Tokyo Trial*, Douban, April 25, 2015, http://movie.douban.com/review/1073963/.
34. Xinxi Wang, October 25, 2007 (5:54 p.m.), review of *Tokyo Trial*, Douban, April 25, 2015, http://movie.douban.com/review/1228549/.

The film also suggests a desire to establish the Chinese narrative as the official global narrative of the memory loop. Indeed, many Chinese scholars have discussed the potential globalization of the Chinese national message in this film.[35] For instance, Fang and Yan argue that Mei is not only a symbol of national sentiment concerning the war but also a humanistic spokesman for the traumatic experience of war itself.[36] *Tokyo Trial* thus imagines a united Chinese diaspora that challenges the Japanese and American narratives of World War II *on a global stage*. Disputing Western domination of the global narrative and the revisionist Japanese narrative, it places Judge Mei at the center of the seating arrangement and declares his position at the center of the memory debate.

"A Continuous Retrial"

While Chinese films have only recently turned to the subject of the trials, since the 1950s the postwar tribunals have inspired a variety of responses in Japanese academic and popular culture. As Madoka Futamura argues, "The Japanese view of the Tokyo Trial consists of a complex mixture of lack of interest, cynicism, sense of 'collective guilt' or 'collective humiliation' and frustration."[37] During the trials, the Japanese side questioned the lack of legal precedent, the hypocrisy of former ally Russia judging Japanese war crimes, issues with translation, and the contradiction of being defined as the sole perpetrator of war crimes despite American use of fire and atomic bombs on Japanese civilians.[38] This debate continued long into the postwar period, spurred onwards by war-related trials of the 1990s and aggregating layers of subsequent history debates. Throughout the postwar period, the postwar tribunals have raised issues of how to address wartime responsibility and questions over who gets to define guilt and innocence within the context of total war.

Generally speaking, there have been three ways that the postwar trials have been described in postwar Japanese discourse among those who dispute their validity: as victor's justice (*shōsha no sabaki*), as the Tokyo Trial view of history (*Tokyo saiban shikan*), and as the masochistic view of history (*jigyaku shikan*). Before 1982, critics used the phrase "victor's justice" or "revenge trial" to argue that the trials were hypocritical punishment from the war's winners. Justice Pal's

---

35. Fu Ma, "Dianying dongjing shenpan de aiguozhuyi sixiang," *Mangzhong* 17 (2012): 156, and Zhao and Tan, *"Dongjing Shenpan."*
36. Fang and Yan, *"Dongjing Shenpan* jiexi," 41–42.
37. Madoka Futamura, *War Crimes Tribunals and Transitional Justice: The Tokyo Trial and the Nuremburg Legacy* (New York: Routledge, 2007), 145
38. See Dower, *Embracing Defeat*, 443–484, and Timothy P. Maga, *Judgment at Tokyo: The Japanese War Crimes Trials* (Lexington: University Press of Kentucky, 2001). For more on the trial in Japanese discourse, see Sandra Wilson, "After the Trials: Class B and C Japanese War Criminals and the Post-war World," *Japanese Studies* 31, no. 2 (2011): 141–149.

rejection of the trials was foundational to this interpretation, which was popularized among the right in the 1960s and 1970s. The expression "Tokyo Trial view of history" entered Japanese public consciousness during the first major textbook dispute in 1982, again emphasizing the constructed nature of the history established at the trials. 1980s interest in the trials was also generated by the declassification of previously unavailable trial records, which allowed the postwar generation of researchers to reassess the significance and meaning of the IMTFE. In the 1990s, there was yet another discursive shift as the trials were described as a "masochistic view of history" as a response to a 1991 trial in which former comfort women filed a lawsuit against the Japanese government. This view of the trials suggests that remembering Japan as perpetrator is harmful to the formation of Japanese national identity.[39]

One of the most comprehensive films on the IMTFE is Kobayashi Masaki's four-and-a-half-hour-long documentary, *The Tokyo Trial* (Tōkyō saiban, 1983), which is constructed almost entirely from edited American military recordings of the trial. Kobayashi's film, while described by a *New York Times* review at the time as "historically empty," both critiques the trial from the Japanese perspective and, to a much lesser extent, documents and bears witness to Japanese wartime violence.[40] Kobayashi's exhaustive film is largely chronological, following the trials from the surrender through the selection of justices, the trial itself, and final sentencing and executions. Like many Japanese war films, the documentary devotes more time to emphasizing Japanese victimhood and suffering than the suffering inflicted on other nations. Several scenes depict starving Japanese soldiers, crashing kamikaze planes, and the bombing of Hiroshima and Nagasaki. The trial promotes the victor's justice narrative by emphasizing the shortcomings of the trial, including translation issues, sleepy justices, and the omnipresent influence of SCAP, with the narrator noting that, upon surrender, "Japan became MacArthur's empire."

Yet unlike many Japanese war films, Kobayashi's documentary also devotes a section to the Nanjing Massacre, which is usually ignored or denied. The film features a long segment of American missionary John Magee's testimony as well as sympathetic scenes of wartime Nanjing projected against a backdrop of sad music. Kobayashi, a pacifist who experienced the war as a soldier and prisoner of war, also famously made the anti-war trilogy *The Human Condition* (1959–1961), one of the few Japanese films to document Japanese brutality toward Chinese people

---

39. See Totani, *Tokyo War Crimes Trial*, 218; Aiko Utsumi, Komori Yōichi, and Narita Ryūichi, "Tokyo saiban ga tsukutta sengonihon," *Gendai Shisō* 35, no. 10 (2007): 44–70; Soh, "Japan's Responsibility toward Comfort Women Survivors."
40. Drew Middleton, "Film: *The Tokyo Trial*," *New York Times*, September 25, 1985, accessed June 12, 2022, https://www.nytimes.com/1985/09/25/movies/film-the-tokyo-trial.html.

during the war. While highly critical of the American dominance of the trials and the uneven application of "justice," his experiences in northeast China during the war potentially shaped his perspective on the violence perpetrated in Nanjing.

The most significant of the fictional trial films, *I Want to Be a Shellfish*, has been remade a staggering five times for film and television (in 1958, 1959, 1994, 2007, and 2008).[41] Based on a novel by Tetsutarō Katō, the 2008 version focuses on Shimizu Toyomatsu, a barber living in a small Japanese town.[42] Drafted by the Imperial Army, Shimizu is a low-level soldier who is forced to bayonet an American soldier to death during wartime. After the war, he is tried in the Yokohama B/C-class war crime trials and sentenced to death. Although his release seems imminent, Shimizu's execution is ultimately carried out. As he walks to the gallows, he laments the cruelty of humanity and prays to be reincarnated as a shellfish in his next life. The film represents one of the more complex depictions of Japanese guilt in these trial films, with Shimizu embodying the postwar narrative of a victimized Japan.

Previous literature on *Shellfish* and similar films has focused on the question of how they deal with Japanese guilt.[43] Sandra Wilson argues that trial films of the 1950s established widespread sympathy among regular Japanese for lower-ranking soldiers.[44] She notes that an essay by Tetsutarō Katō: "create[d] a sort of rough equivalence between Japanese war crimes, which are admitted and regretted, and allegedly cruel Allied treatment of war crimes suspects, which by contrast had not been acknowledged by those responsible. By the end of this essay, everybody—or nobody—is guilty."[45]

Similarly, Kōji Toba compares the film to *The Thick-Walled Room* (produced 1953, released 1956) to explore why *Shellfish* became prominent as *Room* faded into obscurity.[46] *Room* was suppressed when it was first made in October 1953, a

---

41. I saw the Japanese DVD version offered for rental by Universal.
42. Tetsutarō Katō, *Watakushi wa kai ni naritai: Aru BC-kyū senpan no sakebi* (Tokyo: Shunjusha, 1995).
43. Shin Hakyon considers the themes of responsibility and reconciliation by comparing the 1959 and 2008 versions of *Shellfish*, ultimately concluding that while the 1959 version focuses on the theme of compassion, the 2008 version ignores other Asian countries and does not adequately consider Japanese wartime responsibility. Standish views *Shellfish* as a tale of victimization that deploys the "tragic hero" myth to release Japanese society from wartime guilt. Hakyon Shin, "Taishū bunka kara miru BC kyūsenpan saiban to 'sekinin,'" *Nihon Bungakubukai Hōkoku* 4 (2010): 187–191; Isolde Standish, *Myth and Masculinity in the Japanese Cinema: Towards a Political Reading of the Tragic Hero* (London: Routledge, 2000),
44. She prefers the translation *I Want to Be a Limpet*.
45. Sandra Wilson, "War, Soldier and Nation in 1950s Japan," *International Journal of Asian Studies* 5, no. 2 (2008): 201.
46. Kōji Toba, "Eizō no sugamo purizun: Kabe atsuki heya to watashi wa kai ni naritai," *Gendai Shisō* 35, no. 10 (2007): 124–137.

time when war criminals were still a controversial subject and American political pressure still held sway, whereas *Shellfish* was broadcast on television after all the prisoners from Sugamo were released on May 30, 1958.[47] Thus emerging at a time when tension over the image of the prisoners was abating, *Shellfish* became immensely popular. Through the narrative of its "negative hero'" (*fu no hīrō*), or heroic victim, it emphasizes the hero's innocence and suffering, thereby releasing Japanese viewers from a sense of responsibility.[48]

Certainly, the 2008 version avoids discussing the issue of responsibility by presenting Shimizu as a victim. A hardworking family man living in an idealized microcosm of the Japanese hometown, Shimizu is a wronged Everyman who symbolizes Japanese innocence and postwar antimilitarism. Walking with a limp, his physical disability is a symbol of his inherent nonthreatening nature. This limp is also a notable new addition, as in the other four versions Shimizu does not display this physical characteristic. Played by SMAP singer Nakai Masahiro, in his late thirties but still associated with boy bands, Shimizu appears youthful and unthreatening.[49] The camera lingers on the shaving of Nakai's head as he is unwillingly transformed into a soldier. This scene suggests a pacifist message, the loss of both Shimizu's innocence and his hair, and also firmly establishes Shimizu's victimhood in keeping with the postwar narrative of a peaceful, nonviolent Japan. Further, Nakai's star image as a member of a boy band is an integral component of the new version's representation. As Gabriella Lukács describes in her study of fellow SMAP member and idol Kimura Takuya, part of the drama of the haircut scene occurs through the "strategic collapsing of the *tarento*'s public and private personas."[50] Shimizu's haircut—his forced transformation into a soldier—is a striking experience for the viewer familiar with Nakai's stylish boy band image. His "soft" image as an idol serves to further moderate the image of the soldier Everyman, a softening that is reproduced in Nakai's reappearances in magazines and variety shows. Operating thus on both the narrative and the metanarrative level, the film emphasizes Shimizu's pacifism and victimhood through Nakai's transformation.

Perhaps most significantly, the 2008 version demonstrates a subtle attempt to resuscitate the image of the Japanese military. The 1950s versions are highly critical

---

47. Release of prisoners was attained through a complex negotiation process in which the Japanese government had to obtain the approval of the countries in which the soldiers had been convicted. This was in accordance with the San Francisco Peace Treaty and the Taipei Treaty. Wilson, "After the Trials," 144.
48. Toba, "Eizō no sugamo purizun."
49. Other popular recent war films such as *Yamato* (Otokatachi no yamato, 2005) and *Eternal Zero* (Eien no zero, 2013) similarly show a preference for a "feminized" and "pacifist" military composed of idols and reluctant boy soldiers.
50. Gabriella Lukács, *Scripted Affects, Branded Selves: Television, Subjectivity, and Capitalism in 1990s Japan* (Durham, NC: Duke University Press, 2010), 140.

of *both* the Japanese military and the American occupiers, reflecting the betrayal many lower-level soldiers felt during the B/C trials. While the 1958 and 1959 versions reject militarism by depicting the Japanese leadership as cold and uncaring, the 2008 version oscillates between blaming and justifying the actions of the military leadership. On the one hand, Shimizu is beaten by a superior and forced to murder an American soldier; on the other hand, the military leaders attempt to honorably take the blame. In the 1959 version, when Shimizu tells the American judges that he executed a pilot according to the order of the emperor, his compatriots stare back at him apathetically in a scene that could be read as depicting either criticism or nihilism. In the 2008 version, the other Japanese soldiers straighten up in deference at the mention of "his majesty the emperor" (*tennō heika*). Finally, the 1959 Yano emphatically rejects militarism by stating that a democratic army is not possible. This dialogue is completely excised from the 2008 film.[51]

In addition, the murder of the American pilot is justified more forcefully in the 2008 version by shifting the focus to the compassion of the military leadership. The 1959 version criticizes both American bombing and the actions of the Japanese military. First, the film shows stock footage of Japanese cities on fire, followed by a scene with foreboding military leaders discussing the American advance. Finally, there is a much longer scene in which Shimizu is bullied by his superior, followed by the execution scene. The 2008 version downplays the negative imagery of the military by focusing on their emotional response to the bombings and emphasizing the victimization of the Japanese more dramatically. The dry stock footage is replaced by a burning Tokyo juxtaposed with the compassionate gaze of a group of watching soldiers. The next shot focuses on the commander, whose eyes fill with tears at the sight of the burning city. This image is followed by dawn the next morning and a child's body being placed on a mountain of smoking corpses. The execution scene follows. The 2008 version thus downplays the original intention of *Shellfish* by humanizing the military leaders at the top and justifying the later murder of the American pilot. Although Shimizu's death in the 1950s versions was meant to indict both the Americans and the upper echelons of the Japanese military, in this film only the American judges are to blame. Hashimoto Shinobu, the original screenwriter of *Shellfish*, argues that he revised the drama to emphasize Yano, the general, in order to "make another layer of drama."[52] However, the revision comes across not as an artistic choice but as a weakening of the original political critique and a softening of the image of the military.

Like all versions of the film, *Shellfish* attempts to question the American "Tokyo Trial view of history." Because of its focus on the victor's justice at the

---

51. Shin, "Taishū bunka," 190.
52. Katō Masato and Hashimoto Shinobu, "Eiga watashi ha kai ni naritai rimeiku ni atatte no shinario kaitei," *Shinario* 65, no. 1 (2009): 18–27.

trial, the film attempts to downplay or ignore Americans as victims or enemy combatants. In the climactic murder scene the two American pilots are unconscious and hidden in shadows, faces bandaged and turned downward. There is no reverse shot to Shimizu's charge, and when he stabs forward the camera cuts to black. Such imagery obfuscates the victims of Japanese wartime violence, placing Shimizu's violent action in isolation. Through this framing device, the scene also erases evidence of the crime and shifts victimhood to Shimizu. Moreover, in bombing sequences only the bombs and the suffering of the Japanese are shown, with the American planes and pilots either shrouded in fog or off-screen. It is only at the Yokohama trial that the American subject first appears clearly. The three male judges are filmed by a camera placed below, their intimidating and distant forms sitting above and flanked by American flags. A Japanese American and a blond female American secretary sit below, secondary figures who also gaze at Shimizu accusingly. Yet, although the white, male American victors hold power over the Japanese losers, the film also emphasizes that they do not understand Japanese language or culture, thereby suggesting that the trial itself is unjust. The Japanese American translator speaks poorly worded, heavily accented Japanese that Shimizu finds difficult to understand; the lawyers and judges laugh when Shimizu announces that "his majesty the emperor" ordered the war; most of the soldier guards are cruel and forceful. Dismissive and ignorant, these Americans are "winners" by virtue of power only.

At the same time, the film also aches for American understanding and protection. Even though the majority of the male judges, prosecutors, and guards sneer at Japanese culture, the film also emphasizes the affective ties of the US-Japan bond. When Shimizu is led to his death, roughly pushed forward by the rest of the unfeeling American guards, he is caught by a large American soldier. Moved by his charge's plight, the soldier embraces the terrified Shimizu, his chin quivering emotionally as Shimizu is pushed forward to his unhappy fate. This shot of a large American man holding the smaller Shimizu echoes the male US/female Japan narrative of the postwar period (in particular, the image of General MacArthur towering over the diminutive Emperor Hirohito) and also unites the two characters through American compassion for Japanese suffering. This is evocative of both the power of American hegemony and the Japanese desire for American support of their wartime narrative and position in the Pacific.

While *Shellfish* did respectably at the Japanese box office (see Table 1.3), audience reactions tended to be either extraordinarily positive or negative. On the Japanese website Yahoo! Japan, the film has a rating of 3.48/5. The top-rated review (548 votes) gives the film five stars, with user Ted applauding its acting and its humanistic qualities, and particularly its focus on family.[53] The

---

53. Ted, November 19, 2008 (10:08 p.m.), review of *I Want to Be a Shellfish*, Yahoo! Japan, April 25, 2015, http://movies.yahoo.co.jp/movie/私は貝になりたい/327994/review/.

second-highest- and third-highest-rated reviews praise the performance of boyband star Nakai Masahiro for transcending his SMAP persona. The fact that these reviews are highly rated is more likely a testament to the power of Nakai's fans than to historical concern. The top-rated negative review by user Mai (264 votes) gives the film one star, criticizes the corporate packaging of films, and exclaims that Japanese movies emphasize marketing over cinematic excellence.[54] The second-highest-rated critical review notes that the filmmakers scoured Japan to find the most beautiful scenery for the *furusato* scenes—a choice that they argue has absolutely nothing to do with the original anti-war intent of the work and which misses the point entirely. They also criticize the choice of an idol—"Nakai is Nakai. Even if you shave him, he is still Nakai. Even if you put him in an old costume, he is still Nakai."[55] Such responses overall reveal that audience attention is more devoted to star image and narrative quality over historical legitimacy.

The second major Japanese trial film of the early aughts, *Best Wishes for Tomorrow* (Ashita e no yuigon, 2007), similarly approaches the trials from the perspective of the Japanese defendants. Produced by a less prominent studio and starring lesser-known actors, the film came in at number 82 to *Shellfish*'s number 19 at the Japanese box office in 2008.[56] *Best Wishes* centers on the trial of Lieutenant General Okada Tasuku and the Tokai army's execution of eleven American pilots who participated in the bombing of Nagoya. Departing from the mainstream critical or ambiguous depictions of imperial Japanese leadership, *Best Wishes* is a straightforward indictment of American hegemony and an idealization of Japanese nationalism. This rose-colored view of Japanese history extends to the lighting. Compared with the dark and dour cinematography of the other two trial films, *Best Wishes* is relatively brightly lit, matching Okada's optimistic portrayal. Throughout, the film represents the accused Okada as neither perpetrator nor victim: he is a national hero.

Best Wishes must be analyzed not only in contrast to the more mainstream narrative of *Shellfish* but also in relation to *Pride* (Puraido: Unmei no toki, 1998), an earlier film with a similarly idealized hero figure.[57] *Pride* was extremely controversial, inspiring intensive domestic protests and divided critical responses. Emerging in the midst of a renewed international gaze on Japanese history (after the 1991 comfort women trials, the 1997 release of Iris Chang's best-selling book *The Rape of Nanking*, and the 1998 demand for an apology from Chinese leader

---

54. Mai, November 21, 2008 (1:15 p.m.), review of *I Want to Be a Shellfish*, Yahoo! Japan, April 25, 2015, http://movies.yahoo.co.jp/movie/私は貝になりたい/327994/review/.
55. Lem, November 13, 2008 (10:34 p.m.), review of *I Want to Be a Shellfish*, Yahoo! Japan, April 25, 2015, http://movies.yahoo.co.jp/movie/私は貝になりたい/327994/review/.
56. "Japan Yearly Box Office: 2008," *Box Office Mojo*, accessed December 1, 2013, http://http://boxofficemojo.com/intl/japan/yearly/?yr=2008&p=.htm.
57. I saw the Toei rental DVD version offered at Tsutaya.

Jiang Zemin), the film is a mixture of prewar Greater East Asia Co-Prosperity Sphere" justification and 1990s "masochistic history" arguments.[58] Reimagining the role of Tōjō Hideki, *Pride* lionizes him by focusing on his family's postwar suffering and criticizing American hypocrisy. Actor Tsugawa Masahiko, who played Tōjō, appeared with medals and a military uniform to promote the film.[59] He stated: "I am so sad that Japanese people are not allowed to have the pride of their national anthem and flag. War and murder are different. At least in terms of international law, war is legal. There is a difference between Auschwitz, which was ordered by the state, and Nanjing. It is America which dropped the atomic bomb, it is the United States who are the same as Nazis. I want to declare the Tokyo Trial invalid."[60]

Building on a prewar fiction that argued the Japanese nation could stand up to Western power by benevolently leading Asia through a co-prosperity sphere, *Pride* uses images of race and colonialism to displace the narrative of Japanese guilt. It juxtaposes the Indian independence movement and the aggression of British soldiers in India with the entry of the American forces and the beginning of the occupation, using Indian nationalist Subhas Chandra Bose and Japanese defendant Tōjō as its two heroes.

In an early scene, a weakened Tōjō—who has just attempted suicide—is arrested by screaming white American guards in postwar Tokyo; the next shot depicts screaming English soldiers harassing Indian people on a train in 1941 as an Indian narrator mentions that in that year, Japan declared war against both England and the United States. Other scenes similarly link Indian and Japanese experiences, such as a scene in which Indian and Japanese characters bond over August 15—the end of the war and the date of Indian independence. Through such manipulation of time and context, the film implies that the postwar American occupation of Japan and prewar British imperialism in India are similar, with Japan, like India, a victim of Western colonialism. By making this comparison, *Pride* reframes Japanese imperialism as Asian anti-imperialism, a narrative in line with the wartime ideology of the Greater East Asia Co-Prosperity Sphere (Daitōa Kyōeiken). Similar to the Japanese war film *Merdeka 17805* (Murudeka 17805, 2001), which highlights Japanese support of the Indonesian National Revolution, *Pride* compares imperial Japan to colonized nations with

---

58. This is an argument that emerged in the 1990s, particularly among the Atarashii Kyōkasho wo Tsukuru-kai, revisionist movement that aims to "save" Japanese history by fostering a more positive, patriotic view of history. See Marilyn Ivy, "Revenge and Recapitation in Recessionary Japan," *South Atlantic Quarterly* 99, no. 4 (2000): 819–840, and Tessa Morris-Suzuki and Peter Rimmer, "Virtual Memories: Japanese History Debates in Manga and Cyberspace," *Asian Studies Review* 26, no. 2 (2002): 147–164.
59. Tsugawa is a well-known supporter of nationalist causes in Japan.
60. Yoshiyuki Nagaoka, "Eiga *Puraido, Nankin 1937* meguru gekiron no yukue: Rekishi minaoshi ronsō no shin kyokumen ka," *Tsukuru* 28, no. 7 (1998): 94–101.

no reference to Japanese expansionism or its victims. And although Justice Pal's critiques of the trial are movingly read in the film, his critiques of Japanese atrocities committed during the war are excised. In this way, the film appeals to colonial Japan's justification for invading its neighboring nations, ignores the racism and violence of imperial Japanese militarism, and displays an alarming continuity of thought hearkening back to the nationalism of prewar Japan.

Best Wishes emerges from a similar framework that emphasizes American war crimes and the idealized masculinity of its main character.[61] Like *Pride*, the film romanticizes General Okada by depicting him as an icon of nativist notions of Japanese masculinity. Okada is dignified and in control of his emotions. He displays loyalty and leadership toward his men by taking responsibility for the war, singing nostalgic songs about the Japanese *furusato* (hometown), practicing *shiatsu* on injured subordinates, and leading Buddhist prayers. Okada is also represented as an exemplary patriarchal figure often supported at court by his doting wife and respectful children. Even before his execution, Okada marches forward proud and unafraid, pausing only to appreciate the beauty of the moon. To the moment of death, Okada is an icon of Japanese masculinity and nationalism, a perfect soldier who stoically accepts his fate on behalf of his nation. Through these idealized notions of Japaneseness and masculinity, Okada resuscitates the Japanese military leadership and stands up to American power.

Okada's main mission is to expose the hypocrisy of the American "victor's justice," turning the "Japan as perpetrator" narrative on its head. The narrator (whose booming deep voice is also coded as "manly") announces that Okada views the trial as a "legal battle" where his purpose would be to prove America's criminality in the indiscriminate bombing of Japan. Okada asks, "Why should the losing side be held solely responsible for crimes committed?" While Shindō Junko argues that the film represents crimes on both sides—the Japanese killing of prisoners of war and indiscriminate American bombing—it focuses more on the latter.[62] The opening montage presents numerous images of violence across the world that whittle down to those of Japanese suffering. Indiscriminate bombing as a global phenomenon is forgotten, submerged in a narrative of Japanese victimhood. Okada's lawyer argues that the American pilots, as indiscriminate bombers, violated the Geneva Conventions and could not be defined as prisoners of war. This is juxtaposed with the actions of Japanese military leaders who, Okada argues, conscientiously focused on military targets like Pearl Harbor. In *Best Wishes*, Okada rehabilitates the Japanese military leadership by arguing that the Americans themselves were guilty of war crimes. Numerous reviewers were enthusiastic about the film's challenge of accepted narratives, impressed that

---

61. I saw the Kadokawa Entertainment DVD.
62. Junko Shindō, "Sakuhin-hyō: Kantō tokushū ashita e no yuigon," *Kinema Junpō* 1502 (2008): 38–43.

"even when Japan was in a humiliating stage, there was a person who refused to bend to this humiliation."[63]

Yet, like *Tokyo Trial* and *I Want to Be a Shellfish*, *Best Wishes* also appeals to American support for this historical narrative. Although the film ignores Asian victims of imperial Japanese violence, Japanese characters partly recognize and apologize for American victimhood. One Japanese soldier weeps with guilt while describing the execution of an American soldier who "cried like a baby." Moreover, much of the film is in English, with Okada's lawyer a friendly American who even introduces his family to the affable Okada. The antagonistic prosecuting attorney even smiles with pleasure at being bid a good morning by an amiable Okada. The general is even allowed to proudly show his grandchild to the courtroom, his position as (national) patriarch respected by the American judges. Finally, when the judgment is announced, Americans in the court, regardless of affiliation, are saddened by the guilty verdict. Thus, the US-Japan relationship is reaffirmed, all the Americans in the film won over by Okada's patriarchal dignity. Importantly, Okada does not beg for their respect; rather, they give it to him freely as equals. His claim to history is, like Judge Mei's, equal to that of the Americans.

Many Japanese commentators and scholars praised the US-Japan relationship in the film. In the right-wing journal *Seiron*, critics Makino Hiromichi and Hongō Yoshinori emphasize that the films ask for respect and equality by appealing to a sense of "Japaneseness." Similarly, Hongō argues that Okada's identity is based on his personification of *bushidō* (a code of military behavior and masculinity often associated with Japanese nationalism). He continues, "In the relationship with the States, we have this relationship—he is him, I am me . . . the problem is that contemporary Japan doesn't have this—I am me, he is him—point of view."[64] Makino responds, "Was the tragedy of that war that Japan was completely wrong? No. Of course the United States has a responsibility. Through this film, I hope that Japanese people can understand this fact." Thus, in ways parallel to Chinese discourse, the two authors imply that Japan needs to stand up to the American narrative and take a more proactive approach to declaring its own perspective on history.

As for audiences, *Best Wishes for Tomorrow* holds a 3.81/5-star rating on Yahoo out of 241 reviews. The top-rated reviews all give the film five stars, with user Moonlight Sonata (Gekkō no sonata) concluding that Japan can remember peace while also remembering that such Japanese soldiers existed—a view that is increasingly mainstream.[65] The third-highest-rated review notes the film's warm

---

63. Yoshiyuki Uesaka, "Eiga 'ashita e no yuigon' o mite," *Seiron* 433 (2008): 156–160.
64. Hiromichi Makino and Yoshinori Hongō, "Hokori to sekinin kan sōshitsu no jidai ni eiga ashita e no yuigon o kyōō ni kizamu," *Seiron* 433 (2008): 144–151.
65. Gekkō no Sonata, March 5, 2008 (4:21 a.m.), review of *Best Wishes for Tomorrow*, Yahoo! Japan, April 25, 2015, http://movies.yahoo.co.jp/movie/明日への遺言/328955/review.

reception at the Santa Barbara International Film Festival, where "audiences were moved by one man who acted with pride and belief, and to the film's anti-war message," an remark that suggests a desire for international approval of the Japanese narrative.[66] Interestingly, almost all reviewers describe the film as "anti-war" despite its weakening criticism of the military as an institution, focus on Japanese victimhood, and silence on Japanese wartime aggression.

As Dower states, "The contradictions between judicial idealism and plain victor's justice provided fertile soil for the growth of a postwar neonationalism."[67] *Best Wishes* was conceived from this nationalist discourse. Okada, as a high-ranking member of the army and an older patriarchal figure, embodies the masculinist notions of Japanese nationalism. He is bound by duty to his soldiers, family, and nation; he performs Japanese culture through his songs, *shiatsu*, and dignity; he dies in a "manly" way; and he is unapologetic about the war. Through the trial, he provides a Japanese response to the American hegemony on wartime memory, counteracts the American narrative, and articulates a Japanese perspective that the Americans learn to respect. As such, *Best Wishes* rescues Japan's previously despised military leaders and argues for equality in the history debate.

Significantly, *Best Wishes*' clear rejection of the Tokyo Trial view of history is not the dominant discourse in Japan. The ambiguous *I Want to Be a Shellfish* is far more representative of current Japanese views on militarism and nationalism. The difference between the two films is clearest in the execution scenes. In *Best Wishes*, Okada marches proudly to his death, pausing only to comment on the beauty of the moon; Shimizu has to be carried part of the way, limping and terrified, denouncing humanity's propensity for war to the bitter end. While both Japanese films reject the American Tokyo Trial view of history through their heroes' victimhood in the case of Shimizu or heroism in the case of Okada, *Shellfish*'s "negative hero" reveals a far more ambiguous Japanese response to the question of guilt and responsibility. Japan's long postwar period suggests that memory has remained alive, but as with all processes of remembrance, each stage brings new pressures from inside and outside the country. Japanese discourse on the legacy of the war is conflicted, with any unified Japanese "view of history" as yet complicated by the continuing US-Japan military alliance. In both the right and the mainstream, there is a desire to avoid facing others, to be anywhere or be anything other than face the rest of the world. Becoming a shellfish is, in this era, a way to look away, evading responsibility and withdrawing into the Japanese self. It overlaps with the right's "I am me, he is him" argument, which similarly separates Japan from the rest of the world by avoiding the historical views of others.

---

66. Yutake Eve, February 27, 2008 (9:20 p.m.), review of *Best Wishes for Tomorrow*, Yahoo! Japan, April 25, 2015, http://movies.yahoo.co.jp/movie/明日への遺言/328955/review.
67. Dower, *Embracing Defeat*, 444.

Finally, 2017 saw a transnational turn of the memory loop with the release of the four-part miniseries *Tokyo Trial*. Produced by Dutch and Canadian American producers with the participation of Japan's national broadcaster NHK, the series is available widely both on the American streaming service Netflix and on NHK. The production once again tackles the issue of the postwar trials, centering this time on the Dutch justice Röling, a quiet, scholarly man who famously wrote one of the dissenting opinions at the end of the trials. Unlike any other production, the series incorporates multiple national perspectives, albeit in ways that favor the Japanese perspective.

Like other Japanese films on the trials, the miniseries is concerned with the issue of legal precedent and the fairness of the trials themselves. Justice Röling grapples with the then-new legal definition of war crimes, personal and political issues among the justices, translation problems during the proceedings, and prejudicial American influence. While Röling is portrayed as a sensitive and diligent justice largely concerned with the fair application of law, the film is more critical of Lord William D. Patrick, who forms a faction of bullying justices who dominate the proceedings, and of General MacArthur, who interferes by protecting the emperor. Our sympathy thus lies with the main character, Röling, and with his concerns over the impartiality of the trials. The film also emphasizes the Japanese concern with Western colonialism through Justice Pal, who asks Röling, "What gives the Dutch, the English, the French, the Americans, the right to judge the Japanese for their claim that they wanted to free Asia?" Yet unlike other Japanese films, the series also incorporates a critical response to this argument that emphasizes Japanese responsibility. Röling replies, "It didn't sound like they were freeing the people of Nanking, or the rest of Asia."

That said, it must also be noted that while the series discusses the Nanjing Massacre (a rarity in Japanese films), it depicts the proceedings in an emotionally distant way more in line with the murkiness of Japanese discourse. The Nanjing Massacre scene at the beginning of episode 2 juxtaposes actual black-and-white archival footage of Japanese soldiers entering Nanjing and still photographs of two male Chinese witnesses against new black-and-white recordings of the miniseries actors reacting to the testimony. As these images play, an older male American voice reads the translated testimony of the Chinese victims, who recount the mass slaughter of male civilians. The narrator also summarizes the defense's response as they question whether the victims were civilians or "plainclothes troops." This lack of color, use of still frames, lack of visualization of crimes, and unemotional reading by a nonwitness ultimately flatten the emotional impact of the scene, rendering the Chinese victims both invisible and voiceless. Further, by completely avoiding the discussion of sexual violence and questioning the reliability of the Chinese witness's testimony, the scene erases female victims and questions the truth of the massacre itself. This framing of the Nanjing Massacre plays directly into revisionist discourses that aim to deny the violence, and especially the sexual violence, and may be in part due to a desire by NHK or the Western producers to avoid controversy.

The *Tokyo Trial* miniseries is the first of the trial narratives to be widely available due to its distribution via Netflix, part of an intensification of the global mediascape. Produced by an assemblage of filmmakers, albeit in an uneven power structure, the series is broadcast to new audiences via the new medium of digital streaming and incorporates more historical perspectives than ever before. At the same time, the aforementioned uneven power structure and the historical narratives dominant within certain markets mean that producers may self-censor their films, potentially muting certain aspects of history to avoid alienating potential audiences.

Conclusion

As Ian Buruma states, "Political trials produce politicized histories."[68] Recent Chinese and Japanese films reject the perceived "American" Tokyo Trial view of history and present their own images of the war, a new "turn" around the memory loop. China's *Tokyo Trial* is not directed only at the Western Other and the question of historical power but also at Japanese revisionism. The "triumph" of *Tokyo Trial* is therefore not simply the punishment of Japanese crimes but the Chinese judge's ability to demand recognition at the trial and his displacement of the American and Japanese narratives through his unfaltering sense of justice. The film also acknowledges the internationalization of war memory and the continued reality of American power. Establishing a narrative of the war has become increasingly important for the Chinese government both to create a cohesive sense of pan-Chinese nationalism and to strengthen strategic political claims particularly vis-à-vis Japan and the United States.

Japanese films show the disparate narratives of the mainstream and the right, both of which reject the perceived American narrative. The crying, crippled soldier victim of *Shellfish* exculpates Japanese guilt by focusing on Shimizu's victimhood at the hands of the Japanese military, the uneven application of victor's justice, and the unequal balance of power between Japan and the United States. Analysis of the various versions of *Shellfish* reveals a critical change—the critique of the Japanese military is weakening. Rightist films like *Pride* and *Best Wishes for Tomorrow* more boldly challenge the American narrative by rehabilitating the military leadership. They also both argue for more equal footing in terms of the US-Japan relationship—a "Japan That Can Say No"—as mainstream discourse continues to be steeped in an image of pacifism that is hesitant to view the military in terms of the nativist ideals of the right. The emergence of coproduced

---

68. Ian Buruma, *The Wages of Guilt: Memories of War in Germany and Japan* (New York: Farrar, Straus and Giroux, 1994), 166.

miniseries like *Tokyo Trial* (2017) suggests a new potential for transnational memory productions aimed at transnational audiences. Still, their subject matter is limited by the controversy of the topic and may ultimately produce a global memory shared by none.

Though both Chinese and Japanese tribunal films suggest a shift away from the American-dominated narrative, the United States, as a prevailing figure in regional power dynamics, is still an important ally in Chinese and Japanese performances of the past. In the wake of the "Americanization of Japanese war crimes," the American voice is still powerful in the history debate, and the echoes of the IMTFE and the postwar Cold War order are still playing out in Pacific Rim geopolitics. Reactions to the Tokyo Trial in film thus demonstrate the complicated interplay of Chinese, Japanese, and American remembrance of World War II. Changing power balances and other political changes in East Asia will undoubtedly inspire future variations in these narratives.

3
New Heroes in Chinese and Japanese Combat Films

> *Ip Man defeats a group of Japanese soldiers.*
> General Miura: What is your name?
> Ip Man: I am just a Chinese man.[1]

The combat film is the most popular war film genre in both China and Japan, a genre that centers on the trials and tribulations of the male soldier. Chinese combat films famously increased exponentially from the 1990s, with the heroics in television combat dramas so outrageous at one point that the State Administration of Radio, Film and Television (SARFT) ("the censors") issued a warning to production companies in May 2013 admonishing them for "vulgar" depictions of the Second Sino-Japanese War.[2] In Japan, the sixtieth anniversary of the war saw a mini-wave of a new style of heroic combat dramas, including fantasy works like *Lorelei: The Witch of the Pacific* (Rōrerai, 2005), the box-office hit *Yamato* (Otokotachi no yamato, 2005), and less successful films like *Last Operations under the Orion* (Manatsu no orion, 2009) and *Oba: The Last Samurai* (Taiheiyō no kiseki, 2011). Combining drama, action, romance, and national ideology in one entertaining package, these films revolve around the traumas and triumphs of the hero-soldier.

In this chapter, I explore why these films are the most domestically popular cinematic representations of war memory, and further, how they articulate

---

1. From the Hong Kong–PRC coproduction *Ip Man* (Yip man, 2008).
2. Notable shows critiqued include a series in which the female victim of sexual assault manages to dispatch an army of Japanese attackers with superhuman martial arts skills; another series features a leather costume–wearing hero and his Batman-esque room of gadgets. See Cecilia Miao, "Chinese Heroine Gang Raped by Japanese Soldiers Uses Super Move," *China Smack*, March 18, 2013, accessed April 13, 2014, http://www.chinasmack.com/2013/videos/chinese-heroine-gang-raped-by-japanese-soldiers-uses-super-move.html and "China Embarks on Regulating Far-Fetched Anti-Japanese TV Dramas," *Asahi Shimbun*, accessed October 9, 2013, http://ajw.asahi.com/article/asia/AJ201307090012.

and inscribe national identity through stories centered on male soldiers. I also establish how recent memory discourses, geopolitical changes, and economic shifts have led to changing depictions of the Han hero and Yamato warrior in Chinese and Japanese films. I maintain that combat films reveal a departure in the representation of Chinese and Japanese combat masculinities and thus a shift in national identity in this third phase of remembrance. Stories of past heroics formulate new national narratives of the past, part of the discursive process of collective memory. Masculinity, a constructed notion of what it is to be "male," is deeply tied to narratives of nation. As Joane Nagel argues, "Terms like honour, patriotism, cowardice, bravery, and duty are hard to distinguish as either nationalist or masculinist, since they seem so thoroughly tied both to the nation and to manliness."[3] Through the textual analysis of Chinese and Japanese combat films as a site of national memory, I illustrate how the recent nationalist trend in East Asian identity politics is delineated and disseminated through the heroics of such works. However, while I will elaborate on certain trends and tendencies, I do not aim to define a single monolithic image of national masculinity. Rather, I will explore the complex and varied discursive construction of heroic masculinities within each national discourse.

Masculinity and Nationalism

Hegemonic notions of masculinity permeate the nation. This is not to say that the specific whims or personalities of male leaders define the state. Instead, the gendered construction of that system has ensured the dominance of men and masculinities: "The overwhelming majority of top office-holders are men because there is a gender configuring of recruitment and promotion, a gender configuring of the internal division of labour and systems of control, a gender configuring of policymaking, practical routines, and ways of mobilizing pleasure and consent."[4]

The state's protector—the military—also consistently demonstrates "an organizational effort to produce and make hegemonic a narrowly defined masculinity which will make its bearers efficient in producing the organization's effects of violence."[5] Men are thus designated as leaders and soldiers who preside over and safeguard the future of the nation, typically expressed through the equally symbolic figures of women and children.

When nations meet nations, these interactions are often articulated through the idiom of gender. While R. W. Connell's theory of hegemonic masculinity was

---

3. Joane Nagel, "Masculinity and Nationalism: Gender and Sexuality in the Making of Nations," *Ethnic and Racial Studies* 21, no. 2 (1998): 251–252.
4. R. W. Connell, *Masculinities* (Berkeley: University of California Press, 2005), 73.
5. Connell, *Masculinities*, 259.

originally used to refer to normative, idealized images of masculinity within societies, Charlotte Hooper has adapted this concept to refer to international relations. She suggests that Anglo-American culture is hegemonic within that system.[6] Colonialism, its legacies, and continued disparities of economic and military power create national relationships wherein the colonized, dominated, or marginalized nation is "feminized." For example, Carol Cohn discusses the purported usage of the phrase "Bend Over, Saddam" on missiles during the Gulf War, a phrase that suggests male American control over a passive, sexually dominated Iraq.[7] Both China and Japan have been metaphorically "emasculated" by foreign powers: Chinese discourse laments "One Hundred Years of Humiliation" at the hands of foreign invaders; Japan continues to be portrayed as the weaker partner in a military "marriage" with the United States.[8] Colonial masculinity thus represents a standard against which other "peripheral" masculinities are defined. As Ashis Nandy suggests in a frequently quoted passage, colonialism "colonizes minds in addition to bodies and it releases forces within the colonized societies to alter their cultural priorities once for all. . . . The West is now everywhere, within the West and outside; in structures and in minds."[9]

Perceived emasculation is often countered with discourses of masculinity. Susan Jeffords has argued that the imagining of "hard bodies" in 1980s American cinema was to counteract the perceived feminization of America during the 1970s.[10] Gaylyn Studlar and David Desser have further argued that these hard bodies were developed in response to American failure in Vietnam.[11] Similarly, in Chinese literature of the 1980s, *xunzhao nanzihan wenxue* (looking for real men literature) developed in response to *yinsheng yangshuai* (the rise of the feminine and the decline of the masculine).[12] In Japan, the arrival of Western modernity during the Meiji era inspired some Japanese reformers to define a militant,

---

6. Charlotte Hooper, *Manly States: Masculinities, International Relations, and Gender Politics* (New York: Columbia University Press, 2001), 8.
7. Carol Cohn, "Wars, Wimps, and Women: Talking Gender and Thinking War," in *Gendering War Talk*, ed. Miriam Cook and Angela Woollacott (Princeton, NJ: Princeton University Press, 1993), 236.
8. Zheng Wang, "National Humiliation, History Education, and the Politics of Historical Memory: Patriotic Education Campaign in China," *International Studies Quarterly* 52, no. 4 (2008): 788.
9. Ashis Nandy, *The Intimate Enemy* (Oxford: Oxford University Press, 1989), xi.
10. Susan Jeffords, *Hard Bodies: Hollywood Masculinity in the Reagan Era* (New Brunswick, NJ: Rutgers University Press, 1994).
11. Gaylyn Studlar and David Desser, "Never Having to Say You're Sorry: *Rambo*'s Rewriting of the Vietnam War," *Film Quarterly* 42, no. 1 (1988): 9–16.
12. Interestingly, two of the figures deemed manly in this period—Sylvester Stallone and Takakura Ken—were American and Japanese, respectively. Xueping Zhong, *Masculinity Besieged? Issues of Modernity and Male Subjectivity in Chinese Literature of the Late Twentieth Century* (Durham, NC: Duke University Press, 2000), 5.

nativist version of Japanese masculinity.[13] Further, in different eras the masculine concept of *bushidō* (the way of the warrior) has been used to replace perceptions of a feminine or impotent Japan.[14] Thus, the masculinity of the national Other is often juxtaposed with the masculinity of the national Self.

In sum, the male soldier-hero is often depicted as the nation's protector and a symbol of its honor, dignity, and sovereignty. Through his unwavering sacrifice and embodiment of masculinist notions of nation, he represents the defense of the country's territory, culture, and future. It is he who—through his embodiment of these masculine ideals—protects the land, ensures the continued survival of his race, and expels the foreign invaders. New Chinese and Japanese combat narratives are a useful departure point for an examination of recent trends in East Asian nationalism and responses to both the Tokyo Trial narrative and Japanese revisionism. Beginning with Chinese television and film, I will analyze how each specific discourse presents its new images of masculinity.

"Marketized" Socialist Heroes

As the post-Tiananmen "national humiliation" trend matured, the sixtieth anniversary of the end of the war approached, and the 2008 Beijing Olympics grew nearer, heroic war narratives began to shift in tone and style. There are three types of Chinese hero films: the first are known as Red Classic remakes, a trend we see in the early aughts as many Mao-era films were remade in entertaining ways that deviated from the original style. The second is the transnational pan-China film production, similar to *Tokyo Trial*, which employs Hong Kong talent and producers and mainland capital. The third is the "marketized war story," a new trend to meet the demand for characters with more depth for Chinese audiences who are bored by the simplistic socialist hero. Notably, these narratives are all different in form and content—TV dramas, aiming to attract viewers, tend to be more extreme in their depiction of the war. Films, which have higher budgets and transnational aspirations, tend to have better production values and crews/talent drawn from Hong Kong, Taiwan, and Mainland China.

To begin, *Little Solder Zhang Ga* (Xiaobing zhangga, 1963, 2004), part of an early aughts "remake fever" of Red Classic or early Mao-era socialist films, demonstrates several of the Chinese trends toward masculine nationalism.[15] The 1963

---

13. Jason G. Karlin, "The Gender of Nationalism: Competing Masculinities in Meiji Japan," *Journal of Japanese Studies* 28, no. 1 (2002): 41–77.
14. Michele M. Mason, "Empowering the Would-Be Warrior: Bushidō and the Gendered Bodies of the Japanese Nation," in *Recreating Japanese Men*, ed. Sabine Frühstück and Anne Walthall (Berkeley: University of California Press, 2011), 68–90.
15. Chunli Wang, "Guochan dianshiju 'fanpaire' de wenhua genyuan yu chixu fazhan," *Gansu Keji* 3 (2009): 80–81.

version is still taught to this day in Chinese classrooms as a lesson on Japanese aggression, and the figure of Zhang Ga is iconic, appearing in comic books, TV shows, and advertisements. Zhang Ga is directed primarily at child audiences. After-school specials and cartoons use the figure to explore the meaning of war remembrance in contemporary China. Here, I discuss the 2004 version due to its popularity. The TV show was shown across the nation, is widely available online, and has high rankings and positive comments on the Chinese video sites PPTV, Leguan, and CNTV.

Set in 1942 near Baiyangdian Lake in northeastern China, the 1963 film follows Zhang Ga and his grandmother as they harbor a Communist resistance fighter named Zhong Balu. When Zhang Ga's grandmother is murdered by a Japanese officer, he joins a new family (the Communist guerrilla troop) and gains a new ideology (socialism) in the process. Importantly, rather than selfishly avenging himself against the Japanese for personal reasons, Zhang Ga learns the larger ideological significance of resisting the foreign invaders and constructing a strong socialist nation. Although male leadership and male heroism are dominant in the film, children and grandmothers are also icons of powerful national heroism.

The 1963 version and its 2004 television remake reveal differences in terms of heroism and victimhood. As Chinese war films of the 1950s and 1960s aimed to legitimize the CCP's new government, older films emphasized socialist heroism and suppressed narratives of trauma.[16] Heroes in statues, revolutionary operas, and films stand defiant of the colonizers and feudal landlords, gazing upward and onward toward a bright socialist future. In the original *Zhang Ga*, the grandmother dies heroically, her stance before her murder reminiscent of the revolutionary soldiers statue shown at the beginning of the film. In the 2004 version, this socialist heroism is replaced by a hybrid discourse: Zhang Ga's grandmother becomes both victim and hero. While her defiance is still heroic, she is framed as smaller, older, and weaker; the socialist rhetoric is downplayed. Scenes of victimhood also permeate the narrative of the 2004 film. In a scene that recalls the Nanjing Massacre, one woman is nearly raped by Japanese soldiers; in another, peasants are tied up en masse. Such changes mark the return of narratives featuring victimization and trauma after the loosening of state ideology from the 1970s and the emphasis on past humiliation after 1989.[17]

Whereas the original *Zhang Ga* treats the Japanese impersonally as one of many foreign colonizers and internal enemies, the 2004 drama is obsessed with Japanese soldiers. Much of the 1963 version's dialogue implicates Chinese

---

16. Minjie Chen, "From Victory to Victimization: The Sino-Japanese War (1937–1945) as Depicted in Chinese Youth Literature," *Bookbird: A Journal of International Children's Literature* 47, no. 2 (2009): 27–35.
17. William A. Callahan, "National Insecurities: Humiliation, Salvation, and Chinese Nationalism," *Alternatives* 29, no. 2 (2004): 199–218.

traitors (*Hanjian*), while the 2004 version views its sole enemy as the "Japanese devils" (*Riben guizi*). In addition to the nationalist trend that has encouraged the promotion of such demonization, part of the reason for the shift is the country's new political agenda. In establishing its legitimacy in the 1950s and 1960s, the CCP was presented as the sole heroic force during the war, with Chiang Kai-shek's Chinese Nationalist Party relegated to roles of spies and collaborators. Now that PRC war dramas have revised the narratives to promote stories of PRC-Taiwan cooperation, Japanese characters have emerged as the sole enemy. Use of the terms "devil" (*guizi*) and "resist Japan" (*Kangri*) increases from twelve times in the hundred-minute 1963 version to fifty-one times in the forty-four-minute first episode of the 2004 version.[18] Anti-Japanese slogans also pepper the walls of 2004 Zhang Ga's village with phrases like "Unite and Resist the Japanese." This extreme focus on the Japanese enemy has become a national fixation.

However, while the Japanese soldiers are increasingly prominent, they are feminized as ridiculous buffoons or sexual deviants. The 1963 Zhang Ga's youth was primarily intended to simplify the socialist lessons in the original, while the more recent version uses his age to underscore the feminization of the Japanese. In essence, such narratives suggest that even a child could outsmart the foolish, bumbling Japanese soldiers. As in recent comedy war films *Hands Up!* and *Hands Up! 2* (Juqi shoulai!, 2003; Juqi shoulai! 2, 2010)—wherein young Chinese children repeatedly outwit and belittle Japanese soldiers—China's national humiliation is erased by the humiliation of Japan. The popular phrase "little Japanese" (*xiao Riben*) similarly expresses this sentiment.

Another remake of a classic Mao-era film, *Railway Guerrillas* (Tiedao Youjidui, 1956, 1985, 2005, 2011), demonstrates a new kind of heroism through its heroes Liu Hong and Wang Qiang. In analyzing these two characters, the concept of *wen-wu* is a useful framework. Kam Louie explores Chinese masculinity in terms of *wen* (martial) and *wu* (literary)—this can also be seen as *douying* (a battle of courage) and *douzhi* (a battle of wits).[19] While Geng Song argues that this framework can be limiting because of its overreliance on Western binaries, many contemporary films articulate masculinities in ways informed by this binary, especially when juxtaposing Chinese masculinity against a non-Chinese Other.[20]

---

18. Xu argues that the changes after China entered the World Trade Organization actually strengthened the state's control of television productions. Minghua Xu, "Television Reform in the Era of Globalization: New Trends and Patterns in Post-WTO China," *Telematics and Informatics* 30, no. 4 (2012): 370–380.
19. Kam Louie and Morris Low, ed., *Asian Masculinities: The Meaning and Practice of Manhood in China and Japan* (New York: Routledge, 2012), and Kam Louie, *Theorising Chinese Masculinity: Society and Gender in China* (Cambridge: Cambridge University Press, 2002).
20. Geng Song, *The Fragile Scholar: Power and Masculinity in Chinese Culture* (Hong Kong: Hong Kong University Press, 2004).

According to Louie, Chinese masculinity is constructed not only in terms of physical size or toughness but also through intelligence, wit, discipline, self-control, and mastery of skills.[21] The Confucian gentleman-scholar is an icon of *wen*, while the military leader Guan Yu or the monkey king Sun Wukong represents *wu*. Whereas the *wen* fosters "vertical bonds of hierarchy and filiality," the wu fosters "horizontal bonds of brotherhood."[22] In the 2005 version of *Railway Soldiers* (CCTV-3), these concepts define the two main characters. Such Red Classics appear to appeal to older audiences who view the films on television and are familiar with the narrative from seeing the originals, and to younger audiences through the internet, where many younger Chinese access television. Comments online emphasize the nostalgia felt by many viewers for such Red Classics, as well as the entertaining spectacle of bashing Japanese soldiers.[23] On the popular video site PPTV show, user Yesu Wo Ai Ni (Jesus I love you) writes, "I just love to hit those Japanese devils."[24] Meanwhile, user Qiu Zhi Fengye (Maple Leaf in Spring) writes, "(happy) Cherish the Red Classics."[25] This typical drama is useful in showing how Red Classics have been adapted to appeal to new audiences over the years.

Railway is based on the true story of coal miners and railway workers who sabotaged railway tracks during the Second Sino-Japanese War. During the early Mao era, this narrative was used to highlight the heroism of peasant-worker masses and, again, to galvanize popular support for the PRC. Liu Hong, the head of the guerrillas, displays *wu* through his physical strength and mastery of Chinese kung fu; Wang Qiang, a crafty member of the resistance who is originally mistaken for a Chinese collaborator, utilizes his cleverness, or *wen*, to outwit his enemies. These two types of Chinese masculinity are juxtaposed with hypermasculine (rapists, murderers) or hyperfeminine (unarmed, dumb) Japanese soldiers.

In an early scene Liu Hong, the *wu* hero, jumps onto the train by using superhuman kung fu skills. Magically flipping through the air, he consistently

---

21. Louie, *Theorising Chinese Masculinity*, 76.
22. Chris Berry, "Theorising Chinese Masculinity: Society and Gender in China Review," *Intersections: Gender, History and Culture in the Asian Context* 8 (2002), http://intersections.anu.edu.au/issue8/berry_review.html.
23. The socialist education system has become a source of nostalgia both for older Chinese, who felt it was a simpler time, and for younger Chinese, who did not experience the disastrous policies of the 1950s and 1960s. Ironically, CCP projects like "big pot dinners" are now commodified in chain restaurants like Red Classic in Beijing, which offers the Maoist era experience.
24. Yesu Wo Ai Ni, October 13, 2014 (6:06 a.m.), comment on episode 1 of *Railway Guerrillas*, PPTV.com, April 25, 2015, http://v.pptv.com/show/6C9LyTGXB0WoJqo.html.
25. Qiu Zhi Feng Yi, September 19, 2014 (1:47 a.m.), comment on episode 1 of *Railway Guerrillas*, PPTV.com, April 25, 2015, http://v.pptv.com/show/6C9LyTGXB0WoJqo.html.

outmaneuvers the Japanese soldiers by using his superhuman physical abilities and mastery of Chinese martial arts. The sequence is more *wuxia* (martial arts) film than war film. Liu even says "houhuiyouqi" (until we meet again) to his compatriot, a phrase commonly used in *wuxia* dramas between departing heroes. He uses machetes to battle Japanese *katana*, in essence creating a Chinese cultural response to Japanese cultural tropes. Yet his martial abilities are notably hypermasculine and ultraviolent—in one scene he and Wang Qiang massacre a houseful of unarmed Japanese soldiers with machetes, bludgeoning one young soldier to death with a meat cleaver. Such violence is common in PRC World War II narratives, reflecting a strong response to the image of the Japanese enemy. Even in ostensible war comedies like *Hands Up!* there are cringeworthy scenes of violence used for comedic effect, such as a Japanese soldier having teeth knocked out in painful, bloody close-up. The casual production and consumption of these depictions illustrate how the national humiliation narrative—combined with anger over the textbook issue, Yasukuni visits, and the Senkaku/Diaoyu island dispute—has engendered deep anger toward Japan.

Meanwhile, Wang Qiang as *wen* mainly supplements Liu Hong's manly physical heroics by formulating clever plans, infiltrating Japanese defenses, and participating in major attacks on the train system. Additionally, he represents the new trend of rehabilitated *Hanjian*. In recent years, most supposed *Hanjian* renounce their collaboration or are revealed to be secretly working against the Japanese the entire time.[26] This is due to historical changes in the Taiwan-PRC relationship and a desire to represent Chinese unity. While films of the 1950s and 1960s frequently directed much of their invective at Nationalist *Hanjian*, Chinese solidarity over World War II has become one of the main ideologies bringing together the PRC, Hong Kong, and Taiwan.

It is important to note that these Red Classic remakes were heavily scrutinized by the Chinese government, possibly because the *wuxia* elements add a degree of entertaining, ahistorical levity not in keeping with the gravity of the original hero. The government issued two criticisms at the height of the remake fever. Complaints included a lack of understanding of the original's "core spirit," a misunderstanding of the narrative's historical and social background, a "single-minded pursuit of ratings and entertainment," and overemphasis on the humanity of villains.[27] Another critic commented on the depiction of the hero: "Only by grasping the weighty traditional values of the hero, and on that

---

26. Part of the reason Ang Lee's *Lust, Caution* (2007) was so heavily edited was due to its portrayal of loyalty: in the final scene the undercover Wong Chia Chi warns her collaborator lover, betraying all her comrades and her nation. SARFT demanded this betrayal be excised from the PRC version of the film.
27. Wenxiang Peng, "Dianshiju gaibian hongse jingdian de xin weidu he xin changshi: Dianshiju xiaobing zhangga de xushi tese," *Zhongguo Dianshi* 11 (2005): 23–26.

foundation establishing appropriate character development and related richness, can we avoid distorting and smearing the image of the original hero."[28] Such discussions demonstrate the complex and uneasy relationship between the market and government over the issue of remembrance.

A transnational Chinese coproduction, the PRC–Hong Hong film *Ip Man* (Yip man, 2007) also imagines a battle of Chinese *wen-wu* and Japanese hypermasculinity. The film fancifully fictionalizes the life of Bruce Lee's teacher, Yip Man, as he fights against Japanese martial arts expert General Miura. The two men's disparate martial styles represent a battle of Chinese and Japanese masculinities. Yip Man uses softer, more technical Chinese *wing chun*, his hands open and poised; Miura uses hard-hitting and aggressive Japanese karate, his hands clenched and tense. These "native" martial forms represent national masculinities fighting for their respective cultures. Though Miura demonstrates a strong sense of *wu*—he strikes hard and is a diligent fighter—he lacks Yip Man's *wen* (cultivation, diligence, patience). When Yip Man gains the upper hand and strikes Miura against a pole, his strikes are intercut with an earlier scene of training, an edit that stresses that Yip Man's martial arts ability emerges from the more cultured Chinese emphasis on learning. Thus Yip Man is not only physically stronger than Miura but also more principled, cultivated, and refined. It is through his patience and hard work—importantly rooted in Chinese culture and philosophy—that he can overcome the impatient and aggressive Miura. *Ip Man* was massively successful in Mainland China and Hong Kong, earning first place in the box office its first weekend and inspiring praise for its depiction of a Chinese hero and of Donnie Yen in particular for his charismatic acting and physical performance.[29] There were few negative comments on Douban, though some viewers criticized the film's one-dimensional depictions of the Japanese soldiers and its portrayal of women as "flower vases" (*huaping*), that is, pretty to look at but silently placed in the scene with no impact on the narrative.[30]

Finally, the TV show *Drawing Sword* (Liang jian, 2005) is perhaps the most notable PRC war drama in recent years. Rare for Chinese television, the show proved so popular that it was brought back as a second series. It also produced a fair amount of Chinese scholarly interest in the character of Li Yunlong, whose heroics were considered to break with prior models. The majority of the Chinese research on the topic focuses on the individualism of the main character, Li Yunlong, and his ability to promote CCP ideology.[31] According to Minghua Xu:

---

28. Shuo Liu, "Shiting huayu chanshi yu jingshen chuancheng: Dui 'hongse jingdian' gai bianju chuangzuo yanjiu de shuli yu fansi," *Dangdai Dianying* 1 (2007): 73.
29. See Chinese Box Office in Table 1.2.
30. Reviews of *Ip Man*, Douban, April 25, 2015, http://movie.douban.com/subject/3041806/collections.
31. For example, see Yihua Liu, "Xin shiji zhanzheng xiaoshuo de xin tansuo: Cong liangjian tan qi," *Bijie xueyuan xuebao* 2 (2009): 75–78.

Drawing Sword appears interesting to the audiences because it gives a vivid portrayal of CCP heroes who have anxieties, fears, desires and passions just like ordinary persons. It redefines the "CCP hero" and successfully enables audiences to sympathize with him easily and accept what the Mainstream Melody[32] wants the former to know. It does this by making use of the juxtaposition strategy to employ the commercial expression techniques, giving a humanizing image to CCP members.[33]

This emphasis on individualism is in part due to the emergence of "marketized war stories" in China.[34] Originally based on a best-selling novel from 2000 by Du Liang from *tiexue wenxue* (iron-and-blood literature), the book tells the story of military commander Li Yunlong of the Eighth Route Army.[35] It begins with his courageous exploits during the Second Sino-Japanese War and ends with his persecution during the Cultural Revolution and his eventual suicide. The television show's savvy new narrative has been described as a new type of entertainment that has revamped the tired ideological genre. The individuality of the main character; the complex characterization of CCP, KMT, and Japanese forces; and the dramatic story line resonated with many Chinese audiences who, despite taking issue with the changes the TV show made to the original novel, overwhelmingly gave the show four or five stars (out of a possible five) on Douban.

Indeed, Li is portrayed as individualistic and uniquely flawed. He is not always the most strategic commander, often letting his emotions ride over his tactical command. He rashly runs against bullets to break through defenses; he takes care of his men whether or not it will help his cause; he does not always impress his superiors; sometimes he makes precipitous, emotional military decisions; he makes silly jokes; he falls in love and gets married. Yet in battles, he exudes the masculine characteristics of an idealized national hero. Li exemplifies leadership, loyalty, and patriotism, with his ultimate allegiance being to his nation. While superficially encased in a multidimensional persona of humanistic imperfection, Li Yunlong still represents a hyperpatriotic CCP soldier. And through his human flaws, he rehabilitates the image of the CCP hero.

While the quirky Li does get married, the death of his wife, Qiuxin, emphasizes both Li's humanity and his national priorities. When Qiuxin is kidnapped by the Japanese, Li shouts, "I, Li Yunlong, will not exchange the life of my wife for the lives of my soldiers!" His wife affirms his decision in a patriotic speech of self-sacrifice: "You said it well, Troop Leader! It is worth it to trade one Qiuxin for however many Japanese devils!" Li calls for an attack, Qiuxin disappears

---

32. "Mainstream melody" films, or *zhuxuanlü dianying*, are films that represent the CCP's approved ideology or version of historical events.
33. Xu, "Television Reform," 370–380.
34. Rui Chen, "Yi liangjian weilie tan shichanghua xiezuo yu lixiang shenjingde jiehe," *Jiamusi Jiaoyu Xueyuanbao* 4 (2011): 29.
35. Liu, "Xin shiji."

in a fiery explosion, and the battle is won. While Qiuxun's sacrifice is heroic, her death is presented within the narrative as male (national) trauma and the impetus for the ultimate defeat of the Japanese. Stricken with grief, Li clutches at a gun, his duty to his nation still his guiding motivation. Although the series importantly raises the issue of personal loss, the survival of the soldiers (national future) is prioritized over the traumatized woman (national past). In keeping with other CCP dramas, Li chooses his national family over his real family.

As in *Railway Guerrillas*, the sword of the title is also a symbol of Chinese masculinity. The image of the Japanese *katana* is tied to Japanese executions of Chinese soldiers, and specifically the "hundred-man killing contest" in Nanjing. The contest, wherein two Japanese officers allegedly raced to kill one hundred Chinese people with their swords, has been hotly debated by historians. Whether or not the event occurred, it remains an important symbol of Japanese aggression in China.[36] The machete of *Drawing Sword* is thus in part a response to a part of Japanese culture viewed as aggressive and dehumanizing. Since the Japanese have *katana*, the Chinese soldiers use the larger and more impressive machete. The machete also draws from peasant culture and Chinese *kungfu*, both of which feature large knives. Peasants, the icons of socialism, use machetes to harvest; Chinese martial arts utilize weapons to show control and technique. Finally, the film ends with a speech on the "drawing sword" spirit, which is the spirit of acting even when the odds are against you. This is the spirit of Li Yunlong and of China's image of the past—they may have been invaded, but their "drawing sword spirit" means that they were never defeated.

Government regulation ensured that the new creative elements of the show still adhered to the government's nationalist policy, regulation evident in the major changes made to the book's ending.[37] As Liu Fusheng notes, the television series departed significantly from the original novel.[38] This was not ignored by audiences—the top-rated negative comment (as of March 2015) on Douban criticizes the series for departing too much from the book: "The actors are good and it is filmed well. But it is way too different from the book! . . . This isn't *Drawing Sword*."[39] In the book, Li is harassed into killing himself during the Cultural Revolution in 1968, though memories of him are eventually "rehabilitated" by the government in 1978. The thirty-episode television series instead focuses on the Second Sino-Japanese War for roughly twenty of its episodes, downplaying and limiting Li Yunlong's eventual demise. It also replaces his death with

---

36. Joshua A. Fogel, *The Nanjing Massacre in History and Historiography* (Berkeley: University of California Press, 2000), 79–84.
37. Xu, "Television Reform," 372–373.
38. Fusheng Liu, "Cong huanle yingxiong dao lishi shounan zhe: Ping liangjian," *Wenyi Lilun Yu Piping* 6 (2006): 38–42.
39. Biglaity Haihaier, July 12, 2008, comment on *Drawing Sword*, Douban, April 25, 2015, http://movie.douban.com/subject/2254648/comments.

a patriotic speech, titled "The Spirit of Drawing Sword," wherein Li argues that no matter what the odds are, the Chinese must draw their swords and "go down swinging." He connects heroism to the Chinese collective, maintaining that the "military spirit" emerges from Chinese tradition. The TV show ends not with his death but with Li Yunlong saluting the CCP flag. Such changes reveal the limitations of government regulation, which one commentator referred to as "castration."[40]

Thus, Chinese narratives demonstrate a shift in masculine narratives from a monolithic hero to a victim-victor hybrid—a Chinese present avenging a feminized past. Emasculation and abuse of Japanese male characters constitute an increasingly steady trope in these narratives. Further, the individualism of a hero like Li Yunlong shows a market demand for less heroic and more humanistic heroes. The response of the Chinese government reveals conflict between the demand for more complex "marketized war stories" and the political agenda of the state.

"Uneasy Warriors"

With the legacy of the war a far more tendentious issue in Japan, the soldier is a problematic figure in Japanese society. In the immediate postwar period, the mourning of soldiers was complicated by their status as "perpetrators," and in the present, defining heroes of World War II remains a somewhat delicate issue.[41] As noted by Sabine Frühstück,, the Japanese soldier today faces the problematic past of the imperial soldier, an ambiguous love-hate relationship with the American soldier, and conflict with the normative masculinity of the salaryman.[42] Moreover, Self-Defense Force members are problematic individuals whose entry into the force is often marked by marginalization before entering (poverty or failure to enter a company or college) and marginalization after entering (rejection by a society that considers them controversial).[43] Japan's wartime past—seen as traumatic, failed, and wasteful—problematizes the depiction of soldiers.

Even so, 2005 saw the release of three heroic films that all performed respectably at the Japanese box office. *Yamato* (Otokotachi no Yamato, 2005) came in at number 5, *Lorelei: Witch of the Pacific* (Lōrerai, 2005) at 21, and *Aegis* (Bokoku

---

40. Comments on *Drawing Sword*, Douban, April 25, 2015, http://movie.douban.com /subject/2254648/comments.
41. Dower discusses the issues of remembering loss of soldiers during the occupation period. See John Dower, *Embracing Defeat: Japan in the Wake of World War II* (New York: W. W. Norton, 2000).
42. Frühstück, *Uneasy Warriors*, 53.
43. Sabine Frühstück, *Uneasy Warriors: Gender, Memory, and Popular Culture in the Japanese Army* (Berkeley: University of California Press, 2007).

no Aejisu, 2005) at 27.[44] While previous depictions of heroes in Japanese combat films emphasized the victimhood of soldiers and the "bad militant Other" within Japan's predominantly "good Self" (also called the *shidōsha sekinin ron*, or discourse on the responsibility of leaders), new Japanese films do not display such a sharp distinction between the "good" and "bad" sides of the military.[45] These new depictions emerged as the wartime generation—who remembered the destructive nature of the war and pain of defeat—passed away, and as film companies devised new strategies to capitalize on big-budget epics. By exploring the depiction of young soldiers in the most popular of these renditions, *Yamato*, and juxtaposing it against the right wing *For Those We Love* (Ore wa kimi no tame ni koso shi ni iku, 2007), I aim to reveal the differences and overlaps between mainstream and far-right trends in the representation of Japanese heroes.

Aaron Gerow has written extensively on the media that emerged in Japan around 2005, carefully noting that the boom in militaristic films does not connote simplistic nationalism. He reminds us, "This is an audience, we must remember, that supports the Japanese national soccer team and even votes for the 'Koizumi Theater,' but remains unenthusiastic about Security Defense Force deployment in Iraq and other openly militarist moves."[46] In his reading, fantastic representations of victorious war in the films *Lorelei: The Witch of the Pacific Ocean* (Rōrerai, 2005) and *Aegis* (Bōkoku no ījisu, 2005) are related not merely to national feelings but also to the film industry's desire to profit from audience interest in "war spectaculars." While their films echo some of the Japanese right's concerns ("healthy nationalism," a feeling that postwar history has not allowed Japan to be a "normal nation"), the emphasis on life and unclear attitudes toward the meaning of nation render the films ambiguous. Gerow also looks at *Yamato* through his concept of "vicarious trauma," arguing that the film is dealing more with the pre-1989 postwar period than with the war or the present. While films of both the 1950s and the present attempt to forget atrocities committed by Japanese soldiers during wartime, *Yamato* uses the trope of suffering "to forget not only Japanese war responsibility, but also a postwar increasingly defined, especially in contemporary popular culture, by emasculation and hypocrisy, or ahistorical idealization."[47]

Yamato (2005) is the most important of the new combat films to emerge in this period. It was one of the most successful Japanese combat films in decades,

---

44. Box Office Mojo, "Japan Yearly Box Office: 2005," accessed October 9, 2013, http://boxofficemojo.com/intl/japan/yearly/?yr=2005.
45. Lisa Yoneyama, *Hiroshima Traces: Time, Space, and the Dialectics of Memory* (Berkeley: University of California Press, 1999), 10.
46. Aaron Gerow, "Fantasies of War and Nation in Recent Japanese Cinema," *Japan Focus*, February 16, 2006, http://www.japanfocus.org/-Aaron-Gerow/1707.
47. Aaron Gerow, "War and Nationalism in *Yamato*: Trauma and Forgetting the Postwar," *Asia-Pacific Journal* 9, issue 24, no. 1 (2011), http://japanfocus.org/-Aaron-Gerow/3545.

sporting an all-star cast and demonstrating a newfound mixture of respect and nostalgia for Japanese soldiers. The film follows the adopted daughter of a soldier, Uchida Makiko, as she attempts to reach the specific spot where the *Yamato* lies to spread the ashes of her father. With former soldier Kamio Katsumi and his young assistant Atsushi, she travels to the location of the *Yamato*'s demise. During the voyage, Kamio reminisces about his past experience as a soldier on the doomed Yamato and the experiences he had training and fighting on the doomed ship with his friends. In my analysis of *Yamato*, I will expand on how the film's new masculinities displace the Tokyo Trial narrative of Japanese guilt personified in the bad military/good soldier films of the 1950s and 1960s. Through their merging of the good and bad soldiers, they also potentially lay the foundation for normalization in the present.

Masculinity and nationalism begin with the ship itself. The *Yamato* is an important national symbol for Japanese both as nationally produced technology and as a symbol of Japanese ethnic and sovereign identity. For its speed and armaments it was considered a great Japanese technological achievement at the time and has delighted military technology enthusiasts for decades. *Yamato* was the Japanese navy's flagship through 1942, replaced by the *Musashi* after an embarrassing loss during the Battle of Midway. After participating in the Battle of the Philippine Sea and the Battle of Leyte Gulf, the Yamato was sunk by Allied forces near Kyushu on April 7, 1942, during Operation Ten-Go.[48] As for the symbolic meaning of the ship, "Yamato" is a word that denotes the ethnic majority of Japan, as distinct from Japanese minorities like Ainu. This is accompanied by concepts like *Yamato damashi* (Japanese spirit) and *Yamato nadeshiko* (the ideal Japanese woman). The front of the ship even sports the chrysanthemum symbol of the emperor, himself the ultimate representative of Japanese blood and national identity. Finally, the *Yamato*—as an island moving through the ocean, as a small society run by Japanese men, and as a symbol of the protection of Japanese sovereignty—represents the nation itself.

Just as Gerow reads the submarine in *Lorelei* as a microcosm of the Japanese nation, the battleship *Yamato* is also a representation of Japan.[49] The title of the film in Japanese is actually "The Men's Yamato," and indeed the men are deeply tied to the *Yamato*. Led by the emblem of the emperor, they practice Japanese culture through judo, kendo, and other Japanese martial arts on the ship's deck. They use the *Yamato* to protect Japan from the enemy—the ship can only operate through the efforts of the highly trained men, who work in unison aboard the ship. And when the ship dies, the men die, too. The blood of the men splatters against the sides of the ship almost comically, making the ship appear as though

---

48. William Garzke and Robert Dulin, *Battleships: Axis and Neutral Battleships in World War II* (Annapolis, MD: Naval Institute Press, 1985), 43–126.
49. Gerow, "Fantasies of War."

its wounds are bleeding. Finally, Kamio, one of the battle's few survivors, can only escape by abandoning the ship.

While Chinese films directly confront Japanese masculinity, *Yamato* does not attempt to depict American soldiers. Instead, the American Other is conceived as an invisible and hegemonic power. American men do not appear in the film; rather, the nation is presented as planes shrouded in fog and communications scrolling across the screen. Whereas *Yamato* is composed of flesh-and-blood men, America is denoted by technologically advanced machinery and the absence of people. Part of this is due to a historical focus on Japanese suffering in war films—a hermetic focus on the self—and part of this is due to the complex US-Japan relationship. As Frühstück describes in her interviews with Self-Defense Force members, "The American soldier is identified with aggression and violence, but—in the eyes of Self-Defense Forces service members—his modernity releases him from any similarity to the imperial soldier."[50] For example, Frühstück found that Japanese Self-Defense Force members emulated soldiers in American action films.[51] Notably, the masculinity of Hollywood films has often been connected to whiteness and the trivializing of minorities and women.[52] In addition, the US-Japan relationship still retains elements of the postwar "marriage." When *Yamato* appeared in theaters, a popular joke posted to Twitter pointed out the irony of the theme song by manly singer Nagabuchi Tsuyoshi's choice of title. According to this joke, Nagabuchi introduced the theme song to the film as follows: "In Japan there is a rash of using European writing because of American influence. It is destroying the spirits of the dead who guarded our beautiful land and culture. Listen to my memorial to the Japanese men who fought sixty years ago! (Switching to English): *"Close your Eyes!"* The irony here is that the manly Nagabuchi's nationalistic Japanese theme song has an English title, highlighting the US-Japan military relationship and the uncritical absorption of American cultural influence.

Most important, *Yamato* demonstrates a shift in the representation of the Japanese military. Many films of the 1950s and 1960s represented Japanese society as essentially innocent through their feminized passivity and pacifism, such as the character Shimizu in *I Want to Be a Shellfish* (Kai ni naritai, 1958, 1959, 1994, 2007, 2008). The military leadership was depicted as aggressive and destructive, a representation that legitimized *shidōsha sekinin ron* and released the majority of the nation from any sense of guilt. Yet while *Yamato* still features a few scenes of

---

50. Frühstück, *Uneasy Warriors*, 76.
51. Frühstück, *Uneasy Warriors*, 81.
52. Paul Hoch, *White Hero, Black Beast: Racism, Sexism and the Mask of Masculinity* (London: Pluto Press, 1979), and Laura C. Prividera and John W. Howard, "Masculinity, Whiteness, and the Warrior Hero: Perpetuating the Strategic Rhetoric of US Nationalism and the Marginalization of Women," *Women and Language* 29, no. 2 (2009): 29–37.

military brutality, the critical gaze on the military has weakened. For example, in one scene a commanding officer goes too far while physically punishing the soldiers, beating a young man with a pipe. Although that soldier directly disobeys him, there is no punishment from the leadership: the military leadership is uncharacteristically reasonable and fair. The film also begins with a sympathetic image of the real Special Defense Forces returning from an aid mission to the warm reception of family members in Japan. Such a depiction softens their image from that of warrior-soldiers to humanized fathers, brothers, and sons. Finally, Satō criticizes the film for its whitewashing of military leadership, such as its suggestion that Japan passively ended up in war solely due to the economic blockade, and for glossing over the censorship of letters.[53] This weakening of the feminine peaceful/masculine militant divide in essence obfuscates the good/bad narrative and normalizes the image of the Japanese soldier.

While *Yamato* does not criticize military leadership, the men die arbitrary deaths and the meaning of war/military is rendered ambiguous and confusing. As Gerow argues, the men in the film are feminized youths, emasculated and childless, or dead.[54] However, I would argue that the respect displayed toward military figures, the concept of duty, and the ship *Yamato* itself still signifies a weakening of early postwar criticism. While remilitarization is still a contentious issue, the sacrifices of the soldiers of the past—tied to the technology/symbolism of the *Yamato*—are memorialized in a film that romanticizes both the ship and the men. In one of *Yamato*'s final shots, Uchida, Atsushi, and Kamio—the past, present, and future of Japan—salute the fallen *Yamato*. The three are tied together in an act of remembering, gazing not toward a memory of war but toward the future of Japan.

The reception of audiences reveals in many ways how the film's ambiguity led to its success. For example, the top-voted comment on Amazon Japan praises the film's apolitical representation, arguing that it is unnecessary for the audience to talk about aggression or losing, since the film is about the heroes on the *Yamato* and their lives, not about such "political interpretation."[55] Meanwhile, on the film's Yahoo page, where there are more than 1,500 reviews, the top-voted comment by user Pik interpreted the film as specifically anti-war. Pik describes taking their young son to the screening and how they both were profoundly affected by the screening: "Because of the incompetent leaders' stupidity many young people uselessly lost their lives. In a lot of Great East Asia War films soldiers always come out yelling, 'His Majesty the Emperor, Banzai!' but in this film there was not a

---

53. Kōji Satō, "Otokotachi no yamato o megutte: Rekishigaku no shiza kara," *Kikan Sensō Sekinin Kenkyū* 56 (2007): 74–80.
54. Gerow, "War and Nationalism in *Yamato*."
55. Melting, August 18, 2008, comment on DVD of *Yamato*, Amazon.jp, April 25, 2015, http://http://www.amazon.co.jp/男たちの大和-YAMATO-DVD-反町隆史/dp/B000F6RURU.

single one. Certainly many soldiers cried that out, but the film shows that in the hearts of the fallen soldiers there was their family, their lover, their desire to protect their home."[56] Such readings, some of which saw the film as apolitical and humanistic, some of which read the film as specifically anti-war, are in line with Gerow's interpretation. By watering down the historical narrative to its emotional components, and by centering on the uncontroversial notion of Japanese victimhood, the film appeals to audiences across the political spectrum.

The big-budget film *For Those We Love* (Ore wa, kimi no tame ni koso shini ni iku, 2007; literally "I Will Die for You" in Japanese) demonstrates the difference between mainstream and nationalist discourses. While it came in at a disappointing 54 at the box office, the bevy of politicians who supported the film suggest that the right-wing turn in Japanese politics is an important trend that deserves attention.[57] It is also useful to juxtapose this film with *Yamato* to demonstrate the difference between *Yamato*'s more popular ambiguity over the less popular simplicity of a straightforward nationalist representation of the Japanese hero. Coming from a long history of kamikaze films, *For Those* s far more nostalgic than previous kamikaze narratives, whitewashing over the traumatic experiences of the kamikaze.

The film, like *Yamato*, also has a large number of reviews on the website Yahoo (1,162 as of March 2015). Many viewers lamented the sacrifice of so many young people during war and expressed sympathy for the young men. The top-rated comment is also highly critical of the generals of the war for sending young people to die and for surviving the war.[58] Based on the film's nostalgic imagery of soldiers and of the top levels of the military in particular (who honorably commit suicide, following their men to their deaths), this is an oppositional reading. The second-highest review reads the film as a pacifist attempt to deal with memories of war, commending the well-known right-wing politician Ishihara Shintaro (screenwriter and executive producer of the film) for showing the destructive nature of war.[59] Interestingly, this interpretation—that war is negative and that the film is showing the dangers of war—was a common response among viewers.[60]

---

56. Pik, December 19, 2005 (2:18 a.m.), review of *Yamato*, *Yahoo! Japan*, April 25, 2015, http://movies.yahoo.co.jp/movie/男たちの大和/YAMATO/322114/review/.
57. Gerow, "Fantasies of War."
58. Gekkō no Sonata, May 15, 2007 (5:39 p.m.), review of *Best Wishes for Tomorrow*, *Yahoo! Japan*, April 25, 2015, http://movies.yahoo.co.jp/movie/俺は、君のためにこそ死ににいく/324782/.
59. Yutake Eve, May 12, 2007 (11:44 p.m.), review of *Best Wishes for Tomorrow*, *Yahoo! Japan*, April 25, 2015, http://movies.yahoo.co.jp/movie/俺は、君のためにこそ死ににいく/324782/.
60. "Kamikaze Film Sparks Pacifist Response," *New York Times*, May 13, 2007, accessed March 31, 2015, http://www.nytimes.com/2007/05/13/world/asia/13iht-japan.1.5684590.html?_r=0.

Notably, kamikaze occupy a slightly different discursive space in terms of combat narratives. The young *tokkōtai*, or kamikaze pilots, have been heavily symbolized as fireflies, cherry blossoms, and living gods. Yoshikuni Igarashi suggests that their youth and sacrificial deaths have placed them in a different context than other elements of the war, reading the imagination of the pilots as a metaphor for nation and a symbol of war memory closure—just as the kamikaze died in real life, the nation died in defeat. He critiques the easy symbolism of the firefly (men who died as kamikaze were said to return as fireflies), concluding that "the meaning of death, even that of 'heroic' death, emerges only through the living's act of interpretation."[61] Emiko Ohnuki-Tierney examines the writings of kamikaze pilots and the symbolism of the cherry blossom to understand the development, reception, and rejection of nationalism, particularly among these young men. She argues that these highly educated men attached their own meanings to the image of the cherry blossom; in essence, "these men 'volunteered' to reproduce the ideology *in action* while defying it *in their thoughts*."[62] Finally, Nakamura Hideyuki suggests that *tokkōtai* were not represented as young men or heroes who die but rather as *ikiteiru kamisama* (living gods) who "ascend" to the heavens.[63] Nakamura also argues that the final scene of *Yamato*—the blue sea with the white wake of the ship—is reminiscent of the blue sky and white clouds of kamikaze films, a repetition of what he terms the *eigateki girei* (film form) of kamikaze films.[64] These three sets of images all serve to obfuscate the harsh reality of the brutal way in which these young pilots met their deaths.

There has been a change in representation over time. Kamikaze film heroes of the 1950s and 1960s concurrently explored both the good and bad sides of the military, critiquing while concurrently paying homage to the beliefs that promoted the system. Other tropes included ending with the hero's tragic flight into the sunset (*The Last Kamikaze*, 1970) or showing stock footage of the actual kamikaze battles, which were usually short, tragic, and futile (the *Aa* series). There was little dramatization of the battle scenes themselves, with the films focusing instead on the psychological state of the individual kamikaze and the

---

61. Yoshikuni Igarashi, "Kamikaze Today: The Search for National Heroes in Contemporary Japan," in *Ruptured Histories: War, Memory, and the Post–Cold War in Asia*, ed. Sheila Miyoshi Jager and Rana Mitter (Cambridge, MA: Harvard University Press, 2007), 121.
62. Emiko Ohnuki-Tierney, *Kamikaze, Cherry Blossoms, and Nationalisms: The Militarization of Aesthetics in Japanese History* (Chicago: University of Chicago Press, 2010), 300, and Emiko Ohnuki-Tierney, *Kamikaze Diaries: Reflections of Japanese Student Soldiers* (Chicago: University of Chicago Press, 2007).
63. Hideyuki Nakamura, "Tokkōtai hyōshōron," in *Iwanami kōza: Ajia, taiheiyō sensō 5: Senjō no shosō* (Tokyo: Iwanami Shoten, 2006), 306.
64. Hideyuki Nakamura, "Girei toshite no tokkō eiga: Otokotachi no yamato/yamato no baai," *Zen'ya* 7 (2006): 134–137.

society around him However, this was not necessarily unproblematic. As Isolde Standish notes, many early kamikaze films appear to criticize wartime ideology verbally while visually reinforcing the ideologies of that time.[65]

For Those We Love, on the other hand, presents simplistic nationalist narratives of brotherhood, training, and sacrifice framed in terms of nostalgia. Its main difference from both previous kamikaze films and newer mainstream films is its lack of ambiguity. In the first scene, the men work together to climb a large wooden pole. Rather than appearing grueling or difficult as in *Yamato*, such training is a fun and healthy game of masculine bonding with the soldier-brothers striving toward the same goal. When their planes have trouble, the men cheer each other on. They happily do sit-ups in the barracks. The film also features numerous songs and much singing. Even at the end when the men have all died, their spirits are depicted smiling happily against a backdrop of cherry blossoms in the Yasukuni Shrine in a sequence that reduces their suffering to mere ideology. The film continues this emphasis on nostalgic nationalism through the end credits, as photos of youthful kamikaze pilots happily playing with puppies appear next to the titles and in the film's promotional materials. In sum, the film idealizes the youth and innocence of the pilots through repeated images of laughter and play.

However, the boys become men during battle. Instead of victims, the young men are represented as purposeful and honorable, unafraid in the face of death. They are no longer tools used in the war, but weaponized people. In a sequence of shocking images, soldiers pilot their planes into American ships. Their bodies are covered in blood and consumed by fire, yet they grit their teeth, yell, and direct their planes into the American vessels. Despite their youthful faces, the young soldiers are resolute and steadfast. In their patriotic determination—their choice to direct the plane into the enemy's ship—they are heroic men, not boys. Nojima Ryūzō criticizes *For Those We Love* for ignoring the psychological experience of facing death, in terms of the questions these young men must have had or the anger they must have felt. He notes that *Pacchigi: Love & Peace* (2007, which also parodied the rose-colored lens of *For Those*) and *Hotaru* (2001), two films that explored the *Zainichi* (Korean-Japanese) kamikaze experience, were far more critical of the Japanese military and more complex in depicting the individual experiences of these men.[66]

This lack of ambiguity extends to the representation of the military leadership. The leaders are not simply given a pass as in *Yamato*; they are explicitly rehabilitated. In an early scene a general justifies the kamikaze program as a

---

65. Isolde Standish, *Myth and Masculinity in the Japanese Cinema: Towards a Political Reading of the Tragic Hero* (London: Routledge, 2000), 79.
66. Ryūzō Nojima, "Eiga ni egakareta sensō no shinjitsu: Ore wa, kiminotameni koso shini ni iku to Hotaru, Patchigi! LOVE & PEACE" (Tokushū rekishi no shinjitsu o tou), *Minshubungaku* 503 (2007): 140–145.

way to liberate Asia from Western imperialism. This argument was used to defend the invasion of Asian nations during World War II under the concept of the Greater East Asia Co-Prosperity Sphere and continues, in a milder form, as part of mainstream discourse.[67] The American invasion of Okinawa is presented as unprovoked, lending the beginning of the narrative its urgency and supporting the general's "white peril" argument. Further, a *Zainichi* pilot declares that he is dying for the Japanese nation, essentially legitimizing the "Asia for the Asians" narrative of the right and denying Korean (and other Asian) claims to trauma. Finally, the general commits suicide at the end of the film through the ritual of *seppuku*—a performance connected to the masculine concept of *bushidō*.

Like the aforementioned Chinese productions, *Yamato* and *For Those We Love* depict women as figures of trauma, memory, and nostalgia. First, women signify victimhood in the films. In *Yamato*, Kamio's mother and girlfriend are both killed by American bombs; in *For Those* a group of young schoolgirls are massacred by American planes. Second, women are represented as the reason for men to go to war. Wakakuwa Midori argues that, while in reality, Japanese men went to war on behalf of the emperor, in *Yamato* this theme is missing. Thus, in her interpretation of the film, the men are going to war on behalf of their mothers and girlfriends.[68] Third, women are portrayed as the keepers of memory. Uchida reminds everyone that they must commemorate the *Yamato*; *For Those* is narrated by Torihama Tome, a female restaurant owner who comforted young pilots in real life. This smiling, soft-spoken "*tokkō* mother" further legitimizes the sacrifice of the pilots, concealing the loss of real mothers through her easy acceptance of their deaths. As Franziska Seraphim notes, the widows' plight has in many ways been appropriated by and integrated into national narratives, which is traditionally framed by active male nationalists.[69] Like the statue of the war widow at Yushukan—*Haha no zō* (the Mother Statue)—these films use the image of the supportive mother to justify the sacrifice of her son and husband.[70] In essence, women in these films represent nativist notions of culture/land/womb. They

---

67. Lisa Yoneyama notes that the racism that permeated the postwar trials, such as prosecution of crimes against Dutch comfort women and ignoring of Asian comfort women, "created a subtle conflation of Japanese and other Asians, for neither group was granted full membership in the category of 'humanity,' at least within the West-centric discourse of the tribunal." Yoneyama, *Hiroshima Traces*, 12.
68. Midori Wakakuwa, "Jendā no shiten de yomitoku sengo eiga: *Otokotachi no Yamato* wo chūshin ni," *Tōzai Nanboku* (2007): 6–17.
69. Franziska Seraphim, *War Memory and Social Politics in Japan, 1945–2005* (Cambridge, MA: Harvard University Press, 2006), 12–13.
70. Morris Low, "Gender and Representations of the War in Tokyo Museums," in *East Asia Beyond the History Wars: Reconciliation as Method*, ed. Tessa Morris-Suzuki, Morris Low, Leonid Petrov, and Timothy Y. Tsu (Routledge: New York, 2013): 123–143. Films like *Under the Flag of the Rising Sun* (Gunki hatameki motoni, 1972) invert this discourse, demanding the government take responsibility for killing these men.

are the "why men fight" and, like male characters, are often reduced to signs of trauma or nostalgia.

While both mainstream and right-wing films use the innocuous figure of the youthful soldier as their focal point, their representation of masculinity shows disparate visions of Japanese national identity. Although mainstream films no longer demonize the bad militant self and can be read as a metaphor for contemporary Japan's tentative exploration of military normalization, this is by no means a clear-cut affirmation of the military. Attitudes toward Japan's Self-Defense Force continue to be contentious. Right-wing films, meanwhile, display a monolithic masculinity that is idealized nostalgically, though audiences often interpret these films as pacifist. The two films, when read together, reflect the current situation in Japan, wherein the mainstream discourse is still uncertain about the future of the military, and the nationalist minority is increasingly vocal and popular among certain powerful interest groups.

Conclusion

While they are influenced by historical, political, and economic forces, the overall trend in both Chinese and Japanese combat films is toward soldiers who embody rigid notions of national masculinity and male heroism based on myths of race and gender. Chinese soldiers combat the hypermasculine or hyperfeminine Japanese soldier-as-nation; the youthful Japanese soldier gazes in newfound respect at the soldiers of the past. Notably, these combat films are also the dominant war genre domestically and generate less intersecting transnational discourse in terms of the memory loop. Of all the films discussed in this book, combat films perform best at the box office and are the easiest to find in Chinese markets, online, or in the local Japanese video store. Yet while such trends reflect the rising nationalist currents in both nations and the market value of heroic narratives, there are differences in terms of reception as it is unclear to what extent these films appeal to different demographics. In Japan, war narratives are more prominent in theaters; in China, they are more prominent on television and thus are more visible on a daily basis. In both China and Japan, it is believed that older people are the main audience for these films.

Why have these masculinist narratives developed? As socialist ideology loses its significance, Chinese narratives have returned to increasingly nativist *wen-wu* and a loosening of dogmatic heroic narratives. The influence of the market has caused producers to adopt different strategies to appeal to Chinese audiences, with the emergence of magical *wuxia* fantasy elements and the individuality of Li Yunlong part of this market trend. In Japan, there is a similar market trend toward big-budget narratives as Japanese companies attempt to recoup losses by producing big-budget epics. In addition, the Tokyo Trial narrative is being delegitimized to pave the way for Japanese normalization. As such, the dynamic of the postwar period—the hypermasculine leader and the victimized soldier—is undergoing a change. However, that does not mean that these are necessarily "nationalistic" films. Mainstream discourse still suggests an ambiguous narrative due to discomfort over the status of the Self-Defense Force and the legacy of the war.

These combat narratives also reveal a disturbing trend in the representation of women. In China and Japan, women have been returned to increasingly passive figures of trauma who serve only to galvanize or reflect masculinist notions of nation. As will be discussed in the next chapter, Nanjing films in particular demonstrate the appropriation of female trauma to serve national discourses. Yet this is not to say that individual men are not subject to power and control. The traumatic experiences of soldiers—explored brilliantly in anti-war films directed by former soldiers like *The Burmese Harp* (Biruma no tategoto, 1956) and *The Human Condition* (Ningen no jōken, 1959–1961)—are suppressed or ignored in popular combat films. In an era of increasing nationalism, the true nature of combat is concealed by idealized narratives of masculinity.

4
Contested Images of Wartime Rape

> The rape of a motherland is far worse than the rape of actual mothers; the death of a nation is the ultimate tragedy, beyond the death of flesh and blood.[1]

From December 1937 to February 1938, the Imperial Japanese Army committed numerous atrocities against Chinese civilians and prisoners of war in the city of Nanjing, then the capital of China.[2] According to Daqing Yang: "As the verdict of the Tokyo trial put it, the Japanese troops in Nanjing engaged in organized and wholesale murder, committed indiscriminate killing and rape, as well as looting and destruction. Over 200,000 Chinese civilians and POWs were believed to have been murdered in the Nanjing area during a six-week period in the winter of 1937–1938, while approximately 20,000 cases of rape occurred within the city alone. The verdict of the Nanjing trial was similar, except for a higher death toll of over 300,000."[3] The carnage in Nanjing was reported at the time in both Chinese and Western media and later established at the postwar trials in Nanjing and Tokyo, where five officers were executed for their participation in the atrocities.[4]

Due to Cold War relations, the Nanjing Massacre was largely submerged in popular memory until after Sino-Japanese and Sino-American normalization in the 1970s.[5] In Japan, the work of historian Hora Tomio and journalist Honda Katsuichi brought the massacre to widespread attention in the late 1960s and

---

1. Michael Billig, *Banal Nationalism* (London: SAGE, 1995), 4.
2. For collections of essays from scholars based in Asia and the United States, see Joshua Fogel, ed., *The Nanjing Massacre in History and Historiography* (Berkeley: University of California Press, 2000), and Bob Tadashi Wakabayashi, ed., *The Nanking Atrocity, 1937–38: Complicating the Picture* (New York: Berghahn Books, 2013).
3. Daqing Yang, "Convergence or Divergence? Recent Historical Writings on the Rape of Nanjing," *American Historical Review* 104, no. 3 (1999): 844.
4. Yang, "Convergence or Divergence?," 844.
5. Takashi Yoshida, who has analyzed how discourse on Nanjing has emerged in strikingly different ways over different eras, identifies four stages of remembrance (1937–1945; 1945–1971; 1971–1989; 1989–present) and three sections each (China, Japan,

early 1970s.[6] In China, the first historical account of the massacre was compiled locally in Nanjing in the 1960s, becoming more widely known nationally after the first Japanese textbook controversy in the early 1980s. In the United States, Nanjing first emerged in Chinese American communities in the 1980s.[7] It became even more widely well known in the mid-1990s after the publication of Iris Chang's controversial book *The Rape of Nanking* and the efforts of US House of Representatives member Mike Honda to acknowledge wartime sexual violence committed by the Japanese army.[8]

Since the "globalization" of Nanjing discourse in the 1990s, there have emerged nearly as many works on the problems of writing the historiography of Nanjing as actual histories of Nanjing. Contemporary debates have focused on issues including the Tokyo Trial, where the Nanjing Massacre was established as a war crime; the "numbers game," wherein historians and critics fight over the precise number of people killed in Nanjing; debates over whether the "hundred-man killing contest" was propaganda or reality; and arguments over how to refer to the massacre itself (the Rape of Nanjing, the Nanjing Incident, the Nanjing Atrocity, etc.). As historian Joshua Fogel writes in his introduction to a volume on Nanjing: "It is a telling state of affairs historically that I must say

---

and the United States). Takashi Yoshida, *The Making of the "Rape of Nanking": History and Memory in Japan, China, and the United States* (Oxford: Oxford University Press, 2006).

6. Yang notes that the first historical book was written by Japanese historian Hora Tomio in 1967, yet it was reporter Honda Katsuichi's work that brought more widespread exposure in Japanese media and prompted the first wave of debates. Yang, "Convergence or Divergence?," 844.

7. Yoshida, *Making of the "Rape of Nanking,"* 124–125; Fogel, "The Nanking Atrocity and Chinese Historical Memory," in *The Nanjing Massacre in History and Historiography*, 267.

8. Honda has taken up the issue of wartime sexual violence in Asia by supporting American monuments for comfort women and Chang (who committed suicide in 2004) in California and New Jersey. In 1999, Honda passed resolution AJR 27 in the California Assembly, which states that Japan should "finally bring closure to concerns relating to World War II by formally issuing a clear and unambiguous apology for the atrocious war crimes committed by the Japanese military during World War II." See Monsy Alvarado, "Palisades Park 'Comfort Women' Memorial Saluted by Japanese-American Congressman," Northjersey.com, June 27, 2013, accessed June 10, 2014, http://www.northjersey.com/news/palisades-park-comfort-women-memorial-saluted-by-japanese-american-congressman-1.593660; "Bronze Statue of Writer and Journalist Iris Chang Dedicated," Hoover Institute, February 8, 2007, accessed June 10, 2014, http://www.hoover.org/news/bronze-statue-writer-and-journalist-iris-chang-dedicated; "Bill Number: AJR 27," Official California Legislative Information, accessed June 10, 2014, http://www.leginfo.ca.gov/pub/99-00/bill/asm/ab_0001-0050/ajr_27_bill_19990826_chaptered.html; Kinue Tokudome, "The Japanese Apology on the 'Comfort Women' Cannot Be Considered Official: Interview with Congressman Michael Honda," *Japan Focus*, May 31, 2007, accessed June 10, 2014, http://japanfocus.org/-Michael-Honda/2438.

in this introduction that none of us doubts that a great massacre occurred in an around Nanjing from December 1937 through February 1938."[9] Despite these debates and controversies, historians agree that Japanese soldiers committed major atrocities in Nanjing, including the widespread rape and murder of unarmed Chinese civilians and soldiers.

Like other major traumatic events of World War II, the Nanjing Massacre has become the subject of numerous documentaries, feature films, and television dramas and is one of the most dynamic and fraught transnational memory loops. Since the 1980s, producers in China, Hong Kong, and Taiwan have made several major feature films depicting the massacre. From the early aughts (2000–2009), filmmakers in the United States, Germany, and Australia have focused on Western witnesses and the Nanjing Safety Zone. Mainstream Japanese cinema has largely been silent on the subject of wartime sexual violence committed by Japanese forces, with the topic emerging in fringe films of the right and the left from the late aughts. The circumstances of the productions themselves are also useful in revealing the dynamics of remembrance, such as how the massacre is being framed, by whom, and for whom.

Gender is central to these films and to the discourse surrounding Nanjing. As Yuki Tanaka states, "It is imperative to closely analyze the symbolic parallel between the violation of a woman's body and the domination over others (enemies) on the battlefield or through colonial institutions."[10] The rapes of Chinese women are frequently presented in Chinese and American discourse as the rape of the Chinese nation or, as Chinese American writer Iris Chang famously framed it, "the rape of Nanking." In Japan, it is notably the masculinity-preoccupied right wing that responds most vociferously to the specter of Japanese military sexual violence in an attempt to rescue Japan's "besieged" national honor. This chapter draws on arguments developed by Chungmoo Choi and C. Sarah Soh in their analysis of how comfort women discourse in Korea is framed by patriarchal nationalism.[11] It also builds upon Tanya Horeck and Sarah Projansky's work

---

9. Joshua Fogel, "Introduction," in *The Nanjing Massacre in History and Historiography*, ed. Joshua Fogel (Berkeley: University of California Press, 2000), 5. Bob Wakabayashi similarly describes several disagreements over statistics and phrasing over essays published within the same book. Wakabayashi, *Nanking Atrocity*, 20.
10. Yuki Tanaka, *Japan's Comfort Women* (London: Psychology Press, 2002), 4.
11. The comfort women stations were a system of mass sexual slavery created under the direction of the Japanese Imperial Army. Concerned by conflicts with the Chinese populace and widespread venereal disease among the soldiers, Japanese military leaders institutionalized prostitution. Under their purview and with the participation of local prostitution industries, the army regulated the sexual activity of their troops by swiftly expanding the number of stations. Many women in these stations were from occupied nations, coerced into the system by false promises of factory work, sold by struggling family members, or abducted. Meanwhile, comfort women have been variously referred to as prostitutes or slaves, in what Hasegawa and Togo refer to as the

on the issues of representing rape on-screen to examine the dual problems of representing sexual violence both on-screen and as part of a national narrative.[12] Focusing on the subjectivity of the female characters, it argues that Nanjing films often foreground national myths of masculine honor/power, framing the female subject in a transnational dialogue where her rape is ultimately a "conversation between men."[13]

Rape, Gender, Nation

Numerous studies have established the ubiquity of rape during wartime, though scholars differ in their understanding of why it occurs. Some arguments focus on its employment as a systematic weapon to inspire fear and subjugation in the conquered.[14] A second argument suggests that it is a form of genocide to "replace" the

---

"military brothel" and the "rape center" schools of the debate. Hasegawa, Tsuyoshi, and Kazuhiko Togo, *East Asia's Haunted Present: Historical Memories and the Resurgence of Nationalism* (Westport, CT: ABC-CLIO, 2008), 153. For more on comfort women discourse, see Chungmoo Choi, "The Politics of War Memories toward Healing," in *Perilous Memories: The Asia-Pacific War(s)* (Durham, NC: Duke University Press, 2001): 395–410 and Sarah C. Soh, *The Comfort Women: Sexual Violence and Postcolonial Memory in Korea and Japan* (Chicago: University of Chicago Press, 2008).

12. In the analysis of films on sensitive historical events, one runs the risk of appearing insensitive to or even obscuring the traumatic events of the past. This chapter is an analysis of film narratives, not a work of historiography or even a commentary on history, nor does it in any way dispute the violence experienced by Chinese people, the crimes committed by the Japanese army, or the services rendered by Western witnesses who documented and bore witness to these atrocities. Critiques of Chinese and Japanese films are intended to illustrate some of the issues of narrating female trauma as national trauma, particularly via the cinematic medium, not to revise any understanding of the events which occurred in Nanjing. Young deals with similar concerns in the introduction to his book: James Edward Young, *Writing and Rewriting the Holocaust: Narrative and the Consequences of Interpretation* (Bloomington: Indiana University Press, 1990).
13. Zoë Brigley Thompson and Sorcha Gunne, "Introduction: Feminism without Borders: The Potentials and Pitfalls of Retheorizing Rape," in *Feminism, Literature and Rape Narratives: Violence and Violation*, ed. Sorcha Gunne and Zoë Brigley Thompson (New York: Routledge, 2010), 8.
14. According to Jacqui True, "private sphere" crimes against human rights such as rape were not fully recognized until the UN Vienna Conference on Human Rights of 1993. In 2008, the UN Security Council passed resolution 1820, which defines sexual violence as a wartime strategy; in 2009, resolution 1889 declared that quantitative data should be collected on sexual violence. Jacqui True, *The Political Economy of Violence against Women* (Oxford: Oxford University Press, 2012), 114–116. See also Claudia Card, "Rape as a Weapon of War," *Hypatia* 11, no. 4 (1996): 5–18; Nancy Farwell, "War Rape: New Conceptualizations and Responses," *Affilia* 19, no. 4 (2004): 389–403. For a discussion of the different ways rape is employed as a weapon, see Paul Kirby, "How Is Rape a Weapon of War? Feminist International Relations, Modes of Critical Explanation and

ethnic population of the occupied nation.[15] A third theory posits that it is in part a soldier's response to finding themselves powerless within the harsh military system—in effect, they exert power or control over the bodies of the powerless.[16] A fourth suggests that it serves to unite members of the military either through a system of willing "perpetratorhood" or through what Bülent Diken and Carsten Bagge Lausten call a "brotherhood of guilt."[17] There are also many different forms of wartime rape, ranging from highly organized sexual slavery systems, such as Japan's "comfort women" stations, to the strategic revenge kidnapping or rape of women, to rape committed in the midst of battle. Each form suggests different levels of agency and complicity on the part of the military power and the individual soldier.[18] Moreover, it is significant that some armies commit rape, while others do not. According to Susan Brownmiller, it is typically the conquering nations that rape both because of their control over the regions they have invaded and because of the symbolism of the conqueror "penetrating" the conquered nation.[19] Meanwhile, Tanaka ventures that nationalist movements fighting for liberation/independence—being aware of the relationship between colonialism and sexual violence—may be less likely to rape the women of the occupying force.[20]

---

the Study of Wartime Sexual Violence," *European Journal of International Relations* 19, no. 4 (2012), https://doi.org/10.1177/1354066111427614.

15. The employment of "genocidal rape," or rape used in war to eradicate the ethnicity of the dominated group, suggests that the female body is a blank receptacle that can be used to "replace" the population; the woman's own national identity is ignored. Beverly Allen, *Rape Warfare: The Hidden Genocide in Bosnia-Herzegovina and Croatia* (Minneapolis: University of Minnesota Press, 1996). See also Christoph Schiessl, "An Element of Genocide: Rape, Total War, and International Law in the Twentieth Century," *Journal of Genocide Research* 4, no. 2 (2002): 197–210, and Cindy S. Snyder, Wesley J. Gabbard, J. Dean May, and Nihada Zulcic, "On the Battleground of Women's Bodies: Mass Rape in Bosnia-Herzegovina," *Affilia* 21, no. 2 (2006): 184–195.
16. Tanaka, *Japan's Comfort Women*, 180 and 205. Fears about fitting an ideal of masculinity can serve to normalize sexual violence against women. Baaz and Stern argue that wartime rapes are directly affected by notions of masculinity such as the "(hetero) sexually potent male fighter" whose masculinity is imagined as fragile and threatened by a "weak, subordinate, and treacherous" femininity. Maria Eriksson Baaz and Maria Stern, "Why Do Soldiers Rape? Masculinity, Violence, and Sexuality in the Armed Forces in the Congo (DRC)," *International Studies Quarterly* 53, no. 2 (2009): 495–518.
17. Dara Kay Cohen, "Explaining Sexual Violence during Civil War: Evidence from the Sierra Leone War (1991–2002)" (paper presented at the annual convention of the American Political Science Association, Chicago, Illinois, August 16, 2007), and Bülent Diken and Carsten Bagge Laustsen, "Becoming Abject: Rape as a Weapon of War," *Body and Society* 11, no. 1 (2005): 111–128.
18. For instance, a Japanese soldier who visited a "comfort station" was not ordered to do so by his commanders. See Tanaka, *Japan's Comfort Women*, 4.
19. Susan Brownmiller, *Against Our Will: Men, Women and Rape* (New York: Simon and Schuster, 1975).
20. Tanaka, *Japan's Comfort Women*, 179.

The victims of wartime rape are usually women, in part because the rape of a woman symbolizes the rape of the nation. While neither "woman" nor "nation" is a monolithic category, the two are commonly constructed narratively through gendered tropes. One of the first imagined roles of women in nation building is in terms of biological reproduction, which Nira Yuval-Davis argues is tied to issues of ethnic origin, growth of a nation, eugenics, and population control.[21] Yet a woman is not allowed to bear children freely—she must produce the *right kind of citizen*. In Japan and China, for instance, there is a myth of common ethnic origins of Han and Yamato. The "Yamato race" has been associated with Japanese uniqueness, purity, and superiority.[22] In times of war, women's bodies provide the nation with new soldiers: man is the "god of war" (*gunshin*) to the woman's "mother of a god of war."[23]

In addition to being "mother," woman is also imagined as "motherland." Yoshikuni Igarashi has argued that the foundational narrative of postwar Japan was that of a feminized Japan "saved" by the masculine America.[24] As such, the *panpan*, or Japanese sex workers, who often slept with American soldiers, "were striking symbols of the whole convoluted phenomenon of 'Americanization' in which everyone was in some way engaged. The *panpan* openly, brazenly *prostituted* themselves to the conqueror—while others, especially the 'good' Japanese who consorted with the Americans as privileged elites, only did it figuratively."[25] The act of sleeping with American men became a symbol of national defeat and of the dominant US/passive Japan postwar relationship. For this very reason, Japanese prostitutes in northeast China were not allowed to serve non-Japanese clients after Japan invaded Manchuria. According to Tanaka: "In the eyes of Japanese power holders, the bodies of women of their own racial group should not be penetrated by foreigners—an act symbolizing the invasion and deprivation of the motherland."[26] Because women embody national sovereignty, sex with a foreign man represents the subjugation and feminization of the nation.

---

21. Nira Yuval-Davis, *Gender and Nation* (London: SAGE, 1997), 26–37.
22. John Dower, *War without Mercy: Race and Power in the Pacific War* (New York: Random House, 1986), 204–205. The legacy of this concept continues into the present day—while the current Japanese "population crisis" could be solved through immigration, this would not produce the desired "pure" Yamato blood.
23. Chizuko Ueno, *Nationalism and Gender*, trans. Beverley Yamamoto (Melbourne: Trans Pacific Press, 2004): 20.
24. Yoshikuni Igarashi, *Bodies of Memory: Narratives of War in Postwar Japanese Culture, 1945–1970* (Princeton, NJ: Princeton University Press, 2000), 20.
25. John W. Dower, *Embracing Defeat: Japan in the Wake of World War II* (New York: W. W. Norton, 2000), 135.
26. Tanaka, *Japan's Comfort Women*, 180.

Such imagined roles of gender and nation tie into Nanjing discourse. In the case of Nanjing, the power dynamic was between the invading Japanese power and the emasculated Chinese nation. During the first half of the twentieth century, nativist notions of Japanese "purity" and the ideology of the Greater East Asia Co-Prosperity Sphere imagined Japan as the center of Asia. This notion of racial or cultural superiority, with its emphasis on Japanese patriarchy and militarism, facilitated the subjugation and feminization of dominated nations. It is perhaps because of such ideology that the system of military sexual slavery was directed mainly at women of subjugated nations, and particularly large numbers of Korean women, who as colonial subjects were seen as culturally similar yet racially inferior.[27] In China, wartime sexual violence committed against Chinese women existed both in comfort women stations (both officially sanctioned stations and in unapproved stations, particularly in areas perceived to be "hostile"), as well as part of the "Shōdo Sakusen/Sanguang Zuozhan," a kind of scorched-earth policy wherein Chinese areas perceived to be resistant were subjected to indiscriminate looting, burning, killing, and rape.[28]

Zoë Brigley Thompson and Sorcha Gunne, citing the work of Jeffner Allen, suggest that rape is a "conversation between men."[29] It is perhaps for this reason that women are often assaulted in front of their husbands, brothers, or fathers during war, with the act intended to emasculate the men of the invaded nation. As Tamar Mayer states, "Because women's bodies represent the 'purity' of the nation and are thus heavily guarded by men, an attack on these bodies becomes an attack on the nation's men."[30] This leads to problems of telling rape, best described in the work of Soh and Choi.[31] According to Choi in her discussion of the national politics surrounding comfort women in Korea, "Comfort woman discourse displaces the women's subjectivity, which is grounded on pain, and constructs the women only as symbols of national shame. As such, the primacy of the discourse on comfort women attends not to the welfare of women's subjectivity but to the national agenda of overcoming colonial emasculation."[32] As Ueno Chizuko notes, former comfort women have been pressured by the image

---

27. Tanaka, *Japan's Comfort Women*, 45.
28. Tanaka, *Japan's Comfort Women*, 46.
29. Thompson and Gunne, "Introduction," 8.
30. Tamar Mayer, ed., *Gender Ironies of Nationalism: Sexing the Nation* (London: Routledge, 2002), 18.
31. C. Sarah Soh, *The Comfort Women: Sexual Violence and Postcolonial Memory in Korea and Japan* (Chicago: University of Chicago Press, 2008), and Chungmoo Choi, "The Politics of War Memories toward Healing," in *Perilous Memories: The Asia-Pacific War(s)*, ed. T. T. Fujitani, Geoffrey M. White, and Lisa Yoneyama (Durham, NC: Duke University Press, 2001), 395–409.
32. Choi, "Politics of War Memories," 399.

of a "model victim," which prioritizes the narrative of a virgin forcefully kidnapped and raped over other narratives of victimhood.[33] Even the legal measures to address rape are connected to a crisis of masculinity, as they "are almost always framed by a masculine perspective" and based on male fantasies and fears.[34] In sum, the discourse surrounding rape is frequently framed by male politics, even more in the case of wartime rape, which draws from the masculine discourses of the nation and the military.

Watching rape on-screen is inherently problematic. In her analysis of "public fantasies," a term she borrows from Elizabeth Cowie, Tanya Horeck describes how showing, not showing, and deciding how much to show have concerned censors, filmmakers, lawmakers, and academics. Moreover, since the same scene of rape can be interpreted differently depending on the viewer and the context, Horeck suggests that "rape is a battle over the ownership of meaning and of reality, "which "brings questions of audience involvement in onscreen violence to a crisis point."[35] Sarah Projansky also explores the paradox inherent in watching rape. For Projansky, film represents and reveals female trauma while concurrently disseminating images of women being traumatized.[36] Thus the representation of rape mimics what Lynn Higgins and Brenda Silver call the "obsessive inscription" and "obsessive erasure" of the act of rape.[37] Newer works on rape aim to take the discourse beyond second-wave feminism's aim of simply revealing rape to discussions of both *whether* and *how* we should reveal. They explore literary works that attempt to take the rape narrative outside of a hierarchical structure that disenfranchises the female speaker through characterizations as victim/passive; they also discuss the politics both of speaking and of silence, a concept Choi explores in her analysis of how former comfort women verbalized their experiences.[38] In newer literature, such as Dominique Russell's *Rape in Art Cinema*, the discussion switches to the politics of representing rape in an art film that is, by its very nature, ambiguous and pushing boundaries.[39] What is at stake throughout are the politics of representation—of telling, of silence, and of visual and narrative framing.

---

33. Chizuko Ueno, "The Politics of Memory: Nation, Individual and Self," trans. Jordan Sand, *History and Memory* 11, no. 2 (1999): 143.
34. Lynn A. Higgins and Brenda R. Silver, ed., *Rape and Representation* (New York: Columbia University Press, 1991), 2.
35. Tanya Horeck, *Public Rape: Representing Violation in Fiction and Film* (London: Routledge, 2013), 13, 140.
36. Sarah Projansky, *Watching Rape: Film and Television in Postfeminist Culture* (New York: New York University Press, 2001).
37. Higgins and Silver, *Rape and Representation*, 2.
38. Zoë Brigley Thompson and Sorcha Gunne, ed., *Feminism, Literature and Rape Narratives: Violence and Violation* (New York: Routledge, 2010). See also Choi, "Politics of War Memories."
39. Dominique Russell, ed., *Rape in Art Cinema* (New York: Continuum, 2010).

Ultimately, this chapter does not question what constitutes a "good" or "bad" depiction of wartime sexual assault but, rather, how the meaning of such violence is framed by the visual medium of cinema and international discourses. In films about Nanjing, how does the visualization of rape testify to past violence, giving a voice to the voiceless or the deceased? Conversely, how do rigid national narratives constrain the telling of rape, undermining the subjective experience of pain? Finally, how are such images in dialogue with each other, and what do they suggest about the gendered nature of the transnational discourse surrounding the remembrance of Nanjing?

"The Rape of a Motherland"

One of the first films to mention the Nanjing Massacre was a Sino-Japanese coproduction created to commemorate the 1972 diplomatic normalization of relations between the two nations. *The Go Masters* (Yi pan mei xiawan de qi/ Mikan no taikyoku, 1982) follows the lives of two families—the Kuangs and the Matsunamis—as they are united through marriage, separated by war, and reunited by normalization.[40] In one of the film's climactic scenes, the married children of the two families—Kuang A Ming and Matsunami Tomoe—discover an English-language newspaper reporting the massacre. As they read about the atrocities in Nanjing, ecstatic Japanese crowds rejoice outside by singing a nationalistic song. In one sense, the scene appears to acknowledge Chinese victimhood and Japanese responsibility. The English newspaper provides proof of the massacre and further proclaims its global visibility. Yet in another sense, the depiction is in line with the muddled depiction common in Japanese discourse on the massacre. While the scene is certainly critical of the nationalistic cheering outside, textual representation in a foreign language renders the massacre abstract. Moreover, depending on the politics of the viewer, the newspaper could be interpreted as evidence or hearsay.

Go Masters was for the most part successful in both countries upon its release. While contemporaneous Chinese film critics argued that the number dead listed in the newspaper (45,000) critically underestimated the number killed in Nanjing, the film was lauded by the same critics as a momentous step forward in Sino-Japanese reconciliation relations.[41] *Go Masters* won a Japanese Academy Award of Excellence in 1983, though right-wing groups did disrupt screenings at the time. In recent years, however, the film has faded into obscurity in Japan, with contemporary comments on an available YouTube version largely labeling

---

40. I saw the Japanese version in Chinese/Japanese with Japanese subtitles.
41. Mengxi Liu, "Qidao yishu lishi: Yingpian yi pan meiyou xiawan de qi manping," *Dianying Yishu* 10 (1982): 23.

it "anti-Japanese." Many of these comments dispute the Nanjing newspaper, suggesting a popular turn toward atrocity denial.[42]

Massacre in Nanjing (Tucheng xuezheng, 1987), produced by the Fujian and Nanjing film studios, was the first feature film to focus specifically on Nanjing and to depict rape on-screen.[43] This film was produced amid a shift in national discourse from the early 1980s. First, revisionist Japanese textbooks caused a huge controversy in 1982, with Prime Minister Nakasone's official visit to the Yasukuni Shrine in 1985 exacerbating the conflict and inspiring popular protests among Chinese students. Second, authorities concerned by Western "spiritual pollution" began to focus on developing patriotism through nationalist education.[44] Against this backdrop, several monuments and works commemorating the Nanjing Massacre were disseminated throughout China from the late 1980s, including the establishment of the Nanjing Massacre Memorial Hall in 1985. *Massacre in Nanjing* was promoted heavily. It won a national award of excellence in 1987, was viewed by over 1.4 million people in less than a month, and was reported in the press as a cathartic experience for survivors of the war, some of whom shouted at younger viewers for laughing inappropriately at parts.[45] Produced just after the Mao era, the films' reception was also influenced by the ideologies of that period as many audience members shouted slogans during the screening of the film.[46]

Thus, emerging at a time when Nanjing had become increasingly politicized, *Massacre* focuses on establishing the truth of Nanjing. As noted by Michael Berry, the film's rather dramatic Chinese title translates to "The City of Massacre—Evidence in Blood."[47] Photographs permeate the narrative, often punctuating images of violence by materializing with a click over massacre scenes as if to announce their imprint on Chinese memory.[48] Like the later PRC films *Don't*

---

42. Ken'ichi Fujita, September 2014, comment on *The Go Masters*, YouTube, April 26, 2015, https://www.youtube.com/watch?v=4eDO-RoQZNo.
43. I saw a digital transfer of a Chinese VCD, company unknown.
44. Yoshida, *The Making of the "Rape of Nanking,"* 105–106.
45. "Tucheng xuezheng daoyan luoguanqun houhui meiyou liu qunzhong yanyuan di dizhi," *Longhu wang*, June 11, 2013.
46. "Tucheng xuezheng."
47. Michael Berry, "Cinematic Representations of the Rape of Nanking," *East Asia* 19, no. 4 (2001): 85–108, and David Askew, "The Nanjing Incident: Recent Research and Trends," *Electronic Journal of Contemporary Japanese Studies* (2002), http://www.japanesestudies.org.uk/articles/Askew.html.
48. The inclusion of disproven photographs in serious works on Nanjing has been one of the major points of contention in the Nanjing debate. In the late 1990s the Japanese historian Kasahara Tokushi had to apologize for unintentionally using a fabricated photograph in his history of Nanjing. Both Iris Chang's *The Rape of Nanking* and the Nanjing Massacre Memorial have also been criticized for using manipulated photographs.

Cry, Nanking (Nanjing 1937, 1995) and *City of Life and Death* (Nanjing! Nanjing!, 2009), *Massacre* stars an ensemble of Chinese civilians, American observers, and Japanese soldiers, focusing mainly on the Chinese hero Dr. Zhan, the doctor's American love interest Katy, and a sympathetic Japanese soldier. The central drama focuses on atrocities committed against Chinese citizens and the heroic actions of its main male character, Dr. Zhan, as he searches for photographs to prove Japanese crimes.

The actions of Japanese attackers and male Chinese witnesses are featured prominently. Unable to overpower the Japanese forces, Dr. Zhan is forced to witness a Chinese woman's rape. The camera lingers over his horrified expression, the lower half of the woman's body, and the Japanese rapist, but there is no image of the victim's face. The woman is reduced to a symbol, her rape mainly important within the narrative as a catalyst for Dr. Zhan's later heroic actions. Afterward, Zhan escapes the Japanese soldiers and rushes into a river, the water cleansing him of his impotent masculinity and national shame. A similar scene occurs in the latter half of the film when the film's quasi-sympathetic Japanese soldier character executes his Chinese lover. Within the context of the story—after an implied rape or attempted rape—his action is framed as a "mercy killing" that ends her "shame." The deaths of these women thus signify the nation's traumatic past and a crisis of masculinity. Their deaths mark past victimhood and are a catalyst for a powerful, masculine China to emerge.[49] In many ways, *Massacre*'s depiction of rape is primarily framed as "a conversation between men."

Massacre also marks a striking transitional Chinese representation of Western observers and the Nanking Safety Zone. Although the cooperation of Western witnesses was central to the documentation of the massacre and the postwar Tokyo and Nanjing trials, the Cold War saw a reimagining of the role of Westerners. According to Yang, a 1951 article in *Xinhua Yuebao* was "more interested in revealing 'the American crimes' during the Japanese atrocities in Nanjing."[50] Moreover, early Chinese historiographies of the massacre largely omitted mention of the Western-organized Safety Zone.[51] The appearance of Katy, who is central to smuggling out the evidence of the massacre, suggests changing Chinese attitudes toward Western witnesses in the 1980s. Like the English newspaper in *Go Masters*, she signals the increasing transnational visibility of Nanjing

---

49. This appeal to masculinity can also be seen in statues memorializing Nanjing. See Yang's image of fearless, muscular men (and one woman) at the Nanjing Massacre Memorial. Daqing Yang, "The Malleable and the Contested: The Nanjing Massacre in Postwar China and Japan," in *Perilous Memories: The Asia-Pacific War(s)*, ed. T. T. Fujitani, Geoffrey M. White, and Lisa Yoneyama (Durham, NC: Duke University Press, 2001), 71.
50. Yang, "The Malleable and the Contested," 54.
51. Mark Eykholt, "Aggression, Victimization, and Chinese Historiography of the Nanjing Massacre," in *The Nanjing Massacre in History and Historiography*, ed. Joshua Fogel (Berkeley: University of California Press, 2000), 22.

discourse and the importance of Western witnesses at the massacre and Western recognition in the present. In another sense, as Dr. Zhan's unrequited female love interest, Katy is defined by her love of the male hero and serves as a mirror for his heroism. Katy thus signifies both the transnational nature of Nanjing discourse and successful Chinese globalization of the 1980s.

The next major Chinese film, the Taiwan—Hong Kong–PRC coproduction *Don't Cry, Nanking* (Nanjing 1937, 1995) problematizes the nationalist representation of female trauma.[52] This can be partially attributed to the artistic sensibilities of director Wu Ziniu, known for his humanistic approach to narratives, and to the participation of transnational producers from Hong Kong and Taiwan.[53] Before filming, Wu reflected deeply on the meaning of representation: "If I try to present a cinematic record of what actually happened, [the film] will come off too bloody and violent. Then again, using my film as a means to confirm the authenticity of the event is also not what I am interested in—that's work to be left to the historians."[54] As a result, he carefully approaches the representation of rape, also depicting characters from complicated national backgrounds who challenge easy nationalist allegories. *Don't Cry* eloquently shows the massacre from the point of view of an international couple (Chinese husband, Japanese wife), a Chinese teacher, and a Taiwanese draftee in the Japanese army.

Wu avoids the masculine-centered representation of the leering Japanese soldier or the male Chinese witness by emphasizing the chaotic turmoil of the rapes. In the film's climactic massacre scene, the Japanese charge the Safety Zone in darkness. With only parts of arms and legs visible, the audio emerges as the scene's narrative guide. Terrified young women scream, many crying out for their mothers. This emphasis on the voices of the women places their traumatic experience at the center of the narrative. Moreover, not only does the darkness deny the visual spectacle or sexualization of the women, but the disconcerting experience of viewing mimics the shocking experience of violence. When Teacher Liu is assaulted, Wu shows her facial expressions rather than her body or the Japanese soldier. With everything else in shadows, her partially lit face grimacing in pain is the only visible focal point. Liu's expression of suffering—her personal experience of pain—is the only visual marker of the rape. Unlike most women depicted in these films, she survives. Her survival means that she must learn to live and cope with her traumatic experience and further emphasizes the personal nature of her assault; moreover, her rape is not relegated to the distant past or to a national allegory of shame. In other words, the film presents the rape as Teacher Liu's personal experience of pain.

---

52. I saw a DVD version purchased in China, company unknown.
53. Chenying Zheng, "Wei liao buneng wangque de jinian: Cong yingpian *Xin De Lei De Mingdan* dao *Nanjing 1937* you gan," *Zhongguo fu yun* 7 (1995): 44.
54. Quoted in Berry, "Cinematic Representations of the Rape of Nanking," 97.

The depiction of the Japanese characters Rieko and her teenage daughter, Hanako, also provide one of the most unique and humanistic portrayals of sexual violence in Chinese cinema. As Japanese women, they represent the culture and society that male Japanese soldiers are indoctrinated to protect. Faced with this female gaze from home, the Japanese soldiers suddenly become civilized. When Rieko meets the Japanese soldiers the first time, they politely ask her to remain indoors and to keep a Japanese flag hanging overhead. Yet once her husband's Chinese nationality is revealed, she loses the tenuous protection of nationality. Rieko's international marriage and pregnancy are seen as an affront to Japanese masculinity. A Japanese soldier cries out to her husband, "How dare you fuck our women?" Later, the Japanese soldiers kick her in the belly, their attack on her womb a rejection of a compromised symbol of the motherland. Such representation highlights the ways in which national narratives lay claim to the female body.

Sadly, the film was largely a failure in Mainland China upon its release. Fujii Shōzō notes that while *Don't Cry* was heralded in the media as an "anti-Japanese" film, Chinese reception was rather cold. Newspapers were critical of the film; middle-aged people (in their forties and fifties) were the main audiences in the theaters; audiences were small.[55] The film may have resurged somewhat in recent years online as part of the wave of attention on Nanjing after the late 1990s. On the popular Chinese movie site 1905.com, the film currently holds a rating of 7.8/10 from over 40,000 voters, suggesting relatively warm reception among contemporary netizens.

The third major Chinese Nanjing film is Lu Chuan's *City of Life and Death* (Nanjing! Nanjing!, 2009), a highly anticipated production that premiered at film festivals and theaters around the world.[56] Filmed around the aftermath of the 2005 China-Japan history conflict, the director encountered numerous issues with the increasingly sensitive censors of the State Administration of Radio, Film and Television. Like the previous two films discussed here, *City* shows the massacre from a variety of perspectives. The main characters include Lu Jianxiong (a Chinese soldier), Jiang Shuyun (a teacher), Kadokawa Masao (a Japanese soldier), and Xiaojiang (a prostitute). The film narrates the events of several weeks in Nanjing, including the lost battle, the entry of the Japanese troops, mass executions and rapes, the efforts of the Nanking Safety Zone, and the eventual deaths of most of the main characters. Unexpectedly, in terms of screen time and narrative format, the Japanese soldier Kadokawa is the main character. After witnessing the horrors of the massacre, he commits suicide in the final scene.

There are two significant female characters in the film—Xiaojiang and Jiang Shuyun. Xiaojiang, placed in an untenable situation, "volunteers" to become a

---

55. Shōzō Fujii, *Chūgoku eiga: Hyakunen o egaku, hyaku nen o yomu* (Tokyo: Iwanami, 2002), 41–42.
56. I saw the Kino Lorber DVD version.

prostitute for the Japanese soldiers in order to save other refugee women. She quickly dies from the abuse, her naked body tossed onto a wooden cart before Kadokawa's horrified eyes. The teacher Shuyun is captured by Japanese soldiers and begs Kadokawa to shoot her. He complies, killing her to "save" her in a scene reminiscent of the Japanese soldier's execution of his lover in *Massacre in Nanking*. In many scenes, the film movingly focuses on Xiaojiang's and Shuyun's faces, illustrating their subjective feelings of pain and fear. However, the film also implies that Shuyun's chastity is more important than her survival, while Xiaojiang, as a professional sex worker, occupies a marginal position in Chinese society. Shuyun's purity, Xiaojiang's marginalization, and their deaths in the past thus insulate contemporary China from their "shame." Consequently, *City of Life and Death* both bears witness to female pain and concurrently reduces their trauma to political symbolism.

This is not to say that *City of Life and Death* purposely frames wartime rape in a "nationalistic" way. Like most mainland films, *City* came under considerable political pressure from above. Director Lu famously dealt with immense demands from Chinese censors, spending over two years cutting and recutting the film. "Gray," or *huise*, material (narrative elements that are politically suspect) are viewed by censors as historical whitewashing or, at the very least, as confusing for audiences. These audiences are also on "high alert" for perceived betrayal of the nation and have a tendency to label perceived offenders, such as *Lust, Caution*'s (Se, jie, 2007) director Ang Lee, "traitor director[s]."[57] Lu's inclusion of the sympathetic Kadokawa created issues with the censors, generating voluminous discussion and debates among audiences, scholars, and commentators, though the character may have been devised to appeal to transnational audiences.[58] The problems faced by filmmakers in China are thus compounded by popular nationalism and censorship.

---

57. Tim Trausch, "National Consciousness vs. Transnational Narration: The Case of a City of Life and Death," in *Chinese Identities on Screen*, ed. Klaus Mühlhahn and Clemens von Haselberg (Zurich: Lit Verlag, 2012), 41.
58. Guo Songmin argues that Kadokawa was falsely humanistic, suggesting that such a character is merely a product of Lu Chuan's imagination. Yan Hao, while sympathetic to the difficulties Lu Chuan faced in making a film on Nanjing in China's state of heightened nationalism, also critiques Lu's depiction of Kadokawa as not reflecting the historical reality of wartime behavior. Lu Chuan himself spent many of his interviews defending his choice of Kadokawa, suggesting that Kadokawa represents not only himself but all people. He also argued that representing Kadokawa as a human being was more respectful to the Chinese nation, as the popular caricatures of ridiculous Chinese soldiers are in fact "insulting" to Chinese memory. Songmin Guo, "Nanjing! Nanjing! Jiaochuan weisheme shi xujia de?," *Jizhe Guancha* 6 (2009): 60; Hao Yan, "Cuowei de shijiao yu biandiao de qimeng: Lun *Nanjing! Nanjing!* de lishi xushi," *Lilun Yu Chuangzuo* 4 (2009): 32; Qiu Xu, "Luchuan, wo yong wo de fangshi jiyi," *Dianying* 6 (2009): 14–17.

Finally, the most recent depiction of Nanjing in Chinese cinema is Zhang Yimou's *The Flowers of War* (Jinling shisanchai, 2010).[59] The film focuses on John Miller, an alcoholic American mortician, as he transforms from ambivalent Western observer to horrified witness. Despite his efforts to save a group of schoolgirls and prostitutes from marauding Japanese troops, the Chinese prostitutes are finally compelled to sacrifice themselves for the schoolgirls. With Hollywood star Christian Bale portraying John Miller, the film is framed by visual pleasure and national myth centering on the fetishization of the female body. *Flowers* was the top box office earner in China in 2011, mostly due to the controversial subject matter and the popularity of director Zhang Yimou, who had directed the spectacular opening and closing programs of the Beijing Olympics only three years earlier. Although online ratings are generally high, many of the highest-rated comments on Douban and PPTV are highly critical of the visual representation of the massacre and the choice to sacrifice the prostitutes.[60] Western audiences and critics were even more critical of the film, with critics such as Roger Ebert questioning the logic behind placing a Westerner center stage.[61]

The aesthetics of the film and the depiction of female characters are problematic. As Elena Meilicke suggests, it suffers first and foremost from a lack of taste, "It can hardly be called an anti-war film: it takes the same pleasure in exploding bodies as in silken dresses, presenting both in beautiful images that transform the wound inflicted by the 'Rape of Nanking' into a story of heroic and spectacular self-sacrifice."[62] Moreover, it portrays women as madonnas and whores or, as Wang Yaqin phrases it, as "angels" and "witches."[63] The prostitutes, like Xiaojiang in *City*, sacrifice their bodies to protect the future of the Chinese nation—the "pure" schoolgirls. When the Japanese soldiers request thirteen schoolgirls for a party, the prostitutes nobly volunteer by disguising themselves as schoolgirls. The film thus fetishizes both the chastity of the schoolgirls and the sexuality of the prostitutes. Even in the promotion of the film, the actresses playing the schoolgirls and prostitutes appeared in costume, clearly marked in their respective female roles. One of the more contentious reviews on Douban by user

---

59. I saw the Lionsgate DVD version.
60. "Jinling Shisanchai," Douban, April 26, 2015, http://movie.douban.com/subject/3649049/.
61. "One of the ancient ploys of the film industry is to make a film about non-white people and find a way, however convoluted, to tell it from the point of view of a white character.... One of the last places you'd expect to see this practice is in a Chinese film." Roger Ebert, "Flowers of War," RogerEbert.com, January 18, 2012, accessed March 20, 2015, http://www.rogerebert.com/reviews/flowers-of-war-2012.
62. Elena Meilicke, "Big in China: On the Spectacularization of History in the Founding of a Republic, Aftershock and the Flowers of War," *Chinese Identities on Screen* 40 (2012): 61.
63. Yaqin Wang, "Dui 'yan nü' 'bei kan' de dianfu: Dianying *Jinling Shisan Chai* de jiegou zhuyi fenxi," *Xian Jianzhu Keji Daxue Xuebao: Shehui Kexue Ban* 33, no. 1 (2014): 75–80.

Nüquan Zhisheng (Wind of Feminism) points out the film's focus on "consuming virgins" and "consuming prostitutes," criticizing the disservice the film does to female victims by placing them in this national framework of shame, where there is no reason for a woman to survive past her rape.[64] Another reviewer remarks, "What, are prostitutes not Chinese?" Such a depiction does not explore the subjectivity of the female characters and instead categorizes women according to their roles—schoolgirl, prostitute—in a narrative framed by a male gaze and masculinist politics.

The Flowers of War is also significant in terms of its linkage of American and Chinese memory. After the postwar trials, memory of Nanjing lay dormant in mainstream American media until the publication of Iris Chang's book *The Rape of Nanking*, which tied Nanjing to Holocaust discourse, a powerful marker of wartime trauma in American consciousness.[65] Chang references Oskar Schindler and the film *Schindler's List* five times, referring to the Nanking Safety Zone's founder, John Rabe, as the "Oskar Schindler of Nanking" and lamenting the paucity of American films on the massacre.[66] She describes Chinese trauma through the lens of Western experience by prominently featuring the diaries of Americans John Magee and Minnie Vautrin, as well as German John Rabe; such Western witnesses have been increasingly displayed in recent Western films on the massacre.[67] The American docudrama *Nanking* (2007) narrates Chinese trauma from the perspective of Western observers; the German film *John Rabe* (2009) shows Rabe saving mostly silent Chinese victims; *The Children of Huang Shi* (2008), an Australian-Chinese-German coproduction, features a Western male protagonist

---

64. Nuquan Zhisheng, December 23, 2011 (6:05 p.m.), review of *Flowers of War*, Douban, April 25, 2015, http://movie.douban.com/review/5226837/.
65. Yang, "Convergence or Divergence?," 859.
66. Iris Chang, *The Rape of Nanking: The Forgotten Holocaust of World War II* (New York: Basic Books, 2012), 109, 200.
67. Indeed, there is an implicit aligning of Sino-US interests both within these films and in the wider discourse surround the films, particularly through the accounts of American women. Both Minnie Vautrin, the American missionary present at Nanjing, and Iris Chang have been framed by Chinese and American discourse as postwar victims of the massacre. Vautrin, after returning to the United States, committed suicide in 1940. In recent literature, Suping Lu attributes Vautrin's depression and suicide to "the physical and mental stress she had sustained in those months after the Japanese occupation, and her sadness and depression over people's suffering and Japanese atrocities." Hualing Hu also suggests that Vautrin's suicide was a result of the stress of the Nanjing Massacre, thereby suggesting she is a belated casualty of the atrocities. Iris Chang similarly committed suicide in 2004 and has been commemorated at both the Nanjing Massacre Memorial Hall and Stanford University's Hoover Institute in California. Suping Lu, *Terror in Minnie Vautrin's Nanjing: Diaries and Correspondence, 1937–38* (Champaign: University of Illinois Press, 2008), xxvii, and Hualing Hu, *American Goddess at the Rape of Nanking: The Courage of Minnie Vautrin* (Edwardsville: Southern Illinois University Press, 2000).

saving Chinese children from Japanese aggression. *Flowers'* John Miller is thus one of several heroic male observers in Nanjing, part of a wider trend of films on Westerners in Nanjing. These tend to focus on Westerners as individuals, with Chinese victims rendered as silent masses, a depiction revealed in the two posters for Nanking. The explosion of these Schindler-like narratives after the early aughts demonstrates the transnational dimensions of both Nanjing discourse and cinematic expression. Indeed, the American documentary *Nanking* was released widely in China, earning more at the domestic box office than Chinese productions on the massacre (see Table 1.2). However, as Damien Kinney warns, "We should take note of the subthemes of redress, and in extreme cases revenge, which are couched in the rhetoric and ritual of commemoration."[68] The turn toward male Westerners as savior figures—with Chinese women either passive, silent victims or recipients of the Western hero's affections—suggests again that these narratives are framed by discourses that emphasize male heroism and national narratives over the subjectivity of female victims.

As Shuqin Cui and others have commented, women are important symbolic figures for the Chinese nation, often in ways that deny them subjectivity.[69] Chinese women represented the modern in the 1930s, an escape from feudalism in the 1940s and 1950s, and the trauma of the past in the scar cinema of the 1980s. In the 1990s, according to Sheldon Lu, "the male filmmakers of the New Cinema . . . displaced the burden of Chinese history and modernity and . . . replaced them on the shoulders of Chinese women."[70] In Chinese films on Nanjing, the subjective experience of pain is subsumed by the "rape of the nation," isolated in the body of the female victim and banished to the past by her death. Her rape also reveals the crisis of masculinity on which such discourse is based, and which can be employed to justify and encourage aggressive Chinese nationalism. The Westerner—framed by the Schindler narrative—is increasingly significant as witness.

Rape and Japanese Masculinity

Japanese memories of the Nanjing Massacre first resurfaced during the late 1960s when concern over American atrocities in Vietnam and changing cross-strait

---

68. Damien Kinney, "Rediscovering a Massacre: The Filmic Legacy of Iris Chang's *The Rape of Nanking*," *Continuum* 26, no. 1 (2012): 20.
69. Shuqin Cui, *Women through the Lens: Gender and Nation in a Century of Chinese Cinema* (Honolulu: University of Hawai'i Press, 2003). Gail Hershatter similarly states that "the figure of Woman as state subject was ubiquitous in the written record. Named women, however, with personal histories beyond the occasional expression of enthusiasm for Liberation and collectivization, were scare." Gail Hershatter, *The Gender of Memory: Rural Women and China's Collective Past* (Berkeley: University of California Press, 2011), 5.
70. Sheldon Lu, ed., *Transnational Chinese Cinemas: Identity, Nationhood, Gender* (Honolulu: University of Hawai'i Press, 1997), 23.

relations fueled renewed interest in Japanese wartime atrocities. During that period, Ienaga Saburō famously sued the Japanese government over revisionist textbooks, historian Hora Tomio wrote one of the first important Japanese works on Nanjing, and journalist Honda Katsuichi wrote a series of articles in *Asahi Shinbun* based on interviews with Chinese survivors.[71] These accounts prompted several challenges, which were vigorously disputed throughout the 1970s and 1980s by both Hora and Honda.[72] While the 1970s heralded mostly positive Sino-Japanese relations, from the early 1980s textbook controversies damaged relations with both China and Korea.[73] By the early 1990s, neonationalism was on the rise in response to burgeoning redress movements focusing on Nanjing and comfort women, particularly in China and South Korea. Around this time Fujioka Nobukatsu, a professor at the University of Tokyo, founded the Society for Liberal Views of History, a revisionist group that aimed to "rescue" Japanese history from its "self-abuse" and focuses on patriotic history rather than accurate history. As Yoshiko Nozaki notes, "It seems that neonationalists are in the process of reformulating their discursive strategy to appropriate (selectively) certain postmodern concepts such as 'history as story' to serve the purpose of creating an idealized history of a pure Japanese nation. It is a project that resonates with dominant wartime ideologies of empire."[74] From the early 1990s, neonationalism thus entered the elitist sphere in force in a striking continuation of prewar nationalist thought. Nanjing and comfort women became increasingly taboo topics in the mainstream, relegated to the trenches of the right and the left.

Yet while many politicians and right-wing apologists deny atrocities, such claims have not been accepted uncritically among historians and in particular among feminists. Ueno Chizuko, a prominent Japanese feminist, analyzes Fujioka's rise and the right wing's criticism of comfort women. She suggests that the emergence of figures like Fujioka and of right wing revisionism reveals a deeper issue of a fracturing of postwar discourse, noting that intellectuals are arguing from a "positivist" perspective that assumes historical fact is the same for all, facts require evidence, and documentary evidence (testimonies and diaries) is too subjective and unreliable.[75] Ueno strongly criticizes historians who have suggested that it was merely a "product of the times," in effect asking us to "forgive the sexual desire of our fathers who fought for the fatherland."[76] When

---

71. Takashi Yoshida, "A Battle over History: The Nanjing Massacre in Japan," in *The Nanjing Massacre in History and Historiography*, ed. Joshua A. Fogel (Berkeley: University of California Press, 2000), 80–81.
72. Yang, "The Malleable and the Contested," 60–61.
73. Yang, "The Malleable and the Contested," 62–63.
74. Yoshiko Nozaki, "The 'Comfort Women' Controversy: History and Testimony," *Asia-Pacific Journal: Japan Focus* 3, no. 5 (2005), http://japanfocus.org/-Yoshiko-Nozaki/2063.
75. Ueno, "Politics of Memory," 134.
76. Ueno, "Politics of Memory," 141.

Hashimoto Tōru, the mayor of Osaka, caused a controversy by suggesting that a comfort woman system is necessary for armed forces, female Japanese politicians forcefully and publicly rejected his statements, referring to him as the "shame of Osaka."[77]

In approaching the topic of sexual crimes committed during the war, Japanese war films deal with perpetratorhood. As such, there have been very few high-profile representations of wartime rape committed by Japanese soldiers during World War II. Mishima Yukio's short story "Peonies" (1955) describes a commander named Kawamata who has grown 580 peonies, each of them representing a woman he killed during the war. This story did not cause a political scandal at the time, which Irmela Hijiya-Kirschnereit suggests is since such atrocities were then considered historically true and uncontroversial.[78] Endō Shūsaku's novel *Scandal* (1986) also features a Japanese woman recalling her husband's burning of Chinese women and children during the war.[79] However, such narratives are few and far between. Moreover, Chinese films that attempt to enter the Japanese market have been systematically denied distribution. *Don't Cry, Nanking* was attacked by the right wing in Kanagawa in August 1998, with numerous right-wing sound trucks protesting the film's screening.[80] More recently, according to Chinese Radio International, *City of Life and Death* was not released in Japan until 2011; even then, it was shown in a museum rather than a mainstream theater.[81] A search of Tsutaya and Amazon could not reveal a Japanese version of the DVD. Finally, mainstream contemporary Japanese films do not touch the issue: only the films of the far right and the far left deal with the specter of wartime rape.

To be sure, the right wing comments on both the Nanjing and comfort women issues regularly. One of the most active and vocal forces of the right wing is Mizushima Satoru, the director of the right-wing Channel Sakura (Nihon Bunka Chaneru Sakura) and a columnist for the right-wing journal *Seiron*. In January 2007, he announced a three-part film series in response to *Nanking*, an award-winning

---

77. Izumi Sakurai, "Female Lawmakers Blast Hashimoto, Call Him the 'Shame of Osaka,'" *Asahi Shimbun*, May 15, 2013, accessed June 10, 2014, http://ajw.asahi.com/article/behind_news/politics/AJ201305160094.
78. Irmela Hijiya-Kirschnereit, "Hana to gyakusatsu: Nankin jiken to Mishima Yukio no Botan," *Gunzō* 52, no. 8 (1997): 154–159.
79. Chalmers Johnson, "Some Thoughts on the Nanjing Massacre," Japan Policy Research Institute, 2000, accessed June 10, 2014, http://www.jpri.org/publications/critiques/critique_VII_1.html.
80. Yoshiyuki Nagaoka, "Eiga *Nankin 1937* ni futatabi uyoku no mōkōgeki," *Tsukuru* 28, no. 10 (1998): 28–35.
81. The report phrases the release in a diplomatic way, suggesting that the film was an opportunity for dialogue with Japanese viewers. Wu Jia, "*The City of Life and Death* Premieres in Japan," China Radio International, August 23, 2011, accessed June 15, 2014, http://english.cri.cn/7146/2011/08/23/2702s654767.htm.

American documentary on Nanjing. He also began his *Seiron* column, "The Truth of Nanking's Film Production Diary," in October 2007.[82] With only one of the three films completed, Mizushima mostly uses the column to promote his political views through bombastic military jargon. For instance, his column from April 2014 discusses how the right-wing movement's support for the Self-Defense Force officer and mayoral candidate Tamogami Toshio is akin to being a kamikaze pilot—"We knew we would lose but there was a point to the fighting."[83]

Directed by Mizushima, the three parts of *The Truth of Nanking* (2007–) are intended to address the Tokyo Trials, the Nanjing Massacre, and American discourse on Nanjing.[84] The trial film was fully produced and is partially available online or by registering with the Sakura channel (and thus its affiliated right-wing groups). The second part has not yet been produced, and the third part has been adapted into a manga titled *The Truth of Nanking* (1937 Nanking no shinjitsu, 2008–2009). Because the manga is the "script" for the proposed film, and because it encompasses many of the themes that prompt the left-wing response, it is the blueprint for the right wing's proposed Nanjing film and useful in defining the contours of changing Japanese discourse on the massacre.

Truth is constructed around the making of a Hollywood film on Nanjing—an imagined alternative to Western films on Chang and Nanjing. Thus the American interest in these atrocities provides the impetus for the Japanese response. In their preparation of a docudrama, American producer-director Dan Shiotsuki and actress Anna Kinski encounter Chinese propaganda, lies, and intimidation. The manga is a litany of right-wing conspiracy theories, masochism, and xenophobia, with Dan and Anna's "search for the truth" compromised by female Chinese spies and female Chinese American machinations. Their ultimate "discovery": Nanjing simply did not happen. It appears that Mizushima supporters are the primary audience for this book, with mostly positive reviews on Amazon. Critical reviews have been voted down.

Truth constructs the Nanjing issue as an attack on Japanese masculinity, addressing its invective toward Chinese and American women. In a revealing reappropriation of the meaning of Iris Chang's death, it questions her suicide, concluding that she killed herself out of shame in realizing that her book was flawed. It also attacks her choice to commit suicide as she was the mother of a young (male) child, a nationalist appeal to motherhood. Indeed, throughout, Mizushima emphasizes the duplicitous nature of Chinese women and

---

82. Mark Schilling, "Docs Offer Rival Visions of Nanking," *Variety*, January 24, 2007, accessed October 28, 2013, http://variety.com/2007/film/news/docs-offer-rival-visions-of-nanking-2-1117958065/.
83. Satoru Mizushima, "Eiga *Nankin no Shinjitsu* seisaku nisshi: Jōhō-sen no saizensen kara," *Seiron* 480 (2012): 268–273.
84. Satoro Mizushima, *1937 Nanking no shinjitsu* (Tokyo: Asuka Shinsha, 2008).

particularly Chinese American women, depicting them as prostitutes and spies who frequently engage in "honey trap" plots. He represents the American Anna as silent and receptive to her male Japanese American producer-director's lectures on Japanese history. Meanwhile, the film's proposed heroes are Mukai Toshiaki and Noda Takeshi—two soldiers executed for taking part in the purported "hundred-man killing contest" in Nanjing. Their silhouettes are taken from the famed newspaper article in which they were featured for the contest and framed against the rising sun on the book's cover. The book laments their demise and ends with a quote from Mukai's final letter in which he denies atrocities in Nanking but says, "As a Japanese man I will accept this death and become the soil of China.... I hope that by my death the eight-year conflict with China might be wiped away. Long live China, long live Japan!"[85] In other words, the manga, like so many nationalist narratives, denies female trauma, depicts women as conniving sexual predators, and rescues masculine nationalism from the evils of foreigners, women, and especially foreign women. As dignity, honor, racial superiority, and self-control are central to the mythos of the Yamato hero, wartime rape is an affront to the right wing's foundational narrative.

The blueprint for *The Truth of Nanking* also reveals the ways in which Western—and particularly American—attention shapes Japanese discourse on Nanjing. As the directors of the American film *Nanking* (2007) revealed in an interview, "Two days after our premiere at Sundance, a group of conservative politicians and activists in Japan held a press conference announcing plans to rebut our 'fictitious' film with a $2 million documentary entitled *The Truth of Nanking*."[86] Similarly, Mizushima's foreword to the manga rants about the films produced by other countries: "Seventy years after the Nationalist Kai-shek governed Chinese capital Nanking surrendered to the Japanese army, suddenly China's communist government is starting to make 'Nanjing Massacre' films of several hundred million dollars [!] with over ten countries."[87] Such concern with American discourse again suggests the importance of Western witnesses both at Nanjing and in the recent history debates. Without the recognition of other countries, it is doubtful that right-wing groups would break Japanese silence.

Japanese left-wing filmmakers have reacted with equally shocking images of sexual violence. *Caterpillar*, based on a 1929 story by Edogawa Ranpo, relates the downfall of the barbarous Lieutenant Kurokawa, a sexually abusive husband before the war, and a rapist-murderer during the war.[88] Kurokawa is horribly

---

85. Mizushima, *1937 Nanking*.
86. Anne S. Lewis, "Austin Film Society Documentary Tour: 'Nanking,'" *Austin Chronicle*, October 5, 2007, accessed October 28, 2013, http://www.austinchronicle.com/screens/2007-10-05/546606.
87. Mizushima, *1937 Nanking*.
88. I saw the Universal DVD version.

maimed during a battle in China and returns home mute, disformed, quadriplegic, and completely reliant on his wife, Shigeko, for food and sex. The townspeople revere Kurokawa as a "god of war," and Shigeko at first consents to nursing, feeding, and having sex with him, as they are the duties of the "wife of a god of war." Later, she tires of this arrangement and begins to mock his manner of speaking, parade him in front of others, and even sexually assault him. Thus victimized by a woman, Kurokawa starts to feel guilt about the Chinese woman he murdered; eventually, he commits suicide. The film was directed by Wakamatsu Kōji, a former pink (erotic) film director and political provocateur known for his activism and relationship with the Japanese Red Army. It raised the ire of local right-wing groups, resulting in its withdrawal from several Japanese theaters. As for reception, the film received mixed reviews from mainstream audiences in both Japan and the United States, with reviews ranging from euphoric odes to Wakamatsu's bravery to critiques of the political subject matter and unpleasant tone of the film.[89] Overall, the reviews suggest the divisive nature of Wakamatsu's abrasive style and the thrilling draw of his unapologetic political statement.

In an interview with *Kinema Junpō*, the outspoken Wakamatsu noted his concern with the different ways Japanese nationalism framed gender: "In prewar Japan, women did not have the right to vote and were just a machine for having children. Everyone thought that women were just the sexual outlet for men. Men were lied to by the nation and drafted."[90] The film echoes his critique of gender roles and nationalism.

First of all, the film is a relentless mediation on Kurokawa's de-evolution to animal and an attack on the concept of "god of war." Due to his injuries he cannot move, is partially deaf, and cannot speak. So deprived of language and power, Kurokawa becomes increasingly animalistic, biting his wife on the finger when she feeds him or begging for sex. The film's only other supposed "masculine" male, Dr. Okeda, is temporarily impotent, which he laments: "To me, becoming impotent is worse than being crippled." These male authority figures and "gods of war" lack dignity, virility, strength, and honor. The film thus ridicules the militarism of the far right by attacking the masculinity of the hero-soldier.

Caterpillar also reverses the gaze by having female victims look back at their rapists. The film begins with Kurokawa's rape and murder of a Chinese woman.

---

89. For a more positive review, see Andrew Schenker, "Caterpillar," April 29, 2011, *Slant Magazine*, accessed April 25, 2015, http://www.slantmagazine.com/film/review/caterpillar. For a critical review, see Mike Hale, "After the War, a Tense Rehabilitation," May 5, 2011, *New York Times*, accessed April 25, 2015, http://www.nytimes.com/2011/05/06/movies/caterpillar-a-war-story-from-japan-review.html?_r=0.
90. Toshio Takasaki, "Wakamatsu Kōji kantoku intabyū: *Kyatapirā*," *Kinema Junpō* 1563 (2010): 36–40. Wakamatsu touches on similar themes in another interview: Kōji Wakamatsu, "*Kyatapirā* seigi no sensō nado nai koto o tsutaetai," *Sō* 40, no. 6 (2010): 84–87.

Her accusing eye looks directly at the camera lens, the film slowly fading to an image of the Japanese flag. The red circle of the *hinomaru* replaces her eye, indicting the Japanese nation for her murder. Shigeko's reversal of male violence also negates Japanese militant masculinity and avenges the Chinese woman's death. She sexually assaults Kurokawa in anger, an act that forces Kurokawa to remember the rapes he committed in China. He suddenly sees himself from the perspective of the Chinese woman he killed in the first scene, haunted by her screams. Yet it is not simply a reversal, for Shigeko has also been traumatized by assault and is reenacting her traumatic past, too. The rape is thus doubly critical of Japanese male violence directed at both Japanese and Chinese women.

A second left-wing film similarly attacks the right. *A Woman and War* (Sensō to hitori no onna, 2013) was directed by Inoue Junichi, a former student of Wakamatsu.[91] Although it is a lesser version of Wakamatsu's *Caterpillar*, with a smaller release and less fanfare, the politician Tsujimoto Kiyomi from the Social Democratic Party appeared at screenings supporting the film. The film is similarly a radical leftist work based on Sakaguchi Ango's 1946 short story of the same title and also takes a gendered approach to Japan's internal history debate. *Woman* revolves around three characters: a woman, played by Eguchi Noriko, whose husband has abandoned her; Nomura, a writer based on Sakaguchi; and Ohira, an injured soldier. The woman sleeps with other men to get favors and supplies. The writer is jealous of the woman's cavorting while concurrently being fascinated by her sexuality. Meanwhile, Ohira, who has lost an arm, finds himself emasculated and weak after battle. He expresses his frustration with his postwar emasculation by raping and strangling Japanese women.

Similar to *Caterpillar*, *Woman* attacks the masculinity and nationalism represented by the male soldier. Ohira wears his army uniform to gain the trust of his victims. Using his one good arm to strangle the women to unconsciousness, he positions their unconscious bodies and waits for them to awake. He then proceeds to sexually assault and strangle them to death in drawn-out scenes of shocking violence. The "type" of women does not matter—old and young, mothers and schoolgirls. *Woman* takes the sexual violence perpetuated by Japanese soldiers against women in other Asian countries and performs it on the bodies of Japanese women.

Both *Caterpillar* and *Woman* make an astute observation. The nationalism of the right is based on male power/female subordination and has been consistently so from the imperial era to the present, albeit in different ways toward women of different nationalities. This is the same ideology that gave rise to prewar *karayuki-san* systems (Japanese sex workers), wartime comfort stations, and postwar organized prostitution for the American forces. Thus, in attacking the

---

91. I saw the film in the theater at a screening attended by both the filmmaker and the politician Tsujimoto Kiyomi.

right's masculinity, the films are chipping away at the very foundation of nationalist ideology. However, even these leftist films ignore the subjectivity of the Chinese victim by using her rape as a tool to fight the ideology of the right. The individual victims of wartime sexual violence are subsumed by the left's political aims.

In sum, Japanese films on wartime sexual violence reveal the parameters of Nanjing discourse in Japan. The transnational visibility of the discourse has inspired the films of the right, for which wartime rape is a Sino-American fiction intended to emasculate the Japanese nation/military and undermine Japanese sovereignty. For the left, the depiction of wartime sexual violence is intended to criticize radical nationalism, though their pugnacious tone and treatment of female bodies as tools within this debate are problematic. In this way, Nanjing has again become a "conversation between men," but between Japanese men of the right and left. The silence from mainstream cinema is also in and of itself a statement.

Conclusion

Since the 1980s, remembrance of World War II in the Pacific has been dominated by the continuous debate over wartime rape, a highly dynamic memory loop powered by the controversial nature of the event, global visibility, and strong linkages among the three national discourses. When this debate aims to redress past wrongs, reveal subjective pain, or work through feelings of trauma among survivors, it is focused on the experiences of the abused. When represented in popular media, such personal experiences are frequently assimilated by national discourses, reducing the experiences of victims into normative narratives framed by national identity. As works on film, they are also being framed by the narrative structure of the film and the visual medium.

Popular Chinese films often present female trauma through political representations that prioritize male heroism. They reveal problematic nationalist myths of chastity that tend to present women as symbolic rather than real figures. This kind of representation serves to keep the traumatization of Chinese women marginalized—it is often the "indecent" women who are raped, and frequently their deaths mark the "national humiliation" as a distant past. Since the death of the female victim represents the unresolved Chinese past—and since this death is unresolved by the end of the time—it is up to the audience outside to demand retribution. This is suggestive in light of rising Chinese nationalism. These Chinese films also increasingly appeal to and overlap with American narratives as the two national memories are bound together, albeit in slightly different ways. American films have a tendency to reduce female trauma to the Western experience of witnessing or saving people from trauma, inciting a response among the Japanese right.

Japanese right-wing films imagine themselves as a response to the 1990s American acceptance of the Nanjing Massacre. Through images of masculinity, they aim to bolster their attacks not only on Nanjing and comfort women but also on what they perceive to be America's "victor's history" established at the Tokyo Trials. In response, the left wing attempts to deconstruct the right wing's masculinity by portraying Japanese men who bring the violence home to Japanese women. Disturbingly, both Japanese right- and left-wing discourses are ultimately hermetically focused on domestic discourse, with mainstream discourse ignoring the issue of female trauma entirely. This is perhaps unsurprising, considering the current desire of many leaders to normalize the Japanese military. Recognizing past crimes and the Japanese army's complicity in a horrific system of sexual slavery would not help their current agenda of rehabilitating the image of the Japanese military. As perpetrators, it is in their interest to deny guilt, though the left's complicity in framing female trauma is equally problematic.

Nanjing discourse is thus in many ways tied to discourses of national honor and shame that ultimately focus on rescuing the emasculated Chinese nation or rescuing/attacking the honor of the Japanese soldier-nation. During war, rape is a systematically employed form of violence that represents the domination of another person, nation, or race. After war, the remembrance of rape challenges idealized national images of masculine honor and discipline, becoming a site of national contention and an important symbol in the gendered discourse on (trans)national memory. Rape is represented in different ways within each national discourse, often in ways that deny the female subject a voice or that frame her assault as the assault on a territory or a national subject. Throughout the visual representation of the films examined, the rape of a woman is often represented as the rape of culture, of home, of territory, and particularly of masculine honor, for the men who could not protect and the men who chose to rape have both lost their honor. Such symbology often leads to a crisis of national masculinity and the constraint of female trauma narratives in order to foreground masculine national myths of heroism and honor. In examining the narrative portrayal of women who have been sexually abused during World War II, the gendered mechanics of nationalism render the representation of wartime rape inherently problematic.

5
Gender and Reconciliation in Sino-Japanese Melodramas

> Enduring all the calamity brothers have survived / With a smile they bury the hatred.[1]

It has been said that national reconciliation is an emotional process that occurs within the "hearts and minds of the people."[2] If that is the case, it is clear that the past thirty years have seen the hearts and minds of Chinese and Japanese people open once for a brief moment only to close over the ensuing decades.[3] Since the late 1970s, a few Chinese and Japanese coproductions and domestic productions have attempted to construct a unified vision of postwar reconciliation. Appealing to pathos, a narrative's pull on the emotions of the audience, these melodramas reenact collective traumas through the metaphor of the suffering Sino-Japanese family. Within these films, gender-as-nation again emerges as a salient feature: "As a genre occupying the space between history and the unconscious, melodrama offers an imaginary focused on the private sphere of the family—where traumas are secret, hidden—yet an arena structured by male

---

1. Translation by Daqing Yang from "Ti Sanyi Ta," a poem written by Lu Xun for a Japanese doctor after a 1932 battle between Japanese and Chinese forces in Shanghai. Daqing Yang, "Reconciliation between Japan and China: Problems and Prospects," in *Reconciliation in the Asia-Pacific*, ed. Yōichi Funabashi (Washington, DC: United States Institute of Peace Press, 2003), 83.
2. James H. Liu and Tomohide Atsumi, "Historical Conflict and Resolution between Japan and China: Developing and Applying a Narrative Theory of History and Identity," in *Meaning in Action: Constructions, Narratives, and Representations*, ed. Toshio Sugiman, Kenneth J. Gergen, Wolfgang Wagner, and Yamada Yoko (Tokyo: Springer, 2008): 327–344.
3. An overview of several public opinion polls conducted by agencies in China, Japan, Korea, and the United States concludes: "Whereas over 60 percent of Japanese surveyed in the late 1970s felt positively toward China, an equally negative view was presented by 2006. This reversal of goodwill is the same for the Chinese toward Japan." Mindy Kotler, Naotaka Sugawara, and Tetsuya Yamada, "Chinese and Japanese Public Opinion: Searching for Moral Security," *Asian Perspective* 3, no. 1 (2007): 93–125.

power in the public sphere."[4] Melodramas of nations inevitably involve gendered roles, with men and women occupying different symbolic and real roles within the larger imagined family of nation.

The melodramas to be examined here emerged after the Sino-Japanese Joint Statement of 1972. Normalization opened national borders to the movement of people and capital as trade increased between the two nations and Japanese citizens left in China finally returned to Japan. One of the main narratives to emerge out of this era developed from the discourse on Japanese orphans raised by Chinese parents (*Chūgoku zanryū Nihonjin* or *zanryū koji*). These orphans were children of peasant farmers who responded to the Japanese state's call for "One Million Japanese Farm Households to Manchuria" to bolster the Japanese population there in the 1930s.[5] Official repatriation occurred in 1946–1948 and in 1953–1958; then finally, after 1972, it became possible for *zanryū Nihonjin* to return to Japan en masse.[6] In practice, many did not return until the 1980s or 1990s, hence the late emergence of their stories as popular narrative. Sino-Japanese melodramas also developed from cross-border flows of capital and technology. After 1979, China participated in more than 200 coproductions with forty different countries—60 of which were narrative films and 140 of which were documentaries.[7] Positive cinematic images of Sino-Japanese friendship such as *The Go Masters* (1982) were produced amid the Chinese government's interest in strengthening economic ties with Japan.[8] However, these narratives show a distinctive change through the 1990s as the war generation passed away and the initial enthusiasm for the return of the Japanese orphans dampened in the wake of Tiananmen and the rise of Chinese and Korean redress movements.

Sino-Japanese melodramas of the 1980s through the early aughts reenact wartime trauma and postwar uncertainty through the excessive trials and

---

4. E. Ann Kaplan, "Melodrama, Cinema and Trauma," *Screen* 42, no. 2 (2001): 202.
5. Between 1931 and 1933, the Japanese Kwantung Army aggressively expanded their influence in northeast China, culminating in the formation of Japanese-controlled Manchuria in 1932. Poor Japanese farmers were encouraged to populate the area, a move that suddenly put them into a higher socioeconomic class as they became "colonial elite." After the war, these farmers were largely abandoned by the Japanese army. An estimated 11,520 settlers died, the vast majority either by their own hand or in battle. Louise Young, *Japan's Total Empire: Manchuria and the Culture of Wartime Imperialism* (Berkeley: University of California Press, 1997), 401–410.
6. Roughly 100 to 150 people returned per year from 1980 to 1983. Ying Du, "Guanyu riben yigu yu zhongguo yang fumu de guanxi wenti: Jian dui Zhongguo riben yigu yu e sa ha lin riben gui guo zhe zuo bijiao yanjiu," *Xiboliya Yanjiu*, no. 6 (2011): 20.
7. Jindi Yin, "Zhongguo duiwai hepai dianying qianjing kanhao," *Liaowang Zhoukan* 17 (1990): 33.
8. Kinnia Yau Shuk-ting, "Meanings of the Imagined Friends," in *Imagining Japan in Postwar East Asia: Identity Politics, Schooling and Popular Culture*, ed. Paul Morris, Shimazu Naoko, and Edward Vickers (New York: Routledge, 2014), 70.

tribulations of the divided family. Such narratives have the potential to open the temporal, spatial, and social borders of nation, creating a space in which Chinese and Japanese memory can begin to flow, meet, and resolve the dual traumas of war and social change. Conversely, such narratives also have the potential to be warped by national narratives. Building on the work started by Timothy Y. Tsu, this chapter explores five Chinese and Japanese melodramas made for film and television—*The Go Masters* (1982), *The Bell of Purity Temple* (1992), *Son of the Good Earth* (1995), *Autumn Rain* (2005), and *Distant Bonds* (2009)—tracing how such works reflect broader changes in the discourse on Sino-Japanese reconciliation.[9]

Melodrama and Reconciliation

Since these are films of family, tears, trauma, and reconciliation, melodrama theory is a useful departure point. "Melodrama" refers to a film genre that typically focuses on family dilemmas through extreme emotional, musical, and narrative cues such as sentimental music or tears. While such films are often derided for their sentiment, clichés, and sensationalism, in fact melodramatic film is a form of remembrance that is "central to the folklore that inheres in popular culture."[10] Melodrama in many ways parallels and overlaps with cultural trauma, the collective perception of a traumatic event in a group's past.[11] Trauma is a "wound that cries out," a suppressed memory of an overwhelming event that demands to be remembered. Melodrama similarly uses its expressive mode to reveal the characters' suppressed alienation and criticism of society.[12] It is characterized by a sense of the hidden, the "moral occult," or the "domain of operative spiritual values which is both indicated by and masked by the surface of reality."[13] Through its expressive mode, melodrama attempts to reveal the "moral occult" through a "mode of excess."[14] For example, Hollywood melodramas of the 1940s and 1950s

---

9. Tsu focuses on Chinese cinema. See Timothy Y. Tsu, "Reconciliation Onscreen: The Second Sino-Japanese War in Chinese Movies," in *East Asia beyond the History Wars: Reconciliation as Method*, ed. Tessa Morris-Suzuki, Morris Low, Leonid Petrov, and Timothy Y. Tsu (New York: Routledge, 2013), 60–86.
10. Marcia Landy, "Cinematic History, Melodrama, and the Holocaust," in *Humanity at the Limit: The Impact of the Holocaust Experience on Jews and Christians*, ed. Michael A. Signer (Bloomington: Indiana University Press, 2000).
11. Jeffrey C. Alexander, "Toward a Theory of Cultural Trauma," in *Cultural Trauma and Collective Identity*, ed. Jeffrey C. Alexander, Ron Eyerman, Bernard Giesen, Neil J. Smelser, and Piotr Sztompka (Berkeley: University of California Press, 2004), 10.
12. Thomas Elsaesser, "Tales of Sound and Fury: The Family Melodrama," *Monogram* 4 (1972): 2–15.
13. Peter Brooks, *The Melodramatic Imagination: Balzac, Henry James, Melodrama, and the Mode of Excess* (New Haven, CT: Yale University Press, 1976), 4–5.
14. Brooks, *Melodramatic Imagination*, 4–5.

expose the pressures of being a woman in a patriarchy through extreme emotional narratives of thwarted love or marriage, issues between the generations, and motherhood.[15]

Second, melodrama is integral to reconciliation because these narratives force audiences to confront a traumatic past. Watching a melodrama is analogous to the collective experience of experiencing trauma.[16] The excessive sentiment of melodrama reaches outside of the narrative to the audience, inspiring tears, nervousness, or even outrage in the viewer.[17] As Linda Williams elaborates, they are a "body genre" not only within but also outside the narrative, "tearjerkers" that literally force tears from our eyes.[18] Yet, as E. Ann Kaplan points out, while melodramas reenact traumatic events, they differ in one important way. Trauma is a cycle with no closure, a memory that cannot be remembered, and a rupture in identity that cannot be fixed. Melodrama, in contrast, attempts to reconcile the endlessly repeating cycle of trauma. Narrative offers a cure: "The style reassures the viewer, who leaves the cinema believing she is safe and that all is well in her world."[19] Thus, connecting to this book's broader framework of cultural (collective) memory, melodrama is a mode of expression that reenacts collective trauma, appealing to the audience through pathos. These films reconstruct national "memory" by narrating the imagined community's past, instilling in the audience both a sense of the traumatic experience of war and a restorative closure that neatly ties up the nation's past.

One major critique of melodrama theories suggests that they are not historically specific to the Chinese and Japanese context. Lisa Rofel notes that the PRC has a long history of melodramas that were largely class-based—stories of evil landlords and corruption.[20] Nick Brown argues that "political melodrama" might be a more useful term for Chinese melodrama, where "we might treat 'melodrama' as an expression of a mode of injustice whose *mise-en-scène* is precisely the nexus between public and private life, a mode in which gender as a

---

15. See Mary A. Doane, *The Desire to Desire: The Woman's Film of the 1940s* (Bloomington: Indiana University Press, 1987), E. Ann Kaplan, *Motherhood and Representation: The Mother in Popular Culture and Melodrama* (New York: Taylor and Francis, 1992), and Justine Lloyd and Lesley Johnson, "The Three Faces of Eve: The Post-war Housewife, Melodrama, and Home," *Feminist Media Studies* 3, no. 1 (2003): 8.
16. Kaplan, "Melodrama, Cinema and Trauma," 203.
17. Ben Singer, *Melodrama and Modernity: Early Sensational Cinema and Its Contexts* (New York: Columbia University Press, 2001), 39–40.
18. Linda Williams, "Film Bodies: Gender, Genre, and Excess," *Film Quarterly* 44, no. 4 (1991): 5.
19. Kaplan, "Melodrama, Cinema and Trauma," 203.
20. Lisa Rofel, *Desiring China: Experiments in Neoliberalism, Sexuality, and Public Culture* (Durham, NC: Duke University Press, 2007), 48.

mark of difference is a limited, mobile term activated by distinctive social powers and historical circumstances."[21] Emilie Yueh-yu Yeh suggests that Chinese theorists need to abandon the concept of melodrama entirely and return to *wenyi*, the traditional translation of "melodrama" into Chinese and a term that means "letters and arts."[22] Mitsuhiro Yoshimoto, in a highly theoretical work, posits that the emergence of the melodramatic "does not simply designate a literary or cinematic genre but an ideologeme supporting the social formation of postwar Japan." For him, melodrama in Japan signifies the "disparity between modernity and modernization, whose 'synchronic uneven development' has been the sociocultural strain on the Japanese for more than a century."[23] Due to the melodrama's associations with asserting the self, he views melodrama as inescapably connected to a US-Japan binary.[24]

While I agree that any analysis of melodrama must carefully consider the cultural and historical situation of each literature, Chinese and Japanese melodrama do not exist completely outside of Western melodrama traditions. Tony Williams, in his analysis of Hong Kong director Ann Hui's *Song of the Exile* (1992), suggests that the film displays elements of Western and Chinese melodrama, with a Western focus on family and the Chinese melodrama's wider social and historical implications.[25] Jenny Kwok Wah Lau illustrates the ways in which Chen Kaige's *Farewell My Concubine* (1993) performs as a transnational text via its support from Hong Kong–Taiwanese producers and its adoption of narrative elements to attract both Western and Chinese audiences.[26] Moreover, in this chapter, the very fact that many of the films to be examined are coproductions also places their melodramas in an ambiguous transnational framework: while there are different discourses of melodrama influenced by the geographic and political context of their production, films are ultimately part of broader and interrelated global practices of filmmaking. In sum, melodrama and trauma theory, with all their limitations, should be viewed here as a useful tool to explore how

---

21. Nick Browne, "Society and Subjectivity: The Political Economy of the Chinese Melodrama," in *New Chinese Cinemas: Forms, Identities, Politics*, ed. Nick Browne, Paul G. Pickowicz, Vivian Sobchack, and Esther Yau (Cambridge: Cambridge University Press, 1994), 43.
22. Emilie Yueh-yu Yeh, "Pitfalls of Cross-Cultural Analysis: Chinese *Wenyi* Film and Melodrama," *Asian Journal of Communication* 19, no. 4 (2009): 449.
23. Mitsuhiro Yoshimoto, "Melodrama, Postmodernism, and Japanese Cinema," in *Melodrama and Asian Cinema*, ed. Wimal Dissanayake (Cambridge: Cambridge University Press, 1993), 106.
24. Yoshimoto, "Melodrama, Postmodernism and Japanese Cinema," 106.
25. Tony Williams, "Song of the Exile: Border Crossing Melodrama," *Jump Cut* 42 (1998): 94–100.
26. Jenny Kwok Wah Lau, "'Farewell My Concubine': History, Melodrama, and Ideology in Contemporary Pan-Chinese Cinema," *Film Quarterly* 49, no. 1 (1995): 16–27.

melodramas use their mode of excess and family structure to narrate repressed cross-national history.

The Honeymoon Period

The period after normalization has been characterized as the honeymoon phase of Sino-Japanese relations.[27] Although the decade was marred by a few moments of tension, relations between the Chinese and Japanese governments and people were overwhelmingly positive.[28] From 1972 to 1978, China and Japan signed twelve agreements that swiftly increased cultural exchange and bilateral trade.[29] The 1970s also saw the arrival of the "panda boom" in Japan, as China's gift of two Chinese pandas to Tokyo's Ueno Zoo sparked popular Japanese goodwill and cultural interest in China.[30] The goodwill continued into the early 1980s, which saw the establishment of the China-Japan Friendship Committee, the first China-Japan Civilian Meeting, and an increase in students studying abroad in both nations. By 1983, over 72 percent of Japanese people continued to view China in friendly terms.[31] At that time, Hu Yaobang, the general secretary of the Communist Party of China, "compared the PRC and Japan to rival heroes in a Chinese classic tale and stated: 'When they fought both sides were weakened. But when they were united, they were invincible.'"[32]

Against this positive background, several films were made about the Sino-Japanese relationship. In Japan, the late 1970s and early 1980s saw nearly annual documentaries on the return of the Japanese orphans. In China, domestic productions like *So Near Yet So Far* (Ying/Sakura, 1979); *Butterflies Bring Reunion* (Yuse hudie, 1980), and *Bell of Purity Temple* (Qingliangsi de zhongsheng, 1992) portrayed the return of the orphans from the perspective of their adoptive families. The most significant of the reconciliation films made during this era was the coproduction *The Go Masters* (Yipan meiyou xiawan de qi/Mikan no taikyoku, 1982), made to commemorate the ten-year anniversary of normalization. *Go*

---

27. Chalmers Johnson, "The Patterns of Japanese Relations with China, 1952–1982," *Pacific Affairs* 59, no. 3 (1986): 402–428.
28. There were early disputes over the Senkaku islands (1978), Japanese textbooks (1982 and 1986), a Yasukuni shrine visit (1985), and economic setbacks (the "Baoshan shock" of 1981). See Caroline Rose, *Interpreting History in Sino-Japanese Relations: A Case-Study in Political Decision Making* (Routledge: New York, 2005), 50–53.
29. Joseph Cheng, "China's Japan Policy in the 1980s," *International Affairs* 61, no. 1 (1984): 91–107.
30. Ian Jared Miller, *The Nature of the Beasts: Empire and Exhibition at the Tokyo Imperial Zoo*, (Berkeley: University of California Press, 2013): 194.
31. Ryosei Kokubun, "The Current State of Contemporary Chinese Studies in Japan," *China Quarterly* 107 (1986): 505–518.
32. Cheng, "China's Japan Policy," 91.

Masters was crafted with diplomatic precision: not only was the film produced by China's Beijing Film Production Company and Japan's Toko Tokuma Company, but it also shared two teams of illustrious Chinese and Japanese directors, writers, cast, and crew.[33] The final credits sequence is further testament to the carefulness of this coproduction, with the screen evenly split between Japanese and Chinese names. Through swelling music, portrayals of extreme loss, and intense expressions of emotion, the film highlights the heartbreaking experiences of the Matsunamis and the Kuangs, Japanese and Chinese families united through adoption, marriage, and the love of the game of Go.

For the Chinese half of the production team, the film was an important Japanese apology for the past and a glance toward future reconciliation. Describing the process of preparing the script and working with the Japanese directors, then director of the Beijing Film Studio Wang Yang and film director Duan Jishun noted that while the purpose of the film was to foster Sino-Japanese friendship, the Chinese side felt they could not avoid discussing the past suffering that Chinese people experienced at the hands of Japanese imperialism.[34] Chinese reviewers at the time were moved by the apology depicted in the film. Li Mang praises the depiction of the "burning anger" felt by Kuang as a person whose nation was invaded and appreciatively quotes Japanese director Satō Jun'ya's declaration that the film would "never allow this bloodstained history to repeat itself."[35] Xu Ruzhong commends a scene in which Matsunami bows to Kuang, an improvision by actor Mikuni Rentarō meant to represent an apology to the people of China.[36] Yu Qiang applauds director Satō's choice of a nonlinear timeline (a change he apparently made to the original screenplay), arguing that his choice helps juxtapose Sino-Japanese friendship with the dark militaristic past of Japan and force people in both countries to face the reality of the past.[37] Overall, *Go Masters* was a success in China—Chinese spectators watched the film shoots en masse, and the film was broadcast widely to resounding success. Today, it holds a more lukewarm rating online (7.3/10): 16.7 percent of viewers on Douban gave the film five stars, 38.5 percent gave it four stars, and 39.1 percent gave it three stars.[38]

---

33. I saw the Japanese version with Chinese/Japanese dialogue and Japanese subtitles.
34. Yang Wang and Jishun Duan, "Yici bu xunchang de hezuo: Zhongri he she *Yi Pan Meiyou Xia Wan De Qi* de zhuiji," *Jinri Zhongguo* 12 (1982): 61.
35. Mang Li, "Xin lei di yi sheng: *Yi Pan Meiyou Xia Wan De Qi* sixiang qiantan," *Dianying Yishu* 10 (1982): 25.
36. Ruzhong Xu, "Cong *Yi Pan Meiyou Xia Wan De Qi* xiangdao ying," *Dianying Yishu* 1 (1983): 11.
37. Qiang Yu, "Cong *Yi Pan Meiyou Xia Wan De Qi* kan zuoteng fengge," *Dianying Yishu* 11 (1982): 26–32.
38. "Yi pan meiyou xiawan de qi," Douban, accessed April 26, 2015, http://movie.douban.com/subject/1313473/.

Contemporaneous Japanese discourse surrounding the film suggested a desire to atone for the past and to learn more about China. First, filmmaking was a process of getting to know China both economically and culturally after a long period of political estrangement. Japanese production reports describe cross-cultural differences in terms of production and acting style, marveling at the sheer numbers of Chinese (over 30,000 people) who came to view the shooting.[39] Second, apologizing for the past was also a major concern—as many of the filmmakers involved experienced the war, they felt a personal connection to this process. Mikuni Rentarō describes his experiences in Beijing and Nanjing as a soldier during the war. As his Mandarin was rather rough and rude toward Chinese people during the period of colonization, he replicates such mannerisms in his performance. In his view, the film has a responsibility to accurately replicate Japan's dark past to teach the next generation about people from that time.[40] However, as mentioned in Chapter 4, although the film won a Japanese Academy Award prize of excellence, it was somewhat criticized by the right wing upon its release. Moreover, reception has changed over time. On the YouTube version, contemporary Japanese viewers are highly critical of the film's stance on apologizing to China.

Masters begins in a hopeful immediate postwar period with Kuang Yishan, a Chinese Go player, traveling to Japan to meet his son A Ming. As the ship heads toward Tokyo, Kuang reminisces about 1920s China and his first encounter with Matsunami Rinsaku, a deeply respected Japanese player who has adopted A Ming, a Go prodigy, and brought him to Japan. However, Kuang arrives only to discover A Ming dead, A Ming's Japanese wife, Tomoe (Mastunami's daughter), mad with grief, and Matsunami depressed and alcoholic. Enraged and inconsolable, he declares revenge on Matsunami. He is eventually persuaded to return to China, where the years pass. Matsunami eventually discovers that Kuang has founded his own Go school. He sends his granddaughter, A Ming's daughter, to Kuang with the mixed ashes of her parents. Crying over the remains of his son and daughter-in-law, Kuang is finally able to forgive the past and move forward. He and Matsunami reunite to continue their "unfinished game" (the film's original title in both Chinese and Japanese) on the top of the Great Wall.

Throughout this film, sentimental fatherhood—suffering, separation, yearning, love, loss, and anger—provides the basis for the shared Sino-Japanese narrative. The brutality of this time period and postwar misunderstanding are narrated through the patriarchal figures Matsunami and Kuang, the pathos of the melodrama further tying their trauma to Chinese and Japanese audiences. The two men first bond over calligraphy written on a paper fan by Kuang's father,

---

39. Minoru Hachimori, "*Mikan no Taikyoku*: Chūgoku roke repōto," *Kinema Junpō* 6, no. 838 (1982): 106.
40. Hachimori, "*Mikan no Taikyoku*," 105–107.

a renowned player who also competed in Japan. Their relationship deepens as they share A Ming as son and son-in-law. When A Ming's death is revealed, it rips apart the ties between Matsunami and Kuang. They suffer through the remainder of the war and early postwar period, lamenting the loss of A Ming and Tomoe. Eventually they reunite through grief over A Ming's death and their love of their granddaughter. The two men finally reconcile by resuming their Go game from decades earlier. In this way, the trials and tribulations of the two fathers—synecdoches for their two nations—frame the narrative. Through ties of blood and of culture, they are able to reconcile over their traumatic pasts despite the boundaries of nation.

It is also significant that as Go masters, Matsunami and Kuang are cultural rather than militaristic patriarchal figures. The purpose of the game Go (*weiqi* in Chinese or *igo* in Japanese) is to surround the opponent's pieces: the *i* or *wei* means "to surround," and the *go* or *qi* means "go board." It is a territorial game that would, at first sight, be a contentious metaphor for a narrative on Sino-Japanese reconciliation. However, it is presented in the film as a shared cultural marker of Asianness that signifies years of friendly exchange. Although Go emerged in China, Japan has dominated the game for several centuries.[41] Like *Hanzi* or *kanji*, the written language that the two languages share, it has such a long history in both China and Japan that it can no longer be said to be simply Chinese or simply Japanese—the game has developed in both nations and is considered integral to both national cultures. Go also connects to masculinity: historically, it has been dominated by men and imagined as "a decidedly male realm that incorporates historical images of the Confucian gentleman, martial strategists, innate genius, and an unforgiving working ethic."[42] Thus Go is significant for both nations as shared cultural heritage and as urbane cultural masculinity.

The melodramatic format further allows Chinese and Japanese to witness each other's trauma. A Ming observes and experiences Japan's wartime suffering, watching as Japanese friends become unwilling conscripts, and he himself is persecuted for being a Chinese player in a Japanese system. Kuang, meanwhile, sees a Japanese woman lose her child on the ship to Japan, later viewing postwar Tokyo's wasteland of devastated buildings and starving people with sympathy. On the Japanese side, Matsunami watches in horror as Kuang mutilates himself in front of Japanese soldiers, and Tomoe is shocked to read about the atrocities committed in Nanjing.[43] Through all this, cross-cultural gazing is not without its tension.

---

41. Marc L. Moskowitz, *Go Nation: Chinese Masculinities and the Game of Weiqi in China* (Berkeley: University of California Press, 2013), 3.
42. Moskowitz, *Go Nation*, 19.
43. While praising the depiction of Matsunami and Kuang, Liu criticizes the newspaper that announces the Nanjing Massacre. He suggests that the number of deaths listed—45,000—severely underestimates the number killed. Mengxi Liu, "Qidao yishu lishi: *Yingpian Yi Pan Meiyou Xiawan De Qi* manping," *Dianying Yishu* 10 (1982): 23.

Masters justifiably focuses far more on the Chinese side, with much of narrative focusing on Kuang's anger and feeling of betrayal. Matsunami, on the other hand, is portrayed as a slightly more minor character with lesser traumatic experiences. Further, A Ming is depicted at times as a socialist hero, with his emphatic and heroic rejection of Japanese nationalism recalling Chinese films of an earlier era.

Ultimately, *Masters* marks the first time that Chinese and Japanese characters gaze on each other's trauma, as well as the first concerted effort to construct cross-national memory through the trauma of the two fathers. This depiction of the sentimental excess of fatherly love is a metaphor for national reconciliation that directly confronts Chinese and Japanese memory, albeit, at times, in deeply uncomfortable ways. While Matsunami and Kuang do not fully understand each other linguistically or culturally, they can approach each other through their affective ties. The "mode of excess" breaks through boundaries of time and nation to provide a cross-cultural experience of trauma and resolution.

Sino-Japanese Orphans

Sino-Japanese relations soured through the 1980s as historical controversies removed the romantic sheen of cross-border relations. The Chinese popular redress movement emerged around this time as Chinese civilians began to seek damages and apologies from Japan by way of letters, petitions, and lawsuits.[44] The end of the Cold War marked a further change in the US-Japan alliance, and the "disappearance of a Soviet threat removed a bond between Japan and China that had been in place since the early 1970s."[45] The Tiananmen Square massacre prompted a negative turn in Japanese views of the Chinese government and a new Chinese governmental policy—the promotion of national humiliation education focusing on the Japanese war of aggression. By the early 1990s, many scholars were already pointing out the history problem as a major factor in disrupting Sino-Japanese relations.[46]

Amid the decline in Sino-Japanese relations, the 1990s saw two important melodramas enacting the Sino-Japanese relationship. *Bell of Purity Temple* (Qingliangsi de zhongsheng, 1992), a Chinese film directed by one of China's most famous postwar directors, Xie Jin, was produced by the Shanghai Film Studio and shot on location in Japan and China with Japanese and Chinese actors. Xie was a highly political director known for his criticism of the CCP. During the Cultural Revolution, Xie was criticized and then rehabilitated, after which he

---

44. Ming Wan, *Sino-Japanese Relations: Interaction, Logic, and Transformation* (Redwood City, CA: Stanford University Press, 2006), 304–305.
45. Yang, "Reconciliation between Japan and China," 83.
46. Allen S. Whiting and Xin Jianfei, "Sino-Japanese Relations: Pragmatism and Passion," *World Policy Journal* 8, no. 1 (1990): 107–135.

made a series of films showing the destructive nature of the purges. Made to commemorate the twentieth anniversary of Sino-Japanese normalization, the drama follows a Japanese orphan, Gouwa, as he is lost by his Japanese mother, Kazuko, adopted by an elderly Chinese woman named Yangjiao, ordained as a Buddhist monk, and then finally meets his aged Japanese mother after normalization. The film's focus on spiritual elements was considered a departure for director Xie stemming from his desire to transcend simple anti-Japanese slogans to focus on a spiritual kind of human drama.[47] However, while some reviewers praised the film as an "emotional blockbuster" that revealed the "selfless and kind virtue of the Chinese people," the film was received coldly in China.[48] Some reviewers claim that this was due in part to the film's philosophical focus.[49] Others suggest that the Japanese orphan is not considered representative of Chinese culture and thus cannot become a powerful narrative within Chinese society.[50]

Like *Go Masters*, the film is framed between the love of two parental figures: Gouwa's Japanese mother, Kazuko, and his Chinese mother figure, Yangjiao. Mei Duo argues that *Purity Temple*'s main success is Yangjiao's "sublime" representation of motherly love.[51] Although Yangjiao attempts to abandon Gouwa due to the difficulty of the postwar period, it is ultimately impossible for her to leave the child. The film focuses on her gruff but steady parenting—when Gouwa is bullied by other children, she teaches him to fight back by having him practice on her leg. After her death, he expresses his filial piety by visiting her grave. Yet Kazuko's motherhood is equally important. Director Xie emphasizes their bond in a striking close-up on her naked breast as she breastfeeds the infant Gouwa. The climax of the film is when the mother and son finally reunite. While Gouwa first comforts his mother in an impersonal religious way, as he tries on his father's clothing, he transforms from a Buddhist monk into a filial son. Importantly, because Yangjiao is older than Kazuko and is referred to as *nainai*, or "granny," throughout *Purity Temple*, the film makes space for both women—and thus both cultural heritages—in Gouwa's life.

Critic Mei Duo outlines the three main ways the film—and particularly its ending—were interpreted in China. At the end of the film Gouwu removes his father's clothing, dons the robes of a monk, and leaves Kazuko in Japan. The

---

47. Youxun Zhong, "'Chongsujinshen' de changshi: Ping *Qingliangsi Zhongsheng*," *Dianying Yishu* 6 (1992): 70–72.
48. Shunhao Wen, "Duo qingyuan yin shang libie: *Qingliangsi Zhongsheng*," *Dianying Xinzuo* 3 (1992): 62–63.
49. Min Yan, "Xie jin xinzuo *Qingliangsi Zhongsheng* gongying hou weihe fanying lengqing?," *Dianying Pingjie* 4 (1992): 6.
50. Bao Tong and Jiang Yiran, "Riben xiandai wenxue zhong de zhongguo xingxiang: Yi dadi zhizi wei li," *Riyu Xuexi Yu Yanjiu* 3 (2012): 116–123.
51. Duo Mei, "Xie Jin yishu yinqi de quannian pengzhuang: Jian lun yingpian *Qingliangsi Zhongsheng*," *Shehui Kexue* 2 (1992): 69.

first interpretation argues that Gouwa is a negative figure who is detached from love; the second is that the film is primarily concerned with the spiritual; the third is that this film depicts a humanistic and universal love.[52] Following the first line of thought, Tsu notes Gouwa's apparent cold attitude as he leaves.[53] Yet I would argue that while Gouwa is returning to "Chinese" Buddhism, as a Buddhist monk he transcends political boundaries. Chinese culture tends to emphasize marriage, child-rearing, and filial piety, and thus Gouwa's turn toward religion might be interpreted as an escape from the material world—a world steeped in national trauma—and a rejection of national identity. If any critique can be made of the film, it is in the lack of male characters. Yangjiao and Kazuko, as peasant women/farmers, and Gouwa, as a child/Buddhist monk, exist primarily outside of the more economic and political spaces signified by the roles of father/ soldier/leader. Such depiction lacks the clear resolution signified by Kuang and Matsunami and suggests a far more ambiguous approach to the question of national reconciliation. At the same time, such lack can be explained by Xie's concern with the plight of women and the formative influences on his life. Having grown up amid a change in the treatment of women, Xie says, "I often find my female characters better portrayed than the male ones. And naturally this has something to do with my interests, and choices. My childhood memory remains full of oppressed, victimized women. Under feudal oppression, the suffering of men could not be compared to that of women."[54] Moreover, the choice of a monk could be seen as Xie's attempt to avoid a nationalistic frame. In addition, because religion was viewed for a long time as politically suspect in China, the choice of a monk could be seen as keeping with Xie's political resistance to the Communist Party narrative. As Fujii Shōzō notes in his analysis of the film, Buddhism was lambasted by the government, and Red Guards destroyed temples during the Cultural Revolution; even in the 1970s, it was reported that Chinese believers were allowed to pray at the temple only one day a month.[55] Such an issue means that the choice of monks could have been interpreted as somewhat transgressive.

The Japanese production *Son of the Good Earth* (Daichi no ko, 1995) similarly envisions reconciliation through a male child shared by two parents—in this case, two fathers, emphasized by posters and other promotional materials that feature the son flanked by his two fathers.[56] Based on interviews author Yamasaki Toyoko conducted with real *zanryū Nihonjin*, *Child* explores the plight of children left in Manchuria after the war. In 1995 the drama was adapted by NHK and

---

52. Mei, "Xie Jin," 70.
53. Tsu, "Reconciliation Onscreen," 70.
54. Huo'er Da, "Interview with Xie Jin," *Jump Cut* 34 (1989): 107–109, http://www.ejumpcut.org/archive/onlinessays/JC34folder/XieJinInt.html.
55. Shōzō Fujii, *Chūgoku eiga o yomu hon* (Tokyo: Asahi Shimbunsha, 1994), 201–202.
56. I saw the ten-part NHK version offered online through the NHK website.

China's CCTV as a ten-episode TV drama and broadcast to resounding success in Japan on Saturday nights. In fact, the series proved so popular in Japan that it prompted immediate repackaging and rebroadcasting in 1996. Moreover, the book is considered a near classic in Japan, widely available in most bookstores. Unfortunately, the changing political climate in China rendered the TV series a failure: though the film featured numerous notable Chinese actors, CCTV pulled the drama after a few nights.[57] Historian Daqing Yang suggested the series might be introduced to Chinese audience members to promote cultural diplomacy and the potential of reconciliation.[58] However, the book has not been translated into Chinese; indeed, it was reported that some Chinese people who had tried to translate it into Chinese were arrested in the early 1990s.[59] Thus, as *Purity Temple* was made primarily for Chinese audiences, *Good Earth* was made primarily by Japanese filmmakers for a Japanese audience.

The drama was of immense importance in Japan. According to Doi Saisuke, by the 1980s Japanese people had tried to forget the war, but Yamazaki's *Child of the Good Earth* did not let people forget. With large numbers of orphans returning in 1980 and 1981, people who had not experienced the war faced it for the first time. As the book was adapted into drama, new generations of Japanese audiences not only had to face the scars left by the war of invasion but also confront domestic issues such as the difficult acclimation of the Japanese orphans.[60] One theme that resonated was how Chinese parents would sacrifice so much for their adopted children. Yoshie Akio, a University of Tokyo professor, interviewed the actor who played the Chinese father, Zhu Xu, who suggests that such kindness has its roots in Chinese history best exemplified by the idiom "return good for evil" (*yidebaoyuan*).[61] Such images of Chinese kindness toward the "child of their enemy" were an effective emotional bridge for Japanese viewers.

Yet scholars also caution about the discourse surrounding the Japanese orphans. Aragaki Shinzō argues that representations of Japanese orphans can obfuscate historical wrongs by imagining Japan, the more advanced country economically, as a Good Samaritan saving abandoned people from impoverished Chinese villages.[62] Minami Makato also contends that documentaries on Japanese orphans

---

57. *Son of the Good Earth* also touches on the Cultural Revolution and the Chinese government's censorship of its citizens, two politically sensitive topics that may have been deemed too risky to broadcast.
58. Yang, "Reconciliation between Japan and China," 79.
59. Saisuke Doi, "*Daichi No Ko* ni mita shinryaku sensō no kizuato," *Zen'ei* 670 (1996): 89–90.
60. Doi, "*Daichi No Ko* ni mita shinryaku," 84–94.
61. Akio Yoshie, "*Daichi No Ko* to Chūgoku," *UP* 26, no. 8 (1997): 11–17.
62. Shinzō Araragi, "Chūgoku zanryū nihonjin no kioku no katari: Katari no henka to katari no jiba o megutte," in *Manshū: Kioku to rekishi*, ed. Yamamoto Yūzō (Kyoto: Kyōtodaigaku gakujutsu shuppankai, 2007), 212–251.

emerge primarily from domestic discourse—they do not focus on the memories of people left behind (*zanryū koji* literally means "left behind orphan") but rather illustrate the memories of repatriated people (*hikiagesha*) attempting to adapt to Japanese society.[63] Chinese scholars Bao Tong and Jiang Yiran concur—the triumphant focus on the business cooperation of China and Japan also gives the impression that Japan is helping China, not that it has harmed China in the past.[64] Moreover, the book's representation of Japan's rapid postwar progress, Chinese stagnation, and emphasis on Japanese orphans—without focusing on why the Japanese were in China in the first place—elides the real meaning of the war and does not encourage strong consideration of colonialism and war among the Japanese population.

Good Earth, although based on numerous interviews with real orphans, is fictional.[65] It follows a young orphan named Yixin who loses his parents during the madness of battle, is separated from his sister Astuko, and then bounced from Chinese family to family. Yixin is eventually adopted by a kindly Chinese teacher named Lu, suffers through the Cultural Revolution's anti-foreign campaigns, and then chooses to learn about his Japanese heritage. In the 1980s his Japanese-language skills bring him to a Sino-Japanese manufacturing company and into serendipitous contact with his real father, Matsumoto, a broken and family-less man who begs Yixin to return home. However, Yixin, conflicted over his two fathers and two identities, chooses to remain in China. In the end he decides to go to Inner Mongolia to help in developing that region, declaring himself "daichi no ko," or "child of the earth."

Yixin's deeply conflicted sense of cultural identity is the central focus of the melodrama. As a child he begins to lose his memory of Japanese things—his language, his family's faces, and even his own name. Throughout his twenties he defends his Chineseness. However, after being sent to a labor camp, he meets a Chinese man fluent in Japanese who rekindles his interest in Japan. After years of being persecuted for his Japanese blood, Yixin finally accepts that he is also partly Japanese, yet his identity is not posited as simple or clear national identity. Yixin is less certain and more tentative in his exploration of his Chinese and Japanese heritage. Fractured and sentimental memories of his sister, parts of a Japanese farming song, and family words like "mother" and "sister" are his

---

63. Makoto Minami, "Chūgoku zanryū nihonjin no katara re-kata: Kioku hyōshō suru terebi dokyumentarī," in *Manshū: Kioku to rekishi*, ed. Yamamoto Yūzō (Kyoto: Kyōtodaigaku gakujutsu shuppankai, 2007), 252–290.
64. Bao and Jiang, "Riben xiandai wenxue," 121.
65. Liu Ben, a Chinese orphan who was interviewed by Yamazaki with his adoptive father, deeply disliked the series. He argued that her usage of hypothetical questions was confusing and that her work does not represent the real lives of the Japanese orphans. Ben Liu, "Chūgoku zanryū minashigo o makotoni rikai shite iru no wa dare ka," *Kinyōbi* 6 (1998): 26–29.

only connection to his birth country. He wonders to himself, what is his Japanese name? What is the melody of the song he vaguely remembers? Where is his sister? Who is his father? Whereas Japanese orphan series after 2000 feature explicit declarations of nationality, Yixin's identity is very ambiguous. In the final episode, after days of struggling with whether or not to return to Japan, he takes a trip with Matsumoto up the Yangtze River. Overcome by the views of the river and mountains before him, Yixin finally announces to a devastated Matsumoto that he is *daichi no ko* (a child of the earth)—the earth is his mother, the earth is his father, and it is the earth that raised him. His choice of the earth as parent and of Inner Mongolia as his future, far from both of his fathers, is a refusal to choose between China and Japan. By rejecting these two choices but accepting and returning the love of both parents, Yixin rejects simplistic nationalistic binaries.

Like *The Go Masters*, the parallel suffering and love of the two fathers also unites them in a traumatic experience. Lu suffers through the madness of wartime paying for Yixin's medical expenses and protecting him from overzealous soldiers. During the Cultural Revolution, he also petitions for Yixin's release, living in an unheated hovel near the courts for several months through the harsh Beijing winter. His sacrifice and tears parallel those of Yixin's biological father, Matsumoto, who spends much of his time in front of his family shrine lamenting the loss of his wife and children. Lost in his memories, he asks himself, "Am I living?" In one of the most sympathetic scenes in all of these coproductions, Lu and Matsumoto even meet to express their respect for one another and reminisce about Yixin's childhood. Lu asks Matsumoto about how many people are in his family and is very distressed when Matsumoto responds: "one." Matsumoto also shows a great deal of respect and gratitude toward Lu for raising Yixin. With Matsumoto speaking Japanese and the non-Japanese-speaking Lu understanding and responding in Chinese, the scene also has a quasi-surreal and dreamlike quality. Yet as fathers and representatives of their nations, their mutual understanding transcends the barrier of language. *Son of the Good Earth* powerfully uses the triangular relationship between Yixin and his two fathers to construct a shared Sino-Japanese past.

Thus, 1990s discourse suggested a turn toward the self as Chinese and Japanese melodramas narrated cross-border reconciliation in "coproductions" directed primarily at domestic audiences. The character of the Japanese orphan revealed his potential and weakness as both a bridge for Sino-Japanese reconciliation and a self-serving national narrative of condescending benevolence. Finally, while both films suggest the positive image of a transnational or anational child—Gouwa, who has escaped into Buddhism, and Yixin, who has escaped into Mongolia—*Good Earth* more directly and successfully develops a cross-border dialogue via the moving exchange between Yixin's two fathers.

Reconciliation after 2000

The search for national identity in Chinese academic circles after the perceived "national cultural nihilism" of the 1980s and the promotion of nationalism as state policy after Tiananmen had developed into widespread popular nationalism in China by the early late 1990s.[66] In Japan, nationalist movements concurrently emerged within academic circles, popular journals, and online in response to changes in the post–Cold War order, increased focus on the history issue in both Asia and the West, and economic uncertainty after the bursting of the bubble economy.[67] In both countries, the generation that experienced the war had nearly passed away, along with their memories. Against this background, the image of the Sino-Japanese family, relatively pervasive in the late 1970s to early 1990s, underwent another shift. The few films to tackle this topic, such as the Chinese film *Autumn Rain* (Qiuyu, 2005) and the NHK-CCTV coproduction *Distant Bonds* (Harukanaru Kizuna, 2009), were productions of limited success indicative of the increasing marginalization of such projects.

Autumn Rain (Qiuyu, 2005) was a purely domestic feature film that received a fair amount of support from the Chinese government.[68] The film has played on television, is available online, and received generally favorable reviews from Chinese viewers. It currently holds a score of 8/10 on Douban, with many users praising the depiction of the Japanese in the film—particularly the soft, pliant female character Shiko. Made by China Film Group, Movie Channel Program Center, and Beijing Tiege Huayi Film & TV Cultural Development Ltd., *Rain* portrays a romance set in the present between a Chinese and a Japanese character. A Japanese girl named Shiko travels to China to study Peking Opera. As the film progresses, Shiko falls in love with a Chinese student named He Ming but discovers that her grandfather ordered the death of He Ming's grandfather during the war. While He Ming's father, Jichu, cannot forgive Shiko's grandfather (who confesses via email and does not appear in the film), he ultimately blesses the union between He Ming and Shiko.

Timothy Y. Tsu argues that the romantic narrative of films like *Autumn Rain* indicate a positive reconciliation narrative.[69] The final performance of the opera

---

66. Yinan He, "Remembering and Forgetting the War: Elite Mythmaking, Mass Reaction, and Sino-Japanese Relations, 1950–2006," *History and Memory* 19, no. 2 (2007): 43–74.
67. For more on the emergence of East Asian nationalism in the early 1990s, see Caroline Rose, "'Patriotism Is Not Taboo': Nationalism in China and Japan and Implications for Sino-Japanese Relations," *Japan Forum* 12, no. 2 (2000): 169–181, and Yoshimi Shun'ya, "Zasshi media to nashionarizumo no shōhi," in *Nashionaru hisutorii o koete*, ed. Komori Yoichi (Tokyo: Tokyo Daigaku Shuppansha: 1998), 195–212.
68. I saw a version posted on the CCTV online website, CNTV.
69. Tsu, "Reconciliation Onscreen," 72.

Silang Visiting His Mother—the story of a princess from the Liao Kingdom and a prince from the Song Kingdom who marry and fall in love—indicates a kind of reconciliation of the younger generations/future. However, this image of a Chinese male/Japanese female romance also recalls Chinese dramas of the 1990s (*Foreign Babes in Beijing*; *A Beijinger in New York*) wherein the cross-border romance indicated a somewhat condescending Chinese nationalism via the image of masculinity. As Sheldon Lu argues, the "victory that Chinese men are able to score with foreign women symbolizes not only the resurrection of Chinese masculinity but also a triumph of the Chinese nation itself."[70] Similarly, reviewer Du Bule on Douban noted Shiko was a "typical Japanese girl" who was "polite, soft-spoken, simple—almost stupid—innocent, lovely, and gentle."[71] Such a description patronizes the Japanese side by characterizing Japanese as both ignorant and passive.

Thus, while the romance between Shiko and He Ming in one sense suggests reconciliation, in another sense it suggests Chinese "mastery" of the Sino-Japanese relationship. It is Shiko who makes all concessions in this relationship. She moves to China, learns Mandarin, studies Peking Opera, practices making Chinese dumplings, and apologizes for the sins of her grandparents. While her love of Peking Opera is represented as a a bridge for cultural understanding, this image of cultural respect is also tied to a sense of Chinese nationalism. As Caroline Rose notes, in Chinese discourse Japan is seen as "owing" China two historical debts: first, in terms of wrongs committed during the first half of the twentieth century, and second, in terms of thousands of years of Chinese language and culture.[72] Shiko bows to He Ming in her performance, a bow that here represents Japanese acknowledgment of this cultural and historical debt. Finally, the diminutive Shiko is represented as silly and naive, asking He Ming to explain the concept of *Hanjian* (Chinese traitor) in her childlike Mandarin and appearing shocked at the news that Japan invaded China. While the historical ignorance of Japanese youths is a real issue, such a depiction suggests an undercurrent of condescension that has the danger of reproducing nationalist ideologies.

The Japanese television series *Distant Bonds* (Harukanaru kizuna, 2009) also demonstrates a subtle change in the reconciliation narrative in Japan.[73] The show had relatively high ratings, with an average of 7.72 percent in the Kanto region (6.2 to 8.6 percent) and generally positive reviews from viewers and critics, who praised the melodramatic elements of the story and the performance of

---

70. Sheldon H. Lu, "Soap Opera in China: The Transnational Politics of Visuality, Sexuality, and Masculinity," *Cinema Journal* 40, no. 1 (2000): 25–47.
71. Du Bule, February 15, 2009 (3:53 a.m.), review of *Autumn Rain*, Douban, April 25, 2015, http://movie.douban.com/review/1694980/.
72. Rose, *Interpreting History*, 4–5.
73. I saw the rental version offered by NHK.

Anne Suzuki.[74] Like *Child*, the series is also based on a book, an award-winning autobiography by author Kido Hisae about her father experiences growing up in China. Also like *Child*, it is a "coproduction" by NHK and CCTV that ultimately aired on Japanese television. *Bonds* juxtaposes Hisae's journey to China and studies at Northeast China's Jilin University with her father's upbringing and eventual return to Japan. As Hisae learns Mandarin, explores the new culture, and reads her father's old letters, she begins to understand his complicated past more and more. As a child he struggles to learn Chinese, is persecuted during the Cultural Revolution, fights against Chinese bureaucracy to restore his Japanese identity, returns to Japan in the early 1970s, and then struggles to learn Japanese and begin his life again. By the end, Hisae falls in love with a Chinese student and strengthens her relationship with her father, who finally is forced to face his suppressed Chinese past.

Like *Child*, *Bonds* also focuses on Kan's identity, although there is less ambiguity in this telling. Kan is determined to return to Japan and does not question his Japaneseness. For example, the title of the episode in which *Child*'s Yixin returns home is titled "Japan" (*Nihon*) versus the less neutral "homeland" (*sokoku*) of *Distant Bonds*. Furthermore, during the Cultural Revolution, Kan purposely lists his *minzoku* (an ambiguous term that can mean nationality and ethnicity) as "Japanese," a choice that causes him many political issues in China. He inexplicably abandons his loving Chinese mother for his cold and indifferent Japanese parents, rejecting memories of China and his Chinese family until his daughter Hisae forces him to confront them twenty years later. Meanwhile, characters who choose to remain in China, such as an older Japanese woman whom Kan meets in the late 1960s, are portrayed as suspicious and strange.

Bonds also firmly removes the father from the melodrama. All father figures in the drama reject the binational family and display an aversion to memory. Kan's Chinese father beats him for being too Japanese; his Japanese father rejects him for being too Chinese; he himself rejects his Chinese mother and past, and at first does not encourage the determined Hisae to explore Chinese culture. Instead, it is the female characters who demonstrate the ability to cross borders. A Chinese woman named Fu Shuqin raises Kan and is his biggest supporter throughout his life. Hisae bonds with her father's adopted sister, Fu Chunhua, and falls in love with a Chinese man. It is only through Hisae's journey to China, her journey through her father's memories, and her final journey with him to the site of his childhood that Kan remembers his Chinese past.

In recent Japanese media, reconciliation is generally dominated by women. The Korean Wave boom—consumption of Korean popular culture—has been dominated by female consumers. Kaori Hayashi and Eun-Jeung Lee discuss

---

74. Kanto Region, Video Research, Ltd., accessed April 26, 2015, http://www.videor.co.jp/data/ratedata/.

Korean soap operas in Japan and their ability as "soft power" to promote positive national ties. However, this is a limited trend in that such female "reaching across boundaries" has been marginalized in Japanese media and largely ignored in Korean media.[75] Reflecting such "feminization of reconciliation," recent Japanese productions on Manchuria—*The Pioneers* (Kaitakushatachi, 2012), a drama made to celebrate the fortieth year of Sino-Japanese normalization, and *Return Home: The Forgotten Brides* (Kyōkō kikoku: Wasuresarareta hanayometachi, 2012)—similarly show male rejection of border crossing with female characters as the sole agents of reconciliation. Such depictions both elide the brutality of Japanese aggression during the war—by omitting its perpetrators—and marginalize reconciliation.

Finally, 2012 saw the release of a TBS drama-documentary called *Return Home: The Forgotten Brides* (Kyōkō kikoku: Wasuresarareta hanayometachi, 2012), yet another anniversary drama released to celebrate Sino-Japanese normalization.[76] The TV special was a highly anticipated serious acting debut of AKB48 idol Maeda Atsuko after her "graduation" from the popular group. In the drama, she plays the uncontroversial role of the main character's granddaughter. The TV film consists of two parts: a documentary following the real *hanayome* (women who went to Manchuria before the war to marry colonist men and who were left behind in China when their husbands joined the army) and a dramatized version showing their repatriation at a much-publicized protest at Narita Airport in 1993. This drama was not a coproduction and departs significantly from the previously discussed films. Rather than a narrative of reconciliation, the drama portion of the docudrama portrays left-behind Japanese women as victims in need of saving, with clear-cut Japanese national identity as the cure.

Before analyzing the film, it is important to note here that women are treated very differently in "left-behind" narratives. The Japanese government had different policies for the children (*koji*) and the women (*fujin*) until the 1990s, with the *fujin* viewed with more suspicion and distrust. This was because the *fujin*, as adults (thirteen and older was considered "adulthood" according to the policy), were believed to have "chosen" to remain in China. Whereas *zanryū koji* have received financial support since the 1970s, *zanryū fujin* were governed by stricter policies such as a need for a guarantor and a lack of sustained government financial support for travel until the mid-1990s.[77] As such, the Narita conference of 1993 was conducted in an atmosphere of mistrust and was more than likely

---

75. Kaori Hayashi and Eun-Jeung Lee, "The Potential of Fandom and the Limits of Soft Power: Media Representations on the Popularity of a Korean Melodrama in Japan," *Social Science Japan Journal* 10, no. 2 (2007): 197–216.
76. I saw the special when it was broadcast live on TBS.
77. Rowena Ward, "Japanese Government Policy and the Reality of the Lives of the Zanryū Fujin," *Portal Journal of Multidisciplinary International Studies* 3, no. 2 (2006): 1–12.

largely performative. The abandoned *zanryū fujin* had to emphatically declare their Japaneseness to appeal for the same rights and benefits as the perceived "innocent" *zanryū koji*.

The drama portion of *Return Home* is based on the true story of Kunitomo Tadashi, portrayed here as a male "savior" of twelve *zanryū fujin*. Kunitomo, a former colonist and soldier in Manchuria, campaigns with his granddaughter to help left-behind women repatriate to Japan. There is no mention of China or of these women's Chinese families, by implication suggesting that they have no desire to remember those experiences. Rather, the *fujin* become symbolic figures that emphasize Japanese blood, Japanese heritage, and the erasure of Chinese memories. Rather than complex bicultural women, the *fujin* are passive characters who rarely speak except to cry about wanting to come home, to thank Kunitomo for "saving" them, or to express respect for Japanese culture—one woman spends a long time caressing tatami, and another even commits suicide when faced with the prospect of returning to China. Kunitomo thus emerges as a patriarchal figure who can restore their rightful identity to them. What is more, their repatriation erases the uneasy narrative of multiculturalism and forecloses any possible gaze on China.

This is in stark contrast to the exhilaratingly nuanced and complex documentary portion. At variance with the drama's nationalistic take, the real *fujin* were strong women who are shown as survivors who lived through abandonment, a harsh economic and political climate, and twenty years of postnormalization Japanese indifference. One daughter of a *fujin* proudly reminisces about her mother ripping a placard from her Chinese father's neck during the Cultural Revolution. In another scene, the bilingual Chinese grandchild of a living *fujin* marries a Japanese man before the delighted eyes of her elderly grandmother. Thus, in the more realistic world of the documentary, national identity is secondary to the bonds of family. Part of the reason for the difference is possibly due to the two different directors. The drama portion was led by a Japanese director named Miki Shinichi; the documentary was directed by a naturalized Japanese citizen, Kim Buryung. It is likely that Kim, as a naturalized Japanese citizen of Korean descent, would have more understanding of the complexity of national identity.

In sum, while on some levels *Autumn Rain* and *Distant Bonds* display a valiant attempt to approach the memory problem for the new generations via the image of the Sino-Japanese romance, they both demonstrate increasingly internally oriented visions of reconciliation and the marginalization of the discourse. In both Chinese and Japanese narratives, women have become agents of (nonpolitical) reconciliation while men, the leaders and wagers of war, become increasingly bound to rigid notions of national identity. While female reconciliation can be a powerful image, it has been used in *Autumn Rain* to promote the Chinese narrative of cultural superiority and in *Distant Bonds* to elide the specter of wartime

Japanese violence. Meanwhile, *Return Home* marks a disturbing new shift in the discourse—from the hopeful bridge of the 1980s, to the uncertainty of the 1990s, to abandoned Japanese people struggling desperately to come home. In the current climate of anti–North Korean and anti-Chinese sentiment, this conflates their image with the kidnapping of Japanese by North Koreans and ignores the real bicultural lives of actual Japanese women in northeastern China.[78]

Conclusion

In my discussion of films on postwar trials and combat heroics, I have argued that we can trace recent changes in East Asian national identity and nationalism through the new masculinities on display in these narratives. Similarly, images of border crossing and reconciliation have also changed with the recent rise of nationalistic masculinities in both China and Japan. While early melodramas describe reconciliation more productively through the trials and tribulations of a "big Asian family" united by its father figures, recent dramas have isolated male characters from the sentiment and pathos so integral to dealing with traumatic history. With female attempts at border crossing and exchange via popular culture belittled or ignored in mass media, the disappearance of male sentiment from narratives of reconciliation indicates a shift toward the possible marginalization of reconciliation in the wider discourse of China and Japan.[79] Since the father represents authority as head of the family and the national past as soldier/leader, it is important for men to "complete the sentimental gaze"—to recognize and feel sympathy for the Other. Avoiding the normative national categories of politician/soldier/judge, the male characters at the center of these narratives can allow viewers to transcend boundaries of time and space and sympathize with each other. If war is ordered by, waged by, and presided over by men, it is men who must also cry, grieve, and embrace.

The importance of Sino-Japanese coproductions like *The Go Masters* extends beyond their financial or political contexts—as Stephanie DeBoer discusses in her study of East Asian coproductions, coproductions represent a kind of "assemblage" not only in terms of these "material" features (financial [such as markets] or physical [such as locations]) but also in terms of what she calls "articulations

---

78. The abduction of Japanese citizens has been highlighted in recent national campaigns in what some critics believe is an attempt to bolster support for increased militarism. Noromitsu Onishi, "Abduction Issue Used by Japanese Nationalists to Further Their Agenda," *New York Times*, December 17, 2006, accessed November 7, 2014, http://www.nytimes.com/2006/12/17/world/asia/17iht-japan.3928633.html?_r=0.
79. Hayashi and Lee argue that improvements in Japanese female perceptions of Korea were "negated by the male backlash against the Korean Wave in Japan." Hayashi and Lee, "The Potential of Fandom," 213.

here aimed toward knowing and thereby producing the region within the uneven and contingent glows of transnational culture and capital."[80] Through such "assemblages," these melodramas produce—at both a material and an imaginary level—an image of China and Japan reconciled both emotionally (via the narrative) and economically (via the production itself). When a coproduction breaks down, the narrative of reconciliation turns inward. If *The Go Masters*, from 1982, might be viewed as the pinnacle of Japanese reconciliation narratives—in terms of both its production process and its narrative content—recent narratives demonstrate a trend toward the national.

The past thirty years of reconciliation narratives have marked a generational shift from narratives of parental reconciliation to narratives of children and grandchildren in love. The death of the war generation means that new generations with no experience of war must deal with this contentious issue. However, the narratives have become increasingly inward-turning, with recent films imagining reconciliation based on each nation's own terms. We should be suspicious of such love narratives. In many Chinese films, they present an unequal approach to reconciliation based on Chinese masculine leadership and Japanese female compliance, with a strong rejection of the older Japanese generation. In recent Japanese media, women are symbolic figures mobilized to obscure Japan's colonial past. The narrative framings of female Japanese students victimized in Chinese classrooms or of Japanese women desperately fighting to escape China both shift the historical burden to China and avoid taking responsibility for Japan's colonial past. The danger in such narratives is that they ultimately reproduce nationalist ideology through the gendered bodies of their characters.

---

80. Stephanie DeBoer, *Coproducing Asia: Locating Japanese and Chinese Regional Film and Media* (Minneapolis: University of Minnesota Press, 2014), 5.

6
Conclusion

> Don't forget the stench of blood that covered the earth!
> Don't forget the smell of burnt flesh!
> We must not forget . . . for this is what war is.[1]

As a technology of remembrance, Chinese and Japanese war films construct prosthetic memory or "history as identification," identification that is importantly placed within the framework of national memory.[2] Through the analysis of these contemporary films on the Tokyo and Yokohama trials, combat, wartime atrocities, and Sino-Japanese normalization, this book has revealed how these war films construct prosthetic memories of the national past for new audiences. As largely domestically produced narratives of national heroes, victims, and perpetrators, war films promote a sense of national identity through stories that often appeal to gender and race. Yet, at the same time, they are part of a transnational memory loop, one that connects Chinese, Japanese, and American memory discourses. National narratives travel, meet, converge, and diverge. Debates continue to circle over generations around the remembrance of the same event. I have argued that the prosthetic memory produced by these films—particularly

---

1. Kōji Wakamatsu, "Director's Statement," press materials for *Caterpillar*, accessed November 4, 2014, http://www.kinolorber.com/press-detail.php?id=1195.
2. As mentioned in the introduction, films as a site of memory are different from other sites of memory due to their manipulation of time/space and affect. Through their three-dimensional diegetic world of immersive sound, image, and movement, they create a universe of the past *in the present*. Further, through the moving consciousness of the screen, there is a feeling of "being there" and of accessing a world that is not dead, a process called "prosthetic memory." By following the psychological interiority of a nationally situated character, these films enforce the notion of national identity and create a sympathetic view of that character's experience of the war. Alison Landsberg, *Prosthetic Memory: The Transformation of American Remembrance in the Age of Mass Culture* (New York: Columbia University Press, 2004). For more on "history as identification," see Tessa Morris-Suzuki, *The Past within Us: Media, Memory, History* (London: Verso, 2005), 22–23.

films made after 1989—mark a major change in postwar memory and national identity. This is a shift that has been intensifying in recent years in response to changing memory dynamics in East Asia, such as the end of the Cold War, the death of Hirohito, a shift in the American role in the Pacific region, the death of the war generation, and the emergence of new modes of production and distribution. In addition, since new films have been produced in an era wherein national narratives have come under increasing global scrutiny, as well as amid a growing trend in transnational film production and consumption, they demonstrate increasing dialogue with opposing or supporting national narratives.

Perhaps most strikingly, the forms of prosthetic memory constructed by Chinese and Japanese films are fundamentally different not only in terms of narrative content, but also in terms of the temporal and emotional proximity they delineate for their audiences. Mainstream Chinese films depict Han heroes who combat Japanese revisionism and American power by avenging the nation's emasculated past; mainstream Japanese films center on the feminine or masculine Yamato hero-victim who is persecuted by a murky enemy or "victor's history" in an ambiguous conflict. In addition, these films are broadcast and remediated in ways that render the war more or less "visible" and thus temporally/emotionally close or distant in each country. As a result, the forms of prosthetic memory experienced by the two national audiences diverge, with a strong tendency toward clarity/immediacy in China and ambiguity/distance in Japan. These differences, emerging in large part from the different historical and political positioning of the two countries, are one of the main reasons Chinese and Japanese public opinion on war remembrance diverges increasingly as time goes on. In this final chapter I will explore some of my conclusions concerning memory in Chinese and Japanese war films, finishing with some thoughts on the future of the transnational memory loop in the Pacific.

"Tears of Rage"

Chinese films after the 1990s reproduce the political narrative of "national humiliation" through the figure of the masculine Han hero avenging a feminized Chinese past. The saturation, clarity, and continuity of these narratives compress the sense of time for Chinese audiences, fomenting an urgent desire for a strong response to perceived attacks on the nation. In other words, the increasing visibility of such texts, the mixture of such texts with contemporary discourse, and the unity of these narratives produce a communal sense of humiliation and anger for Chinese audiences and the feeling that the past is still alive.

In terms of visibility, Chinese war films and television shows have high broadcast rates on television and in theaters and, as mentioned in the case of *Little Soldier Zhang Ga* (Xiaobing zhangga, 1963) in Chapter 3, are occasionally taught in schools. Many of these films are also uploaded freely to the internet, thereby exposing a large portion of the country to narratives of the war. Broadcasting of such narratives has accelerated in post-Tiananmen China due to post-1980s economic development (which has allowed Chinese audiences access to more media through TV, cinema, and the internet), the post-1990s humiliation campaign (which has encouraged producers to film "safe" topics like the war), and the increasing marketization of Chinese television (which aims to capitalize on the popularity of the war genre). As a result, on television, computer, and film screens across the nation, Japanese soldiers continue to charge into Chinese villages. Furthermore, like Hollywood World War II films, the vast amount of television programs and films produced on the war have developed into a genre and industry. In addition to disseminating easily recognizable archetypal characters such as the comedic Japanese soldier and the indefatigable Chinese hero, the Chinese war film has evolved into numerous subgenres, including Red Classic remakes, "marketized" narratives, comedic war films, and *wuxia* war films, among others. Chinese audiences are thus exposed to images of the war across multiple platforms yet in a somewhat standardized and regulated genre format. This has created an oversaturation of anti-Japanese hero narratives. As author Yu Hua sardonically notes, "There's a joke that more Japanese have been 'killed' at Hengdian (a film studio in Zhejiang that specialized in war dramas) than at all the actual battlefields put together. More, even, than the total population of Japan."[3]

Second, the ways that these films interact with the contemporary discourse outside the narrative have also heightened the sense of immediacy in China. Narrative television shows emphasize stories of past Japanese invasions while concurrently broadcasting news reports that focus on Japanese revisionism or Japanese claims to the Senkaku/Diaoyu islands. Such broadcasting creates a sense of continuity by mixing remembrance of the past with issues of the present. Many Chinese films also blend the past and present within their narratives, citing crimes of the past alongside contemporary debates. For instance, the World War II comedy *Hands Up! 2* (Juqi shoulai 2 2010) ends with an ahistorical scene of a Chinese farmer proudly protecting the Senkaku/Diaoyu islands from a Japanese soldier. In the worst case, this diegetic world's sense of immediacy—and its overlap with news and other stories from "real life"—creates a sense of national peril. The impression of a continuous historical stream of Japanese wrongs is thus a dominant trope in Chinese films and a defining feature of Chinese nationalism.

Third, Chinese war films demonstrate a clear narrative of the past that underlines the unity of the discourse. Chinese films, as opposed to mainstream Japanese films, appeal to historical truth. Films like *Tokyo Trial* (Dongjing shenpan,

---

3. Hua Yu, "China Waits for an Apology," *New York Times*, April 9, 2014, accessed April 15, 2014, http://www.nytimes.com/2014/04/10/opinion/yu-hua-cultural-revolution-nostalgia.html?_r=0.

Conclusion   123

2006), *Massacre in Nanjing* (Tucheng xuezheng, 1987), and *City of Life and Death* (Nanjing! Nanjing! 2009) often emphasize evidence or testimony and are advertised as reenactments of the true historical past; director Lu Chuan also repeatedly cited the "historical truth" of his film as he made the rounds promoting *City*.[4] In part, this is due to the subject positioning of the nation. Many Chinese people, as citizens of the invaded/colonized nation and descendants of the war's victims, rightly regard historical remembrance of victimization as an issue of paramount collective importance. This is also partly due to censorship. Television series that deviate from collectively approved narratives have been censored by the government for being seen as making light of a serious topic.[5] Moreover, when Chinese war narratives veer too far away from being what audiences and critics regard as "truthful," they are criticized for their lack of historical authenticity or the directors are lambasted as "traitor directors."[6] Since such censorship and policing silences or limits the distribution of many narratives, there is a far more unified expression of the war being disseminated in China than in Japan.

Chinese films also extend this unified narrative across the "three Chinas." Many World War II films employ stars from Taiwan, Mainland China, and Hong Kong, uniting contested areas of China under the umbrella of one memory. In one way, this is an unintentional side effect of transnational filmmaking, as Hong Kong and Taiwanese producers aim for mainland funding and markets. In another, it demonstrates a shift in the CCP narrative, which previously avoided war narratives showing the Kuomintang (KMT) in a positive light. Especially after 2000, such films have served to smooth over the Taiwanese–Mainland China conflict through narratives that emphasize CCP and KMT collaboration in the fight against Japanese aggression. Like Marianne Hirsch's process of postmemory, which transmits traumatic memory from the older generation to the younger via the family photo, the transnational movie or television screen is a window into remembering a unified Chinese past.[7] The humiliation/"never forget" narrative has become a way to unite pan-Asian Chinese diasporas, and in particular the three Chinas, through a solidarity of remembrance.

---

4. "Lu chuan tan nanjing: Xifang zhuliu meiti guanzhu dechu hu yiliao," *Zhongguo Xinwenwang*, October 30, 2009, accessed November 4, 2014, http://media.people.com.cn/GB/40606/10289472.html.
5. "China Embarks on Regulating Far-Fetched Anti-Japanese TV Dramas," *Asahi Shimbun*, accessed October 9, 2013, http://ajw.asahi.com/article/asia/AJ201307090012, and Philip J. Cunningham, "China's TV War Machine," *New York Times*, September 11, 2014, accessed November 4, 2014, http://www.nytimes.com/2014/09/12/opinion/chinas-tv-war-on-japan.html?_r=0.
6. "China Embarks on Regulating Far-Fetched Anti-Japanese TV Dramas."
7. Marianne Hirsch, *Family Frames: Photography, Narrative, and Postmemory* (Cambridge, MA: Harvard University Press, 1997).

Daqing Yang writes that the Chinese have a saying: "Luohou jiu yao ai da" (If you are backward, you will be beaten).[8] In the rise of popular nationalism from the 1980s to 1990s, this has emerged as a saying to mark the "lesson" of Japanese imperialism—the "lack of resolution provides justification enough to strengthen China economically and militarily."[9] To be certain, the pervasive image of the unapologetic Japanese perpetrator committing continued wrongs inspires anger in many Chinese and prompts responses in real life. Although China's humiliation campaign was originally intended to fill the void left by the decline in dogmatic Maoist socialism and focus the collective focus on 20th century Chinese trauma that emerged in the 1980s away from the government, the media produced in its aftermath has also resulted in unintended consequences. A group often derogatorily referred to as *fenqing*, or "angry youths," express their Chinese nationalism virulently on the internet.[10] Chinese boats rush en masse toward the Senkaku/Diaoyu islands, sudden mass migration that is not entirely welcome in a country that micromanaged population movement just twenty years ago.[11] A Chinese man was brutally assaulted for owning a Toyota during the 2012 anti-Japanese riots.[12] Many Chinese citizens feel visceral anger even seventy years after the war: "We hate Japan. We've always hated Japan. Japan invaded China and killed a lot of Chinese. We will never forget."[13]

Thus, produced after the rise in "national humiliation" narratives after Tiananmen—a rise due to both encouragement from the top and civilian redress movements from below—Chinese films show a turn toward increasingly bombastic heroic narratives that demonstrate a profound sense of urgency and continuity. The narrative is as follows: China as a nation was abused by numerous foreign powers for over a hundred years; this abuse of national sovereignty is crystallized by the emasculation of the Nanjing Massacre and current Japanese

---

8. Daqing Yang, "Reconciliation between Japan and China: Problems and Prospects," in *Reconciliation in the Asia-Pacific*, ed. Yōichi Funabashi (Washington, DC: United States Institute of Peace Press, 2003), 66.
9. Yang, "Reconciliation between Japan and China," 66.
10. Xu Wu, *Chinese Cyber Nationalism: Evolution, Characteristics, and Implications* (Lanham, MD: Lexington Books, 2007).
11. The *hukou* or household registration system has been explored as a policy that regulated Chinese movement. Kam Wing Chan and Li Zhang, "The Hukou System and Rural-Urban Migration in China: Processes and Changes," *China Quarterly* 160 (1999): 818–855.
12. Amy Qin and Edward Wong, "Smashed Skull Serves as Grim Symbol of Seething Patriotism," *New York Times*, October 10, 2012, accessed April 13, 2014, http://www.nytimes.com/2012/10/11/world/asia/xian-beating-becomes-symbol-of-nationalism-gone-awry.html.
13. Sui-Wei Lee and Maxim Duncan, "Anti-Japan Protests Erupt in China Over Islands Row," Reuters, September 15, 2012, accessed November 4, 2014, http://www.reuters.com/article/2012/09/15/us-china-japan-idUSBRE88E01I20120915.

revisionism; now, China will heroically challenge American hegemony and Japanese power to avoid being humiliated again. Like Li Yunlong, who sacrifices his wife for the Chinese nation in *Drawing Sword* (Liang jian, 2005), or Mei Ru'ao, who avenges the Chinese nation on the global stage in *Tokyo Trial* (Dongjing shenpan, 2006), victimization of the past is often the justification for a strong expression of Chinese nationalism in the present. Chinese war films thus compress the sense of time and space for Chinese audiences and produce a sense of immediacy and danger—the threat of victimization, or victimization gone unpunished—which can serve as the foundation for aggressive and angry nationalism. These narratives, in effect, produce "tears of rage," which are magnified and extended through their visibility, continuity, and clarity.[14]

"I Am Me, He Is Him"

While Chinese war films demonstrate a clear narrative of the war, Japanese films tend toward solipsism, ambiguity, and divisiveness, as seen in the disparate depictions of the feminized victim-soldier and idealized *Yamato* hero. The sense of time delineated by Japanese films is also more distant from the past. These narratives suggest temporal distance, a lack of clarity, and a lack of unity, which allows for a range of audience interpretations across the political spectrum. This also has the consequence, intended or not, of eliding wartime responsibility and of potentially paving the way toward military normalization.

As opposed to the nonstop visibility of Chinese films, recent Japanese war films are almost exclusively broadcast around major anniversaries, such as the anniversaries of Sino-Japanese normalization and the end of the war. Both of these trends increased through the 1990s as a framing device to link younger viewers to the past, though such broadcasting trends mark remembrance of the war as a special occasion and not an ever-present reality, as it is represented in China. Many Japanese narratives produced after 1990 also contain a flashback or past/present framing device that isolates contemporary audiences from the past. Movies like *Yamato* (Otokotachi no yamato, 2005), the film *Winds of God* (Za uinzu obu goddo, 1995), and the blockbuster *The Eternal Zero* (Eien no zero, 2014) begin and end with a framing story in the present or, in the case of *Winds*, time travel. Although such structuring appears to create a linkage between the younger generation and the older generation in the film, in another sense the flashback in fact separates Japanese audiences from the past. It creates a border between the two worlds by creating a filmic "present tense" and "past tense." Even in dramas like *The Pioneers* (Kaitakushatachi, 2012), the audience is reminded that they are contemporary viewers witnessing the past through the framing devices showing the main actress,

---

14. I take this title from an article by Peter Gries: "Tears of Rage: Chinese Nationalist Reactions to the Belgrade Embassy Bombing," *China Journal* 46 (2001): 25–43.

Mitsushima Hikari, visiting the real locations depicted in the film. In Chinese films, by contrast, there is no border between the past and the present. Everything occurs in "present tense," transporting the viewer to the past with no flashback framing device to demarcate the past from the present. Japanese films thus make it clear that Japan of the present is not entirely the same as Japan of the past—there is a rupture in this continuity. While this is partly done to appeal to contemporary Japanese who do not feel a sense of connection to their past, it also separates Japanese audiences from the past and creates a feeling of distance from wartime Japan.

Furthermore, Japanese narratives lack the clarity of Chinese narratives. First, Japanese films appeal to relative truth rather than absolute truth. Films like *Best Wishes for Tomorrow* (Ashita e no yuigon, 2008) and *I Want to Be a Shellfish* (Watashi wa kai ni naritai, 2007) propose the "I am me, he is him" narrative, wherein America has America's point of view, and Japan has Japan's point of view.[15] Second, mainstream films tend to focus on the victimized Japanese victim-soldier, a figure who can be interpreted as anti-war or pro-military depending on the political leaning of the viewer, as discussed in Chapter 3. Third, many Japanese narratives emphasize subjective emotional experience over objective historical reality. Television shows like *Distant Bonds* (Harukanaru kizuna, 2009) are based on autobiographies of children remembering their parents; in an interview promoting *The Eternal Zero* (2013), the author framed his story in terms of his connection to his father's and grandfather's memory.[16] Such personal narratives appeal to audiences who want to remember their grandparents and great-grandparents without providing a comprehensive national narrative or addressing difficult questions of collective guilt and responsibility.

This ambiguity is compounded by solipsistic representation. In the majority of Japanese war films, the rest of Asia is primarily invisible, the enemy is unclear, and only suffering Japanese characters are depicted. And although viewers can experience the blue skies and white clouds of flying kamikaze pilots and the blue seas of the *Yamato* in an increasingly visceral way, these are abstract images with no clear referent. The war takes place for unknown reasons against unclear enemies in the abstract space of the skies and sea. By the 1990s, partly due to the desire to benefit from war spectaculars and partly from the desire to avoid offending a divided audience, mainstream films no longer made clear claims about perpetrators or any real attempt to address victims of Japanese imperialism.[17] This

---

15. Hiromichi Makino and Yoshinori Hongō, "Hokori to sekinin kan sōshitsu no jidai ni eiga ashita e no yuigon o kyōō ni kizamu," *Seiron* 433 (2008): 144–151.
16. "'Okubyōna reisen sōjū shi ni kometa omoi hyakuta naoki san ni kiku eiga eien no zero gensakusha," Nikkei, December 20, 2013, accessed November 4, 2014, http://www.nikkei.com/article/DGXBZO63257680Y3A121C1000000/.
17. Aaron Gerow makes a similar point. Aaron Gerow, "War and Nationalism in *Yamato*: Trauma and Forgetting the Postwar," *Asia-Pacific Journal* 9, issue 24, no. 1 (2011), http://japanfocus.org/-Aaron-Gerow/3545.

was compounded by the "idolization" of the soldier, which serves to soften the image of the Japanese soldier, as Okada Jun'ichi and Nakai Masahiro bring their innocuous boy-band images to their performances as kamikaze pilots and war criminals.

The rise in ambiguity is in large part due to the divisive nature of remembrance in Japan. Undoubtably, the right is on the rise. In the 1990s, as Japanese soldiers became rapists and revisionists in the Western imagination and the country slumped into a recession, there was a backlash among elites who termed memories of Japanese atrocities "masochistic history"; this movement was supplemented by the increase in neonationalism online among young people who had only vicarious memories of the war. However, although Japanese surveys show a popular trend toward constitutional change, revision of Article 9 continues to be controversial. Only 38 percent of respondents of a Nikkei survey in 2013 argued that that provision should be rewritten.[18] Also, in April 2014, thousands of protesters, including the Nobel Prize winner Ōe Kenzaborō, contested what they perceived as dangerous moves toward militarization, including Prime Minister Abe Shinzō's intention to change Article 9 of the Japanese Constitution. At the protest, Ōe warned, "I'm afraid that Japan's spirit is approaching the most dangerous stage over the past 100 years."[19] Finally, although it has been a continuous project among the right since the beginning of the postwar period, Japanese heroes are still "uneasy warriors" in terms of both filmic representation and real life.[20]

In sum, the closed and ambiguous narrative of Japanese war films creates an unclear war memory and an indistinct relationship with the past that is epitomized by the figure of the feminized victim-soldier cut off from the present in flashback. The suffering and death of these victim-soldiers, and their framing within sentimental stories in abstract locations create an open text that can be filled by the political orientation of the viewer. This ambiguity and its lack of continuity obscure remembrance of the suffering Japan inflicted on the rest of Asia and relieves Japan of its uncomfortable sense of wartime guilt.[21] Alleviating

---

18. Takashi Mochizuki, "Most Japanese Support Change to Postwar Charter," *Wall Street Journal*, May 5, 2013, accessed April 13, 2014, http://online.wsj.com/news/articles/SB10001424127887323372504578464622440869226.
19. "Pacifists Rally as Poll Shows Japan Is Uneasy over Abe's Military Aims," *Japan Times*, April 8, 2014, accessed April 13, 2014, http://www.japantimes.co.jp/news/2014/04/08/national/pacifists-rally-as-poll-shows-japan-is-uneasy-over-abes-military-aims/#.U0n22cdGEWU.
20. See Franziska Seraphim, *War Memory and Social Politics in Japan, 1945–2005* (Cambridge, MA: Harvard University Press, 2006); Sabine Frühstück, *Uneasy Warriors: Gender, Memory, and Popular Culture in the Japanese Army* (Berkeley: University of California Press, 2007).
21. Kōji Toba, "Eizō no sugamo purizun: Kabe atsuki heya to watashi wa kai ni naritai," *Gendai Shisō* 35, no. 10 (2007): 124–137.

this guilt and rejecting the label of perpetrator may help galvanize more popular support for normalization of the military and undoubtably creates an growing chasm between Japan and the rest of Asia in terms of reconciling war memory.

The Future of Remembrance

In this book, I have examined how film as a site of popular memory uses gendered and racial motifs of nationalism to articulate new narratives of Chinese and Japanese nationalism, suggesting that each reassessment of the past marks a significant shift in the present. Popular memory, like Joseph Roach's concept of surrogation, is performed to substitute, to fill in the "actual or perceived vacancies [that] occur in the network of relations that constitutes the social fabric."[22] Chinese and Japanese war films, in participating in the ceaseless turning of the transnational memory loop, articulate an identity that is meant to smooth over these transitions, to create a sense of continuity and stability *in a time of transition*. This process of "circling back" to remember particular events of World War II through narratives of gender, race, and nation are ultimately a mobilization of memory/identity in response to Japanese normalization, the rise of China, and the uncertain presence of the United States in the Pacific. Unfortunately, they reveal a disturbing trend toward increasingly irreconcilable positions.

This process is hardly a stable one. "National identity" is a fraught nexus of competing voices, and these popular narratives reveal a tension among the local, the national, and the global. As Aleida Assmann and Sebastian Conrad note, we have moved from eras of stability to motion. Nation-states are still important, but the "global audience has an important impact on political action and on the interpretation and evaluation of historical events."[23] Locally produced narratives are translated and disseminated globally, creating the potential for either the homogenization of memory or its opposition. In many ways the globalization of memory has only exacerbated national responses, as national crisis—such as the threat of historical revisionism or the perception of foreign-imposed "masochistic history"—can serve to reinforce national identity.[24]

Due to the increasingly global nature of historical discourse, and due to what I have envisioned here as a memory loop, Chinese and Japanese filmmakers

---

22. Joseph Roach, *Cities of the Dead: Circum-Atlantic Performance* (New York: Columbia University Press, 1996), 2.
23. Aleida Assmann, "Introduction," in *Memory in a Global Age: Discourses, Practices and Trajectories*, ed. Aleida Assmann and Sebastian Conrad (London: Palgrave Macmillan, 2010), 5.
24. For more on this, see Shun'ya Yoshimi, "Television and Nationalism: Historical Change in the National Domestic TV Formation of Postwar Japan," *European Journal of Cultural Studies* 6, no. 4 (2003): 483.

not only reinforce national identity through the narratives of their films but also show increasing interest in showing their national vision to the world. Of late, many Chinese directors have announced plans to broadcast their war films globally.[25] Moreover, many recent Chinese and Japanese war films have enlisted American production companies and American actors. They face a challenge—mainstream films like *Yamato*, *The Eternal Zero*, *Tokyo Trial*, and *The Message* were highly successful in China and Japan but are viewed as average or subpar by critics in other nations, possibly because such national narratives simply do not travel well.[26] The future will tell whether Chinese and Japanese filmmakers attempt to take their narratives global.

Would a unified global memory even be possible? Jan Assmann notes, "Memory functions in the direction of identity which, in all of its fuzziness, always implies a notion of difference. Globalization, on the other hand, works in the direction of diffusion, blurring all boundaries and bridging all differences."[27] Indeed, cosmopolitan or global memory is homogeneous and "flat": "a timeless global culture answers to no living needs and conjures no memories."[28] Rather, it is through the constant questioning of war and nationalism that filmmakers of today might engage in a more useful discussion of the past. As Michel Foucault wondered, "How is this particular reality on film to be reactivated as an existing, historically important reality?"[29] In my opinion, this is only possible through the interrogation of the past and active resistance of frameworks that limit the representation of individual experience. By questioning the dominant ideologies that impact the ways we construct the past, we come closer to understanding why and how such events occur, and what the impact is on the people who experience such events. The statement of the belated Japanese director Wakamatsu quoted at the beginning of this chapter—the staunchly leftist filmmaker who

---

25. See, for example, Chen Lu, "'Donjing shenpan' daoyan: Xiwang shiren dou zhidao zhejian shiqing," *Nanjing Zhoumo*, August 16, 2006, accessed November 4, 2014, http://news.sina.com.cn/c/cul/2006-08-16/141510742488.shtml; "Lu chuan tan nanjing."
26. Russell Edwards, "Review: 'Yamato,'" *Variety*, March 28, 2006, accessed November 4, 2014, http://variety.com/2006/film/reviews/yamato-1200517376/; Maggie Lee, "Review: 'The Eternal Zero,'" *Variety*, April 12, 2014, accessed November 4, 2014, http://variety.com/2014/film/reviews/film-review-japanese-hit-the-eternal-zero-1201155266/.
27. Jan Assmann, "Globalization, Universalism, and the Erosion of Cultural Memory," in *Memory in a Global Age: Discourses, Practices and Trajectories*, ed. Aleida Assmann and Sebastian Conrad (London: Palgrave Macmillan, 2010), 123.
28. Anthony D. Smith, *Nations and Nationalism in a Global Era* (Cambridge: Polity Press, 1995), 22–23.
29. Michel Foucault, "From 'Film in Popular Memory: An Interview with Michel Foucault,'" in *The Collective Memory Reader*, ed. Jeffrey K. Olick, Vered Vinitzky-Seroussi, and Daniel Levy (Oxford: Oxford University Press, 2011), 253.

constantly questioned dominant ideologies throughout his lifetime—demands this type of "combative" remembrance.

Only a few Chinese and Japanese war films have effectively interrogated memory and provide a more reflective gaze at the past. Hara Kazuo's documentary *The Emperor's Naked Army Marches On* (Yuki yukite shingun, 1988) challenges the silence of the 1980s in a shocking exposé of suppressed wartime secrets. Jiang Wen's *Devils on the Doorstep* (Guizi laile, 2000) presents a biting commentary on both war and nationalism. Guan Hu's film *Cow* (Douniu, 2009) is a humanistic look at wartime suffering from the perspective of a peasant and a cow. Finally, *The Wind Rises* (Kaze tachinu, 2013) warns the new generation against repeating dangerous mistakes of the past. Critics and academics may fight over the precise meaning or artistic choices of these complex works, but they nonetheless mark intriguing possibilities for a discussion of East Asian memory. Such unique and varied voices can explore remembering in a critical and useful way.

To conclude, I end with an image of such "critical" remembrance. In the independent Chinese film *Cow*, a Chinese peasant is entrusted with a Dutch cow imported to help the Chinese war efforts, a "stranger than fiction" story based on an actual event during the Sino-Japanese War. His entire village decimated by a Japanese bomb, only the peasant, Niu'er, and the cow survive. Niu'er decides it is his duty to deliver the cow to the Eighth Route Army, traveling across the mountains to find it. As he makes his journey, Niu'er encounters starving deserters, guerrilla soldiers, and other villagers, all of whom attempt to steal his cow. Coming across a wounded Japanese soldier, he decides to carry the injured man to safety. A Chinese soldier unexpectedly arrives, leading to a hysterical confrontation. When the chaos subsides, both the Chinese and the Japanese soldier dead by the side of the road. Niu'er buries them together in a shallow grave, unceremoniously tossing their bodies into a pit. National disputes mean nothing to the dead.

Niu'er's rejection of nationalism represents an alternative view of remembrance. This film is both a warning for the future and a commentary on the current state of war remembrance in China and Japan. In this highly charged political atmosphere, filmmakers should question the ideologies on which their films are based and consider the future paths their narratives will foster. Remembrance is a process, and like the memory loop, it will always return. For humanist narratives of personal trauma and national reconciliation to be heard, they must join this process of remembering.

Tables

Table 1.1: International box office for World War II films

Rank	Movie Title	Country	Lifetime Gross (Worldwide)	Release
1	*Dunkirk*	United Kingdom United States France Netherlands	$527,016,307	7/21/2017
2	*Saving Private Ryan*	United States	$482,349,603	7/24/1998
3	*Pearl Harbor*	United States	$449,220,945	5/25/2001
4	*Captain America: The First Avenger*	United States	$370,569,774	7/22/2011
5	*Schindler's List*	United States	$322,161,245	12/15/1993
6	*Inglourious Basterds*	United States	$321,457,747	8/21/2009
7	*The Imitation Game*	United States	$233,555,708	11/28/2014
8	*Life Is Beautiful*	Italy	$230,098,753	10/23/1998
9	*Fury*	United States	$211,822,697	10/17/2014
10	*Valkyrie*	United States	$201,545,517	12/25/2008
11	*Hacksaw Ridge*	United States	$180,563,636	11/4/2016
12	*Unbroken*	United States	$161,459,297	12/25/2014
13	*The Monuments Men*	United States	$156,706,638	2/7/2014
14	*U-571*	United States	$127,666,415	4/21/2000
15	*Midway*	United States	$127,420,861	11/8/2019

Source: Box Office Mojo by IMDb Pro, April 18, 2022, https://www.boxofficemojo.com/.

Table 1.2: Pacific War films at the Chinese box office (2005–2012)

Rank	Movie Title	Distributor	Domestic Box Office	Lifetime Gross (Worldwide)	Release Date in China
1	Mei Lanfang (Forever Enthralled)	China Film	$16,507,195	$17,773,395	12/4/2008
2	Jip Man (Ip Man)	Mandarin Films	$13,728,640	$22,108,789	12/12/2008
3	Shanghai	China Film	$6,721,903 for original release; $46,425 for 2015 rerelease	$15,302,850	6/17/2009
4	Se, Jie (Lust, Caution)	China Film	$4,604,982	$67,091,915	11/01/2007
5	Nanking (American documentary)	THINKFilm	$1,315,650	$1,566,248	07/06/2007
6	The Children of Huang Shi	Huaxia	$1,031,872	$7,785,975	4/3/2008
7	The Flowers of War (Jinling shisan chai)	EDKO Film	$311,434	$2,855,644	01/20/2012
8	City of Life and Death (Nanking! Nanking!)	China Film Group	$122,558	$10,687,316	05/11/2009

Source: Box Office Mojo by IMDb Pro, April 18, 2022, https://www.boxofficemojo.com/.

Table 1.3: Pacific War films at the Japanese box office (2005–2012)

Rank	Movie Title	Distributor	Domestic Box Office	Lifetime Gross (Worldwide)	Release
1	*Kaze tachinu* (*The Wind Rises*)	Toho	$119,513,192	$136,533,257	7/20/2013
2	*Eien no zero* (*Eternal Zero*)	Toho	$82,652,465	$82,879,386	12/21/2013
3	*Letters from Iwo Jima*	WB	$42,911,049	$68,673,228	12/9/2006
4	*Otoko-tachi no Yamato* (*Yamato*)	Toei	$39,287,114	$39,287,114	12/17/2005
5	*Lorelei*	Toho	$19,787,866	$19,806,585	3/5/2005
6	*Watashi wa kai ni naritai* (*I Want to Be a Shellfish*)	Toho	$18,502,784* ($24.5 billion yen)	No data	11/22/2008
7	*Rengō kantai shirei chôkan: Yamamoto Isoroku* (*Isoroku Yamamoto, the Commander-in-Chief of the Combined Fleet*)	Toei	$17,969,314	$18,110,621	12/23/2012
8	*Taiheiyou no kiseki: Fokkusu to yobareta otoko* (*Oba: The Last Samurai*)	Toho	$17,737,092	$17,737,092	2/11/2011
9	*Flags of Our Fathers*	WB	$13,100,000	$65,900,249	10/28/2006
10	*Ore wa, kimi no tame ni koso shini ni iku* (*For Those We Love*)	Toei	$7,769,311	$7,769,311	5/12/2007
11	*Ashita e no yuigon* (*Best Wishes for Tomorrow*)	Asmik Ace	$5,308,952	$5,309 1,137	3/1/2008

Sources: Box Office Mojo by IMDb Pro, April 18, 2022, https://www.boxofficemojo.com/. The box office statistics from *Watashi wa kai ni naritai* are from the Motion Picture Producers Association of Japan and were originally calculated in yen, June 8, 2022, http://www.eiren.org/toukei/img/eiren_kosyu/data_2009.pdf.

Glossary

aiguozhuyi jiaoyu	爱国主义教育	patriotic education
Atarashii Kyōkasho o Tsukuru-kai	新しい歴史教科書をつくる会	Japanese Society for History Textbook Reform
bainian guochi	百年国耻	100 Years of National Humiliation
bushidō	武士道	the way of the warrior
Chogukhaebangŭi nal	조국해방의 날	"Liberation of Fatherland Day"
Chūgoku zanryū koji	中国残留孤児	Japanese orphans left in China after the war
daichi no ko	大地の子	child of the earth
Daitōa Kyōeiken	大東亜共栄圏	Greater East Asia Co-Prosperity Sphere
dongyabingfu	东亚病夫	sick man of Asia
douzhidouyong	斗智斗勇	a battle of wits and courage
fenqing	愤青	angry youths
fujin	婦人	wife, woman
fu no hīrō	負のヒーロー	negative hero
furusato	故郷	hometown
gong'an	公案	desk of the magistrate
gong'an xiaoshuo	公案小说	crime fiction
gunshin	軍神	god of war
Gwangbokjeol	광복절	"Restoration of Light Day"
hanayome	花嫁	bride
Hanjian	汉	Chinese traitors
Hanminzu	汉民族	Chinese race

Hanzi	汉字	Chinese characters
Hikiagesha	引揚者	returnee, repatriated person
hinomaru	日の丸	the Japanese flag
houhuiyouqi	后会有期	until we meet again
huaping	花瓶	flower vase, a female character who is pretty but has no impact on the narrative
huise	灰色	gray or pessimistic (when used in reference to political content)
ianfu	慰安婦	comfort women
igo	囲碁	Go
ikiteiru kamisama	生きている神様	living gods
jigyaku shikan	自虐史観	masochistic view of history
kang Ri	抗日	resist Japan
karayuki-san	唐行きさん	Japanese woman who works as a prostitute in China literally, "Miss Goes-to-China"
katana	刀	Japanese sword
koji	孤児	orphan
luohou jiu yao ai da	落后就要挨打	If you are backward you will be beaten
minzoku	民族	race, people
nainai	奶奶	grandmother
nanzihan	男子汉	manly man
Nihon	日本	Japan
panpan	パンパン	postwar prostitute
Riben guizi	日本鬼子	Japanese devils
seppuku	切腹	ritual suicide
shiatsu	指圧	finger massage
shidōsha sekinin ron	指導者責任論	discourse on the responsibility of leaders
shōdo sakusen	焦土作戦	scorched-earth policy
shōsha no sabaki	勝者の裁き	victor's justice
Shūsen-kinenbi	終戦記念日	"Memorial Day for the End of the War"
sokoku	祖国	native country, motherland, fatherland

Glossary

tennō heika	天皇陛下	his majesty the emperor
tiexue wenxue	铁血文学	iron-and-blood literature
tokkōtai	特攻隊	special attack unit, kamikaze unit
Tōkyō saiban shikan	東京裁判史観	Tokyo Trial view of history
weiqi	围棋	Go
wen	文	literary
wenyi	文艺	letters and arts, also melodrama
wu	武	martial
wuwang guochi	勿忘国耻	Never Forget National Humiliation
wuxia	武侠	martial arts narrative
xunzhao nanzihan wenxue	寻找男子汉文	looking for real men literature
Yamato	大和	ancient Japan/Japanese race
Yamato damashī	大和魂	Japanese spirit
Yamato minzoku	大和民族	Japanese race, Yamato race
Yamato nadeshiko	大和撫子	an ideal Japanese woman
yidebaoyuan	以德报怨	return good for evil
yinsheng yangshuai	阴盛阳衰	the rise of the feminine and the decline of the masculine
Zainichi Kankokujin or *Zainichi*	在日韓国人	person of Korean descent living in Japan
zanryū koji	残留孤児	left-behind orphans
zanryū Nihonjin	残留日本人	left-behind Japanese
zhuxuanlü	主旋律	mainstream melody, a work that upholds the CCP dogma

Bibliography

Alcoff, Linda Martin. *Visible Identities: Race, Gender, and the Self*. Oxford: Oxford University Press, 2005.
Alexander, Jeffrey C. "Toward a Theory of Cultural Trauma." In *Cultural Trauma and Collective Identity*, edited by Jeffrey C. Alexander, Ron Eyerman, Bernard Giesen, Neil J. Smelser, and Piotr Sztompka, 1–30. Berkeley: University of California Press, 2004.
Allen, Beverly. *Rape Warfare: The Hidden Genocide in Bosnia-Herzegovina and Croatia*. Minneapolis: University of Minnesota Press, 1996.
Anand, Dibyesh. "Anxious Sexualities: Masculinity, Nationalism and Violence." *British Journal of Politics and International Relations* 9, no. 2 (2007): 257–269.
Anderson, Benedict. *Imagined Communities: Reflections on the Origin and Spread of Nationalism*. London: Verso, 1991.
Anthias, Floya, and Nira Yuval-Davis. *Woman-Nation-State*. New York: Macmillan, 1989.
Apel, Dora. "The Tattooed Jew." In *Visual Culture and the Holocaust*, edited by Barbie Zelizer, 300–322. New Brunswick, NJ: Rutgers University Press, 2001.
Araragi, Shinzō. "Chūgoku zanryū nihonjin no kioku no katari: Katari no henka to katari no jiba o megutte." In *Manshū: Kioku to Rekishi*, edited by Yūzō Yamamoto, 212–251. Kyoto: Kyōtodaigaku gakujutsu shuppankai, 2007.
Armstrong, John Alexander. *Nations before Nationalism*. Chapel Hill: University of North Carolina Press, 1982.
Ashplant, Timothy G., Graham Dawson, and Michael Roper, eds. *Commemorating War: The Politics of Memory*. London: Routledge, 2004.
Askew, David. "The Nanjing Incident: Recent Research and Trends." *Electronic Journal of Contemporary Japanese Studies* 2, no. 1 (2002). http://www.japanesestudies.org.uk/articles/Askew.html.
Assmann, Aleida. "Introduction." In *Memory in a Global Age: Discourses, Practices and Trajectories*, edited by Aleida Assmann and Sebastian Conrad, 1–16. London: Palgrave Macmillan, 2010.
Assmann, Jan. "Globalization, Universalism, and the Erosion of Cultural Memory." In *Memory in a Global Age: Discourses, Practices and Trajectories*, edited by Aleida Assmann and Sebastian Conrad, 121–127. London: Palgrave Macmillan, 2010.
Assmann, Jan, and John Czaplicka. "Collective Memory and Cultural Identity." *New German Critique* 65 (1995): 125–133.
Aumont, Jacques, ed. *Aesthetics of Film*. Austin: University of Texas Press, 1992.

Baaz, Maria Eriksson, and Maria Stern. "Why Do Soldiers Rape? Masculinity, Violence, and Sexuality in the Armed Forces in the Congo (DRC)." *International Studies Quarterly* 53, no. 2 (2009): 495–518.

Bao, Tong, and Jiang Yiran. "Riben xiandai wenxue zhong de zhongguo xingxiang: Yi dadi zhizi wei li." *Riyu Xuexi Yu Yanjiu* 3 (2012): 116–123.

Barthes, Roland. *Mythologies*. New York: Macmillan, 1972.

Bass, Gary. *Stay the Hand of Vengeance: The Politics of War Crimes Tribunals*. Princeton, NJ: Princeton University Press, 2000.

Berry, Chris. "Theorizing Chinese Masculinity: Society and Gender in China Review." *Intersections: Gender, History and Culture in the Asian Context* 8 (2002): http://intersections.anu.edu.au/issue8/berry_review.html.

Berry, Michael. "Cinematic Representations of the Rape of Nanking." *East Asia* 19, no. 4 (2001): 85–108.

Berry, Michael. *A History of Pain: Trauma in Modern Chinese Literature and Film*. New York: Columbia University Press, 2011.

Bhatia, Vijay, John Flowerdew, and Rodney H. Jones. "Approaches to Discourse Analysis." In *Advances in Discourse Studies*, edited by Vijay K. Bhatia, John Flowerdew, and Rodney H. Jones, 1–18. New York: Routledge, 2008.

Billig, Michael. *Banal Nationalism*. London: SAGE, 1995.

Bordwell, David. *Narration in the Fiction Film*. New York: Routledge, 2013.

Braester, Yomi. "Tracing the City's Scars: Demolition and the Limits of the Documentary Impulse in the New Urban Cinema." In *The Urban Generation: Chinese Cinema and Society at the Turn of the Twenty-First Century*, edited by Zhen Zhang, 161–180. Durham, NC: Duke University Press, 2007.

Brockmeier, Jens. "Remembering and Forgetting: Narrative as Cultural Memory." *Culture and Psychology* 8, no. 1 (2002): 15–43.

Brooks, Peter. *The Melodramatic Imagination: Balzac, Henry James, Melodrama, and the Mode of Excess*. New Haven, CT: Yale University Press, 1976.

Browne, Nick. "Society and Subjectivity: The Political Economy of the Chinese Melodrama." In *New Chinese Cinemas: Forms, Identities, Politics*, edited by Nick Browne, Paul G. Pickowicz, Vivian Sobchack, and Esther Yau, 40–56. Cambridge: Cambridge University Press, 1994.

Brownmiller, Susan. *Against Our Will: Men, Women and Rape*. New York: Simon and Schuster, 1975.

Burch, Noël. *Life to Those Shadows*. Berkeley: University of California Press, 1990.

Burgoyne, Robert. "Prosthetic Memory/Traumatic Memory: *Forrest Gump*." *Screening the Past* 6 (1999). Accessed November 4, 2014. http://tlweb.latrobe.edu.au/humanities/screening thepast/firstrelease/fr0499/rbfr6a.htm.

Buruma, Ian. *The Wages of Guilt: Memories of War in Germany and Japan*. New York: Farrar Straus and Giroux, 1994.

Callahan, William A. "National Insecurities: Humiliation, Salvation, and Chinese Nationalism." *Alternatives* 29, no. 2 (2004): 199–218.

Card, Claudia. "Rape as a Weapon of War." *Hypatia* 11, no. 4 (1996): 5–18.

Chan, Kam Wing, and Li Zhang. "The Hukou System and Rural-Urban Migration in China: Processes and Changes." *China Quarterly* 160 (1999): 818–855.

Chang, Iris. *The Rape of Nanking: The Forgotten Holocaust of World War II*. New York: Basic Books, 2012.

Chen, Lu. "'Donjing shenpan' daoyan: Xiwang shiren dou zhidao zhejian shiqing." *Nanjing Zhoumo*, August 16, 2006. Accessed November 4, 2014. http://news.sina.com.cn/c/cul/2006-08-16/141510742488.shtml; "Lu chuan tan nanjing."

Chen, Minjie. "From Victory to Victimization: The Sino-Japanese War (1937–1945) as Depicted in Chinese Youth Literature." *Bookbird: A Journal of International Children's Literature* 47, no. 2 (2009): 27–35.

Chen, Rui. "Yi liangjian weilie tan shichanghua xiezuo yu lixiang shenjingde jiehe." *Jiamusi Jiaoyu Xueyuanbao* 4 (2011: 40–41.

Cheng, Joseph. "China's Japan Policy in the 1980s." *International Affairs* 61, no. 1 (1984): 91–107.

Cheng, Zhaoqi. "Cong *Dongjing Shenpan* dao dongjing shenpan." *Shi Lin* 5 (2007): 19–33.

Choi, Chungmoo. "The Politics of War Memories toward Healing." In *Perilous Memories: The Asia-Pacific War(s)*, edited by T. T. Fujitani, Geoffrey M. White, and Lisa Yoneyama, 395–410. Durham, NC: Duke University Press, 2001.

Cohen, Dara Kay. "Explaining Sexual Violence during Civil War: Evidence from the Sierra Leone War (1991–2002)." Paper presented at the annual convention of the American Political Science Association, Chicago, Illinois, August 16, 2007.

Cohn, Carol. "Wars, Wimps, and Women: Talking Gender and Thinking War." In *Gendering War Talk*, edited by Miriam Cook and Angela Woollacott, 227–246. Princeton, NJ: Princeton University Press, 1993.

Confino, Alon. "Collective Memory and Cultural History: Problems of Method." *American Historical Review* 102, no. 5 (1997): 1386–1403.

Connell, R. W. "Globalization, Imperialism, and Masculinities." In *Handbook of Studies on Men and Masculinities*, edited by Michael S. Kimmel and Jeff R. Hearn, 71–89. London: SAGE, 2005.

Connell, R. W. *Masculinities*. Berkeley: University of California Press, 2005.

Connerton, Paul. *How Societies Remember*. Cambridge: Cambridge University Press, 1989.

Crary, Jonathan. "Spectacle, Attention, Counter-memory." *October* 50 (1989): 97–107.

Cui, Shuqin. "Negotiating In-Between: On New-Generation Filmmaking and Jia Zhangke's Films." *Modern Chinese Literature and Culture* 18, no. 2 (2006): 98–130.

Cui, Shuqin. *Women through the Lens: Gender and Nation in a Century of Chinese Cinema*. Honolulu: University of Hawai'i Press, 2003.

Culbertson, Roberta. "Embodied Memory, Transcendence, and Telling: Recounting Trauma, Re-establishing the Self." *New Literary History* 26, no. 1 (1995): 169–195.

Curtin, Michael. *Playing to the World's Biggest Audience: The Globalization of Chinese Film and TV*. Berkeley: University of California Press, 2007.

Custen, George F. "Making History." In *The Historical Film: History and Memory in Media*, edited by Marcia Landy, 67–97. New Brunswick, NJ: Rutgers University Press, 2001.

Da, Huo'er. "Interview with Xie Jin." *Jump Cut* 34 (1989): 107–109. http://www.ejumpcut.org/archive/onlinessays/JC34folder/XieJinInt.html.

Davis, Natalie Zemon. "'Any Resemblance to Persons Living or Dead': Film and the Challenge of Authenticity." *Historical Journal of Film, Radio and Television* 8, no. 3 (1988): 457–482.

DeBoer, Stephanie. *Coproducing Asia: Locating Japanese and Chinese Regional Film and Media*. Minneapolis: University of Minnesota Press, 2014.

Deleuze, Giles. *Masochism: Coldness and Cruelty & Venus in Furs*. New York: Urzone, 1999.

Diken, Bülent, and Carsten Bagge Laustsen. "Becoming Abject: Rape as a Weapon of War." *Body and Society* 11, no. 1 (2005): 111–128.

Dissanayake, Wimal. "Globalization and the Experience of Culture." In *Globalization, Cultural Identities, and Media Representations*, edited by Natascha Gentz and Stefan Kramer, 25–44. Albany, NY: SUNY Press, 2012.

Doane, Mary A. *The Desire to Desire: The Woman's Film of the 1940s*. Bloomington: Indiana University Press, 1987.

Doane, Mary Ann. *The Emergence of Cinematic Time: Modernity, Contingency, the Archive*. Cambridge, MA: Harvard University Press, 2002.
Doi, Saisuke. "*Daichi No Ko* ni mita shinryaku sensō no kizuato." *Zen'ei* 670 (1996): 89–90.
Dower, John. *War without Mercy: Race and Power in the Pacific War*. New York: Random House, 1986.
Dower, John W. *Embracing Defeat: Japan in the Wake of World War II*. New York: W. W. Norton, 2000.
Du, Ying. "Guanyu riben yigu yu zhongguo yang fumu de guanxi wenti: Jian dui zhongguo riben yigu yu e sa ha lin riben gui guo zhe zuo bijiao yanjiu." *Xiboliya Yanjiu*, no. 6 (2011): 19–21.
Dyer, Richard. *Stars*. London: British Film Institute, 1979.
Ebert, Robert. "Flowers of War." RogerEbert.com, January 18, 2012. Accessed March 20, 2015. http://www.rogerebert.com/reviews/flowers-of-war-2012.
Edgerton, Gary Richard. "Introduction." In *Television Histories: Shaping Collective Memory in the Media Age*, edited by Gary Edgerton and Peter C. Rollins, 1–18. Lexington: University Press of Kentucky, 2001.
Elsaesser, Thomas. "Tales of Sound and Fury: The Family Melodrama." *Monogram* 4 (1972): 2–15.
Enloe, Cynthia. *Bananas, Beaches and Bases: Making Feminist Sense of International Politics*. Berkeley: University of California Press, 1989.
Erll, Astrid. "Literature, Film, and the Mediality of Cultural Memory." In *Cultural Memory Studies: An International and Interdisciplinary Handbook*, edited by Astrid Erll and Ansgar Nünning, 389–398. Berlin: Walter de Gruyter, 2008.
Erll, Astrid, and Ann Rigney, eds. *Mediation, Remediation, and the Dynamics of Cultural Memory*. Berlin: Walter de Gruyter, 2009.
Evangelista, Matthew. *Gender, Nationalism, and War: Conflict on the Movie Screen*. Cambridge: Cambridge University Press, 2011.
Eykholt, Mark. "Aggression, Victimization, and Chinese Historiography of the Nanjing Massacre." In *The Nanjing Massacre in History and Historiography*, edited by Joshua Fogel, 11–69. Berkeley: University of California Press, 2000.
Fang, Qingqing, and Yan Jun. "Dongjing Shenpan jiexi." *Dianying Pingjie* 17 (2007): 41–42.
Fanon, Frantz. *The Wretched of the Earth*. New York: Grove Press, 1961.
Farwell, Nancy. "War Rape: New Conceptualizations and Responses." *Affilia* 19, no. 4 (2004): 389–403.
Felman, Shoshana. "The Return of the Voice: Claude Lanzmann's *Shoah*." In *Testimony: Crises of Witnessing in Literature, Psychoanalysis, and History*, edited by Shoshana Felman and Dori Laub, 204–283. New York: Routledge, 1992.
Felski, Rita. *The Gender of Modernity*. Cambridge, MA: Harvard University Press, 2009.
Fogel, Joshua A. "Introduction: The Nanjing Massacre in History." In *The Nanjing Massacre in History and Historiography*, edited by Joshua A. Fogel, 1–10. Berkeley: University of California Press, 2000.
Fogel, Joshua, ed. *The Nanjing Massacre in History and Historiography*. Berkeley: University of California Press, 2000.
Foucault, Michel. "From 'Film in Popular Memory: An Interview with Michel Foucault.'" In *The Collective Memory Reader*, edited by Jeffrey K. Olick, Vered Vinitzky-Seroussi, and Daniel Levy, 252–253. Oxford: Oxford University Press, 2011.
Frühstück, Sabine. *Uneasy Warriors: Gender, Memory, and Popular Culture in the Japanese Army*. Berkeley: University of California Press, 2007.
Fu, Hualing. "Television in Post-reform China: Serial Dramas, Confucian Leadership and the Global Television Market." *China Quarterly* 201 (2010): 195–227.

Fujii, Shōzō. *Chūgoku eiga: Hyakunen o egaku, hyaku nen o yomu*. Tokyo: Iwanami, 2002.
Fujii, Shōzō. *Chūgoku eiga o yomu hon*. Tokyo: Asahi Shimbunsha, 1994.
Fujiwara, Kiichi. *Sensō o kioku suru Hiroshima horokōsuto to genzai*. Tokyo: Kōdansha, 2001.
Fukuma, Yoshiaki. *"Hansen" no media-shi: Sengonihon ni okeru yoron to yoron no kikkō*. Kyoto: Sekai shisō-sha, 2006.
Fukuyama, Francis, and Kongdan Oh. *The US-Japan Security Relationship after the Cold War*. Santa Monica: National Defense Research Institute, 1993.
Futamura, Madoka. *War Crimes Tribunals and Transitional Justice: The Tokyo Trial and the Nuremburg Legacy*. New York: Routledge, 2007.
Garzke, William, and Robert Dulin. *Battleships: Axis and Neutral Battleships in World War II*. Annapolis, MD: Naval Institute Press, 1985.
Gerow, Aaron. "Fantasies of War and Nation in Recent Japanese Cinema." *Japan Focus*, February 16, 2006. http://www.japanfocus.org/-Aaron-Gerow/1707.
Gerow, Aaron. "War and Nationalism in *Yamato*: Trauma and Forgetting the Postwar." *Asia-Pacific Journal* 9, issue 24, no. 1 (2011). http://japanfocus.org/-Aaron-Gerow/3545.
Gilman, Sander L. "Is Life Beautiful? Can the Shoah Be Funny? Some Thoughts on Recent and Older Films." *Critical Inquiry* 26, no. 2 (2000): 279–308.
Gray, Jonathan. *Show Sold Separately: Promos, Spoilers, and Other Media*. New York: New York University Press, 2010.
Gries, Peter Hays. "Tears of Rage: Chinese Nationalist Reactions to the Belgrade Embassy Bombing." *China Journal* 46 (2001): 25–43.
Guo, Songmin. "*Nanjing! Nanjing!* Jiaochuan weisheme shi xujia de?" *Jizhe Guancha* 6 (2009): 60.
Hachimori, Minoru. "*Mikan no Taikyoku*: Chūgoku roke repōto." *Kinema Junpō* 6, no. 838 (1982): 105–107.
Halbwachs, Maurice. "The Collective Memory." In *The Collective Memory Reader*, edited by Jeffrey K. Olick, Vered Vinitzky-Seroussi, and Daniel Levy, 139–140. Oxford: Oxford University Press, 2011.
Hansen, Miriam Bratu. "'Schindler's List' Is Not 'Shoah': The Second Commandment, Popular Modernism, and Public Memory." *Critical Inquiry* 22, no. 2 (1996): 292–312.
Hasegawa, Tsuyoshi, and Kazuhiko Togo. *East Asia's Haunted Present: Historical Memories and the Resurgence of Nationalism: Historical Memories and the Resurgence of Nationalism*. Westport, CT: ABC-CLIO, 2008.
Hashimoto, Akiko. "Divided Memories, Contested Histories: The Shifting Landscape in Japan." In *Cultures and Globalization: Heritage, Memory and Identity*, edited by Helmut Anheier and Yudhishthir Raj Isar, 239–244. London: SAGE, 2011.
Hayashi, Kaori, and Eun-Jeung Lee. "The Potential of Fandom and the Limits of Soft Power: Media Representations on the Popularity of a Korean Melodrama in Japan." *Social Science Japan Journal* 10, no. 2 (2007): 197–216.
He, Yinan. "Remembering and Forgetting the War: Elite Mythmaking, Mass Reaction, and Sino-Japanese Relations, 1950–2006." *History and Memory* 19, no. 2 (2007): 43–74.
Hein, Laura Elizabeth, and Mark Selden, eds. *Censoring History: Citizenship and Memory in Japan, Germany, and the United States*. Armonk, NY: M. E. Sharpe, 2000.
Hershatter, Gail. *The Gender of Memory: Rural Women and China's Collective Past*. Berkeley: University of California Press, 2011.
Higbee, Will, and Song Hwee Lim. "Concepts of Transnational Cinema: Towards a Critical Transnationalism in Film Studies." *Transnational Cinemas* 1, no. 1 (2010): 7–21.
Higgins, Lynn A., and Brenda R. Silver, eds. *Rape and Representation*. New York: Columbia University Press, 1991.

Hijiya-Kirschnereit, Irmela. "Hana to gyakusatsu: Nankin jiken to Mishima Yukio no *Botan.*" *Gunzō* 52, no. 8 (1997): 154–159.

Hirsch, Marianne. *Family Frames: Photography, Narrative, and Postmemory.* Cambridge, MA: Harvard University Press, 1997.

Hoch, Paul. *White Hero, Black Beast: Racism, Sexism and the Mask of Masculinity.* London: Pluto Press, 1979.

Hooper, Charlotte. *Manly States: Masculinities, International Relations, and Gender Politics.* New York: Columbia University Press, 2001.

Horeck, Tanya. *Public Rape: Representing Violation in Fiction and Film.* London: Routledge, 2013.

Hoskins, Andrew. "Signs of the Holocaust: Exhibiting Memory in a Mediated Age." *Media, Culture and Society* 25, no. 1 (2003): 7–22.

Howard, Keith. *True Stories of the Korean Comfort Women.* London: Cassell, 1995.

Hu, Hualing. *American Goddess at the Rape of Nanking: The Courage of Minnie Vautrin.* Edwardsville: Southern Illinois University Press, 2000.

Huyssen, Andreas. "Monument and Memory in a Postmodern Age." *Yale Journal of Criticism* 6 (1993): 249–261.

Huyssen, Andreas. "Of Mice and Mimesis: Reading Spiegelman with Adorno." *New German Critique* 81(2000): 65–82.

Igarashi, Yoshikuni. *Bodies of Memory: Narratives of War in Postwar Japanese Culture, 1945–1970.* Princeton, NJ: Princeton University Press, 2000.

Igarashi, Yoshikuni. "Kamikaze Today: The Search for National Heroes in Contemporary Japan." In *Ruptured Histories: War, Memory, and the Post–Cold War in Asia,* edited by Sheila Miyoshi Jager and Rana Mitter, 99–121. Cambridge, MA: Harvard University Press, 2007.

Ivy, Marilyn. "Revenge and Recapitation in Recessionary Japan." *South Atlantic Quarterly* 99, no. 4 (2000): 819–840.

Iwasaki, Minoru. "Higashiajia no kioku no ba no kanōsei: Piēru Nora e no hihanteki ōtō no kokoromi to shite." *Quadrante* 11 (2009): 47–54.

Jauss, Hans Robert, and Elizabeth Benzinger. "Literary History as a Challenge to Literary Theory." *New Literary History* 2, no. 1 (1970): 7–37.

Jeffords, Susan. *Hard Bodies: Hollywood Masculinity in the Reagan Era.* New Brunswick, NJ: Rutgers University Press, 1994.

Johnson, Chalmers. "The Patterns of Japanese Relations with China, 1952–1982." *Pacific Affairs* 59, no. 3 (1986): 402–428.

Johnson, Chalmers. "Some Thoughts on the Nanjing Massacre." Japan Policy Research Institute. (2000) Accessed June 10, 2014. http://www.jpri.org/publications/critiques/critique_VII_1.html.

Jones, Rodney H., and Sigrid Norris. *Discourse in Action: Introducing Mediated Discourse Analysis.* New York: Routledge, 2005.

Kaes, Anton. "History and Film: Public Memory in the Age of Electronic Dissemination." *History and Memory* 2, no. 1 (1990): 111–129.

Kaes, Anton. *Shell Shock Cinema: Weimar Culture and the Wounds of War.* Princeton, NJ: Princeton University Press, 2009.

Kaplan, E. Ann. "Melodrama, Cinema and Trauma." *Screen* 42, no. 2 (2001): 201–205.

Kaplan, E. Ann. *Motherhood and Representation: The Mother in Popular Culture and Melodrama.* New York: Taylor and Francis, 1992.

Karlin, Jason G. *Gender and Nation in Meiji Japan: Modernity, Loss, and the Doing of History.* Honolulu: University of Hawai'i Press, 2014.

Karlin, Jason G. "The Gender of Nationalism: Competing Masculinities in Meiji Japan." *Journal of Japanese Studies* 28, no. 1 (2002): 41–77.
Katō, Masato and Hashimoto Shinobu, "Eiga watashi ha kai ni naritai rimeiku ni atatte no shinario kaitei." *Shinario* 65, no. 1 (2009): 18–27.
Katō, Tetsutarō. *Watakushi wa kai ni naritai: Aru BC-kyū senpan no sakebi.* Tokyo: Shunjusha, 1995.
Kilbourn, Russell. *Cinema, Memory, Modernity: The Representation of Memory from the Art Film to Transnational Cinema.* Vol. 6. New York: Routledge, 2013.
Kinkley, Jeffrey C. *Corruption and Realism in Late Socialist China: The Return of the Political Novel.* Stanford, CA: Stanford University Press, 2006.
Kinney, Damien. "Rediscovering a Massacre: The Filmic Legacy of Iris Chang's *The Rape of Nanking*." *Continuum* 26, no. 1 (2012): 11–23.
Kirby, Paul. "How Is Rape a Weapon of War? Feminist International Relations, Modes of Critical Explanation and the Study of Wartime Sexual Violence." *European Journal of International Relations* 19, no. 4 (2012). https://doi.org/10.1177/1354066111427614.
Klein, Kerwin Lee. "On the Emergence of Memory in Historical Discourse." *Representations*, no. 69 (2000): 127–150.
Kleinman, Arthur, and Joan Kleinman. "How Bodies Remember: Social Memory and Bodily Experience of Criticism, Resistance, and Delegitimization Following China's Cultural Revolution." *New Literary History* 25, no. 3 (1994): 707–723.
Kokubun, Ryosei. "The Current State of Contemporary Chinese Studies in Japan." *China Quarterly* 107 (1986): 505–518.
Kong, Shuyu. "Genre Film, Media Corporations, and the Commercialisation of the Chinese Film Industry: The Case of 'New Year Comedies.'" *Asian Studies Review* 31, no. 3 (2007): 227–242.
Kotler, Mindy, Naotaka Sugawara, and Tetsuya Yamada. "Chinese and Japanese Public Opinion: Searching for Moral Security." *Asian Perspective* 3, no. 1 (2007): 93–125.
Kress, Gunther, and Theo Van Leeuwen. *Multimodal Discourse.* London: Arnold, 2001.
Kushner, Barak. "Pawns of Empire: Postwar Taiwan, Japan and the Dilemma of War Crimes." *Japanese Studies* 30, no. 1 (2010): 111–133.
LaCapra, Dominick. "Lanzmann's *Shoah*: Here There Is No Why." *Critical Inquiry* 23, no. 2 (1997): 231–269.
Lacy, Mark J. "War, Cinema, and Moral Anxiety." *Alternatives* 28, no. 5 (2003): 611–636.
Landsberg, Alison. "America, the Holocaust, and the Mass Culture of Memory: Toward a Radical Politics of Empathy." *New German Critique*, no. 71 (1997): 63–86.
Landsberg, Alison. *Prosthetic Memory: The Transformation of American Remembrance in the Age of Mass Culture.* New York: Columbia University Press, 2004.
Landy, Marcia. "Cinematic History, Melodrama, and the Holocaust." In *Humanity at the Limit: The Impact of the Holocaust Experience on Jews and Christians*, edited by Michael A. Signer, 376–390. Bloomington: Indiana University Press, 2000.
Landy, Marcia. "Introduction." In *The Historical Film: History and Memory in Media*, edited by Marcia Landy, 1–24. New Brunswick, NJ: Rutgers University Press, 2001.
Lau, Jenny Kwok Wah. "'Farewell My Concubine': History, Melodrama, and Ideology in Contemporary Pan-Chinese Cinema." *Film Quarterly* 49, no. 1 (1995): 16–27.
Levy, Daniel, and Natan Sznaider. "Memory Unbound: The Holocaust and the Formation of Cosmopolitan Memory." *European Journal of Social Theory* 5, no. 1 (2002): 87–106.
Li, Mang. "Xin lei di yi sheng: *Yi Pan Meiyou Xia Wan De Qi* sixiang qiantan." *Dianying Yishu* 10 (1982): 24–26.

Ling, Jinqi. "Identity Crisis and Gender Politics: Reappropriating Asian American Masculinity." In *An Interethnic Companion to Asian American Literature*, edited by King-Kok Cheung, 312–337. Cambridge: Cambridge University Press, 1997.

Liu, Ben. "Chūgoku zanryū minashigo o makotoni rikai shite iru no wa dare ka." *Kinyōbi* 6 (1998): 26–29.

Liu, Fusheng. "Cong huanle yingxiong dao lishi shounan zhe: Ping liangjian." *Wenyi Lilun Yu Piping* 6 (2006): 38–42.

Liu, James H., and Tomohide Atsumi. "Historical Conflict and Resolution between Japan and China: Developing and Applying a Narrative Theory of History and Identity." In *Meaning in Action: Constructions, Narratives, and Representations*, edited by Toshio Sugiman, Kenneth J. Gergen, Wolfgang Wagner, and Yamada Yoko, 327–344. Tokyo: Springer, 2008.

Liu, Jin. "The Rhetoric of Local Languages as the Marginal: Chinese Underground and Independent Films by Jia Zhangke and Others." *Modern Chinese Literature and Culture* 18, no. 2 (2006): 163–205.

Liu, Mengxi. "Qidao yishu lishi: Yingpian *Yi Pan Meiyou Xiawan De Qi* manping." *Dianying Yishu* 10 (1982): 20–23, 30.

Liu, Shuo. "Shiting huayu chanshi yu jingshen chuancheng: Dui hongse jingdian gai bianju chuangzuo yanjiu de shuli yu fansi." *Dangdai Dianying* 1 (2007): 69–74.

Liu, Yihua. "Xin shiji zhanzheng xiaoshuo de xin tansuo: Cong liangjian tan qi." *Bijie xueyuan xuebao* 2 (2009): 75–78.

Lloyd, Justine, and Lesley Johnson. "The Three Faces of Eve: The Post-war Housewife, Melodrama, and Home 1." *Feminist Media Studies* 3, no. 1 (2003): 7–25.

Louie, Kam. *Theorising Chinese Masculinity: Society and Gender in China*. Cambridge: Cambridge University Press, 2002.

Louie, Kam, and Morris Low, eds. *Asian Masculinities: The Meaning and Practice of Manhood in China and Japan*. New York: Routledge, 2012.

Low, Morris. "Gender and Representations of the War in Tokyo Museums." In *East Asia beyond the History Wars: Reconciliation as Method*, edited by Tessa Morris-Suzuki, Morris Low, Leonid Petrov, and Timothy Y. Tsu, 107–127. New York: Routledge, 2013.

Lu, Sheldon H. "Soap Opera in China: The Transnational Politics of Visuality, Sexuality, and Masculinity." *Cinema Journal* 40, no. 1 (2000): 25–47.

Lu, Sheldon, ed. *Transnational Chinese Cinemas: Identity, Nationhood, Gender*. Honolulu: University of Hawai'i Press, 1997.

Lu, Suping. *Terror in Minnie Vautrin's Nanjing: Diaries and Correspondence, 1937–38*. Champaign: University of Illinois Press, 2008.

Lukács, Gabriella. *Scripted Affects, Branded Selves: Television, Subjectivity, and Capitalism in 1990s Japan*. Durham, NC: Duke University Press, 2010.

Ma, Fu. "Dianying dongjing shenpan de aiguozhuyi sixiang." *Mangzhong* 17 (2012): 156–157.

Machura, Stefan, and Stefan Ulbrich. "Law in Film: Globalizing the Hollywood Courtroom Drama." *Journal of Law and Society* 28, no. 1 (2001): 117–132.

MacKinnon, Catharine A. "Rape, Genocide, and Women's Human Rights." *Harvard Women's Law Journal* 17 (1994): 5–16.

Maga, Timothy P. *Judgment at Tokyo: The Japanese War Crimes Trials*. Lexington: University Press of Kentucky, 2001.

Makino, Hiromichi, and Hongō Yoshinori. "Hokori to sekinin kan sōshitsu no jidai ni eiga ashita e no yuigon o kyōō ni kizamu." *Seiron* 433 (2008): 144–151.

Marchetti, Gina. *Romance and the "Yellow Peril": Race, Sex, and Discursive Strategies in Hollywood Fiction*. Berkeley: University of California Press, 1993.

Mason, Michele M. "Empowering the Would-Be Warrior: Bushidō and the Gendered Bodies of the Japanese Nation," In *Recreating Japanese Men*, edited by Sabine Frühstück and Anne Walthall, 68–90. Berkeley: University of California Press, 2011.

Mayer, Tamar, ed. *Gender Ironies of Nationalism: Sexing the Nation*. London: Routledge, 2002.

McIntyre, Stephen. "Courtroom Drama with Chinese Characteristics: A Comparative Approach to Legal Process in Chinese Cinema." *East Asia Law Review* 8 (2013): 1–19.

Mei, Duo. "Xie Jin yishu yinqi de quannian pengzhuang: Jian lun yingpian *Qingliangsi Zhongsheng*." *Shehui Kexue* 2 (1992): 66–70.

Meilicke, Elena. "Big in China: On the Spectacularization of History in the Founding of a Republic, Aftershock and the Flowers of War." In *Chinese Identities on Screen*, edited by Klaus Mühlhahn and Clemens von Haselberg, 56–61. Zurich: Lit Verlag, 2012.

Meron, Theodor. "Reflections on the Prosecution of War Crimes by International Tribunals." *American Journal of International Law* 100, no. 3 (2006): 551–579.

Metz, Christian. *Film Language: A Semiotics of the Cinema*. Chicago: University of Chicago Press, 1974.

Miller, Ian Jared. *The Nature of the Beasts: Empire and Exhibition at the Tokyo Imperial Zoo*. Berkeley: University of California Press, 2013.

Minami, Makoto. "Chūgoku zanryū nihonjin no katara re-kata: Kioku hyōshō suru terebi dokyumentarī." In *Manshū: Kioku to rekishi*, edited by Yūzō Yamamoto, 252–290. Kyoto: Kyōtodaigaku gakujutsu shuppankai, 2007.

Minear, Richard. "'The Trial of Mr. Hyde' and Victors' Justice by Takeyama Michio." *Japan Focus*, August 11, 2006. Accessed November 4, 2014, http://www.japanfocus.org/-Takeyama-Michio/2192.

Mitter, Rana. *Forgotten Ally: China's World War II, 1937–1945*. New York: Houghton Mifflin Harcourt, 2013.

Mizushima, Satoru. "Eiga *Nankin no Shinjitsu* seisaku nisshi: Jōhō-sen no saizensen kara." *Seiron* 480 (2012): 268–273.

Mizushima, Satoru. *1937 Nanking no shinjitsu*. Tokyo: Asuka Shinsha, 2008.

Morrell, Robert, and Sandra Swart. "Men in the Third World: Postcolonial Perspectives on Masculinity." In *Handbook of Studies on Men and Masculinities*, edited by Michael S. Kimmel and Jeff R. Hearn, 90–113. London: SAGE, 2005.

Morris-Suzuki, Tessa. *The Past within Us: Media, Memory, History*. London: Verso, 2005.

Morris-Suzuki, Tessa, and Peter Rimmer. "Virtual Memories: Japanese History Debates in Manga and Cyberspace." *Asian Studies Review* 26, no. 2 (2002): 147–164.

Moskowitz, Marc L. *Go Nation: Chinese Masculinities and the Game of Weiqi in China*. Berkeley: University of California Press, 2013.

Moss, Mark. *Toward the Visualization of History: The Past as Image*. Oxford: Oxford University Press, 2008.

Nagaoka, Yoshiyuki. "Eiga *Nankin 1937* ni futatabi uyoku no mōkōgeki." *Tsukuru* 28, no. 10 (1998): 28–35.

Nagaoka, Yoshiyuki. "Eiga *Puraido, Nankin 1937* meguru gekiron no yukue: Rekishi minaoshi ronsō no shin kyokumen ka." *Tsukuru* 28, no. 7 (1998): 94–101.

Nagel, Joane. "Masculinity and Nationalism: Gender and Sexuality in the Making of Nations." *Ethnic and Racial Studies* 21, no. 2 (1998): 243–269.

Nakamura, Hideyuki. "Girei toshite no tokkō eiga: Otokotachi no yamato/yamato no baai." *Zen'ya* 7 (2006): 134–137.

Nakamura, Hideyuki. "Tokkōtai hyōshōron." In *Iwanami kōza: Ajia, taiheiyō sensō 5: Senjō no shosō*, 301–330. Tokyo: Iwanami Shoten, 2006.

Nandy, Ashis. *The Intimate Enemy*. Oxford: Oxford University Press, 1989.

Nietzsche, Friedrich. "On the Uses and Disadvantages of History for Life." Translated by R. J. Hollingdale, 57–123. Cambridge: Cambridge University Press, 1983.

Nojima, Ryūzō. "Eiga ni egakareta sensō no shinjitsu: Ore wa, kiminotameni koso shini ni iku to Hotaru, Patchigi! LOVE & PEACE (Tokushū rekishi no shinjitsu o tou)." *Minshubungaku* 503 (2007): 140–145.

Nora, Pierre. "Between Memory and History: Les Lieux de Mémoire." *Representations*, no. 26 (1989): 7–24.

Nora, Pierre. "Reasons for the Current Upsurge in Memory." *Eurozine*, April 19, 2002. Accessed April 13. 2014, http://www.eurozine.com/articles/2002-04-19-nora-en .html.

Norris, Sigrid. *Analyzing Multimodal Interaction: A Methodological Framework*. New York: Routledge, 2004.

Nozaki, Yoshiko. "The 'Comfort Women' Controversy: History and Testimony." *Asia-Pacific Journal: Japan Focus*. 3, no. 5 (2005). http://japanfocus.org/-Yoshiko-Nozaki /2063.

Ohnuki-Tierney, Emiko. *Kamikaze, Cherry Blossoms, and Nationalisms: The Militarization of Aesthetics in Japanese History*. Chicago: University of Chicago Press, 2010.

Ohnuki-Tierney, Emiko. *Kamikaze Diaries: Reflections of Japanese Student Soldiers*. Chicago: University of Chicago Press, 2007.

Olick, Jeffrey K., and Joyce Robbins. "Social Memory Studies: From "Collective Memory" to the Historical Sociology of Mnemonic Practices." *Annual Review of Sociology* 24, no. 1 (1998): 105–140.

Olick, Jeffrey, Vered Vinitzky-Seroussi, and Daniel Levy. "Introduction." In *The Collective Memory Reader*, edited by Jeffrey K. Olick, Vered Vinitzky-Seroussi, and Daniel Levy, 3–62. Oxford: Oxford University Press, 2011.

Ouzgane, Lahoucine, and Daniel Coleman. "Postcolonial Masculinities: Introduction." *Jouvert: A Journal of Postcolonial Studies* 2, no. 1 (1998): 1–10.

Owen, Susan A. "Memory, War and American Identity: Saving Private Ryan as Cinematic Jeremiad." *Critical Studies in Media Communication* 19, no. 3 (2002): 249–282.

Paltridge, Brian. *Discourse Analysis: An Introduction*. London: Bloomsbury, 2012.

Pence, Jeffrey. "Postcinema/Postmemory." In *Memory and Popular Film*, edited by Paul Grainge, 237–256. Manchester: Manchester University Press, 2003.

Peng, Wenxiang. "Dianshiju gaibian 'hongse jingdian' de xin weidu he xin changshi: Dianshiju xiaobing zhangga de xushi tese." *Zhongguo Dianshi* 11 (2005): 23–26.

Pierson, Michelle A. "Production Designer's Cinema: Historical Authenticity in Popular Films Set in the Past." In *The Spectacle of the Real: From Hollywood to "Reality" TV and Beyond*, edited by Geoff King, 139–149. Bristol: Intellect, 2005.

Pinchevski, Amit. "Archive, Media, Trauma." In *On Media Memory: Collective Memory in a New Media Age*, edited by Motti Neiger, Oren Meyers, and Eyal Zandberg, 253–264. London: Palgrave Macmillan, 2011.

Pritchard, John R. "International Military Tribunal for the Far East and Its Contemporary Resonances." *Military Law Review* 149 (1995): 25–36.

Prividera, Laura C., and John W. Howard. "Masculinity, Whiteness, and the Warrior Hero: Perpetuating the Strategic Rhetoric of US Nationalism and the Marginalization of Women." *Women and Language* 29, no. 2 (2009): 29–37.

Projansky, Sarah. *Watching Rape: Film and Television in Postfeminist Culture*. New York: New York University Press, 2001.

Qi, Jin. "The Politics of History and Historical Memory in China-Japan Relations." *Journal of Chinese Political Science* 11, no. 1 (2006): 25–53.

Radstone, Susannah. "What Place Is This? Transcultural Memory and the Locations of Memory Studies." *Parallax* 17, no. 4 (2011): 109–123. http://www.tandfonline.com /doi/full/10.1080/13534645.2011.605585.

Reading, Anna, "Memory and Digital Media: Six Dynamics of the Globital Memory Field." In *On Media Memory: Collective Memory in a New Media Age*, edited by Motti Neiger, Oren Meyers, and Eyal Zandberg, 241–252. London: Palgrave Macmillan.

Ricoeur, Paul. *Time and Narrative*. Chicago: University of Chicago Press, 2010.

Roach, Joseph. *Cities of the Dead: Circum-Atlantic Performance*. New York: Columbia University Press, 1996.

Roberts, Luke. "Empowering the Would-Be Warrior: Bushidō and the Gendered Bodies of the Japanese Nation." In *Recreating Japanese Men*, edited by Sabine Frühstück and Anne Walthall, 68–90. Berkeley: University of California Press, 2011.

Rofel, Lisa. *Desiring China: Experiments in Neoliberalism, Sexuality, and Public Culture*. Durham, NC: Duke University Press, 2007.

Rose, Caroline. *Interpreting History in Sino-Japanese Relations: A Case-Study in Political Decision Making*. New York: Routledge, 2005.

Rose, Caroline. "'Patriotism Is Not Taboo': Nationalism in China and Japan and Implications for Sino-Japanese Relations." *Japan Forum* 12, no. 2 (2000): 169–181.

Rosen, Stanley. "Foreword." In *Television in Post-reform China*, edited by Zhu Ying, xiii–xxii. London: Routledge, 2008.

Rosenstone, Robert. "History in Images/History in Words: Reflections on the Possibility of Really Putting History onto Film." *American Historical Review* 93, no. 5 (1988): 1173–1185.

Rosenstone, Robert A., ed. *Revisioning History: Film and the Construction of a New Past*. Princeton, NJ: Princeton University Press, 1995.

Russell, Dominique, ed. *Rape in Art Cinema*. New York: Continuum, 2010.

Sakurai, Izumi. "Female Lawmakers Blast Hashimoto, Call Him the 'Shame of Osaka.'" *Asahi Shimbun*, May 15, 2013. http://ajw.asahi.com/article/behind_news/politics /AJ201305160094.

Satō, Kōji. "Otokotachi no yamato o megutte: Rekishigaku no shiza kara." *Kikan Sensō Sekinin Kenkyū* 56 (2007): 74–80.

Schiessl, Christoph. "An Element of Genocide: Rape, Total War, and International Law in the Twentieth Century." *Journal of Genocide Research* 4, no. 2 (2002): 197–210.

Sedgwick, James Burnham. "Memory on Trial: Constructing and Contesting the 'Rape of Nanking' at the International Military Tribunal for the Far East, 1946–1948." *Modern Asian Studies* 43, no. 5 (2009): 1229–1254.

Seraphim, Franziska. *War Memory and Social Politics in Japan, 1945–2005*. Cambridge, MA: Harvard University Press, 2006.

Shek, Yen Ling. "Asian American Masculinity: A Review of the Literature." *Journal of Men's Studies* 14, no. 3 (2006): 379–391.

Shimizu, Celine. *Straitjacket Sexualities: Unbinding Asian American Manhoods in the Movies*. Stanford, CA: Stanford University Press, 2012.

Shin, Hakyon. "Taishū bunka kara miru BC kyūsenpan saiban to 'sekinin.'" *Nihon Bungakubukai Hōkoku* 4 (2010): 187–191.

Shindō, Junko. "Sakuhin-hyō: Kantō tokushū ashita e no yuigon." *Kinema Junpō* 1502 (2008): 38–43.

Shohat, Ella. "Gender and Culture of Empire: Toward a Feminist Ethnography of the Cinema." *Quarterly Review of Film and Video* 13, no. 1–3 (1991): 45–84.

Silberschmidt, Margrethe. *"Women Forget That Men Are the Masters": Gender Antagonism and Socio-economic Change in Kisii District, Kenya*. Copenhagen: Nordic Africa Institute, 1999.

Singer, Ben. *Melodrama and Modernity: Early Sensational Cinema and Its Contexts.* New York: Columbia University Press, 2001.
Smith, Anthony D. *The Ethnic Origins of Nations.* Oxford: Basil Blackwell, 1988.
Smith, Anthony D. "Memory and Modernity: Reflections on Ernest Gellner's Theory of Nationalism." *Nations and Nationalism* 2, no. 3 (1996): 371–388.
Smith, Anthony D. *Nations and Nationalism in a Global Era.* Cambridge: Polity Press, 1995.
Snyder, Cindy S., Wesley J. Gabbard, J. Dean May, and Nihada Zulcic. "On the Battleground of Women's Bodies: Mass Rape in Bosnia-Herzegovina." *Affilia* 21, no. 2 (2006): 184–195.
Soh, C. Sarah. *The Comfort Women: Sexual Violence and Postcolonial Memory in Korea and Japan.* Chicago: University of Chicago Press, 2008.
Soh, C. Sarah. "Japan's Responsibility toward Comfort Women Survivors." Japan Policy Research Institute Working Paper No. 77. 2001. http://www.jpri.org/publications/workingpapers/wp77.html.
Song, Geng. *The Fragile Scholar: Power and Masculinity in Chinese Culture.* Hong Kong: Hong Kong University Press, 2004.
Stam, Robert, and Louise Spence. "Colonialism, Racism and Representation." *Screen* 24, no. 2 (1983): 2–20.
Standish, Isolde. *Myth and Masculinity in the Japanese Cinema: Towards a Political Reading of the Tragic Hero.* London: Routledge, 2000.
Stoller, Paul. *Embodying Colonial Memories: Spirit Possession, Power, and the Hauka in West Africa.* New York: Psychology Press, 1995.
Studlar, Gaylyn, and David Desser. "Never Having to Say You're Sorry: *Rambo*'s Rewriting of the Vietnam War." *Film Quarterly* 42, no. 1 (1988): 9–16.
Sztompka, Piotr. "Cultural Trauma: The Other Face of Social Change." *European Journal of Social Theory* 3, no. 4 (2000): 449–466.
Takasaki, Toshio. "Wakamatsu Kōji kantoku intabyū: *Kyatapirā.*" *Kinema Junpō* 1563 (2010): 36–40.
Tanaka, Yuki. *Japan's Comfort Women.* London: Psychology Press, 2002.
Taylor, Diana. *The Archive and the Repertoire: Performing Cultural Memory in the Americas.* Durham, NC: Duke University Press, 2003.
Terdiman, Richard. *Present Past: Modernity and the Memory Crisis.* Ithaca, NY: Cornell University Press, 1993.
Teshome, Gabriel. *Third Cinema as Guardian of Popular Memory: Towards a Third Aesthetics.* London: British Film Institute, 1989.
Thompson, Zoë Brigley, and Sorcha Gunne. "Introduction: Feminism without Borders: The Potentials and Pitfalls of Retheorizing Rape." In *Feminism, Literature and Rape Narratives: Violence and Violation,* edited by Sorcha Gunne and Zoë Brigley Thompson, 1–20. New York: Routledge, 2010.
Toba, Kōji. "Eizō no sugamo purizun: Kabe atsuki heya to watashi wa kai ni naritai." *Gendai Shisō* 35, no. 10 (2007): 124–137.
Tokudome, Kinue. "The Japanese Apology on the 'Comfort Women' Cannot Be Considered Official: Interview with Congressman Michael Honda." *Japan Focus,* May 31, 2007. Accessed June 10, 2014. http://japanfocus.org/-Michael-Honda/2438.
Totani, Yuma. *The Tokyo War Crimes Trial: The Pursuit of Justice in the Wake of World War II.* Cambridge, MA: Harvard University Asia Center, 2008.
Trausch, Tim. "National Consciousness vs. Transnational Narration: The Case of a City of Life and Death." In *Chinese Identities on Screen,* edited by Klaus Mühlhahn and Clemens von Haselberg, 38–55. Zurich: Lit Verlag, 2012.

True, Jacqui. *The Political Economy of Violence against Women*. Oxford: Oxford University Press, 2012.
Tsu, Timothy Y. "Reconciliation Onscreen: The Second Sino-Japanese War in Chinese Movies." In *East Asia beyond the History Wars: Reconciliation as Method*, edited by Tessa Morris-Suzuki, Morris Low, Leonid Petrov, and Timothy Y. Tsu, 60–86. New York: Routledge, 2013.
"Tucheng xuezheng daoyan luoguanqun houhui meiyou liu qunzhong yanyuan di dizhi." *Longhu wang*. June 11, 2013.
Ueno, Chizuko. *Nationalism and Gender*, translated by Beverley Yamamoto. Melbourne: Trans Pacific Press, 2004.
Ueno, Chizuko. "The Politics of Memory: Nation, Individual and Self." Translated by Jordan Sand. *History and Memory* 11, no. 2 (1999): 129–152.
Uesaka, Fuyuko. "Eiga 'ashita e no yuigon' o mite." *Seiron* 433 (2008): 156–160.
Utsumi, Aiko, Komori Yōichi, and Narita Ryūichi. "Tokyo saiban ga tsukutta sengonihon." *Gendai Shisō* 35, no. 10 (2007): 44–70.
Vautrin, Minnie. *Terror in Minnie Vautrin's Nanjing: Diaries and Correspondence, 1937–38*. Edited by Suping Lu. Champaign: University of Illinois Press, 2008.
Wakabayashi, Bob Tadashi, ed. *The Nanking Atrocity, 1937–38: Complicating the Picture*. New York: Berghahn Books, 2013.
Wakakuwa, Midori. "Jendā no shiten de yomitoku sengo eiga: *Otokotachi no Yamato* wo chūshin ni." *Tōzai Nanboku* (2007): 6–17.
Wakamatsu, Kōji. "*Kyatapirā* seigi no sensō nado nai koto o tsutaetai." *Tsukuru* 40, no. 6 (2010): 84–87.
Wan, Ming. *Sino-Japanese Relations: Interaction, Logic, and Transformation*. Redwood City, CA: Stanford University Press, 2006.
Wang, Chunli. "Guochan dianshiju 'fanpaire' de wenhua genyuan yu chixu fazhan." *Gansu Keji* 3 (2009): 80–81.
Wang, Yang, and Duan Jishun. "Yici bu xunchang de hezuo: Zhongri he she *Yi Pan Meiyou Xia Wan De Qi* de zhuiji," *Jinri Zhongguo* 12 (1982): 61–64.
Wang, Yaqin. "Dui 'yan nü' 'bei kan' de dianfu: Dianying *Jinling Shisan Chai* de jiegou zhuyi fenxi." *Xian Jianzhu Keji Daxue Xuebao: Shehui Kexue Ban* 33, no. 1 (2014): 75–80.
Wang, Zheng. "National Humiliation, History Education, and the Politics of Historical Memory: Patriotic Education Campaign in China." *International Studies Quarterly* 52, no. 4 (2008): 783–806.
Ward, Rowena. "Japanese Government Policy and the Reality of the Lives of the Zanryū Fujin." *Portal Journal of Multidisciplinary International Studies* 3, no. 2 (2006): 1–12.
Wen, Shunhao. "Duo qingyuan yin shang libie: *Qingliangsi Zhongsheng*." *Dianying Xinzuo* 3 (1992): 62–63.
Wertsch, James, and Doc M. Billingsley. "The Roles of Narratives in Commemoration." In *Cultures and Globalization: Heritage, Memory and Identity*, edited by Helmut Anheier and Yudhishthir Raj Isar, 25–38. London: SAGE, 2011.
Whiting, Allen S., and Xin Jianfei. "Sino-Japanese Relations: Pragmatism and Passion." *World Policy Journal* 8, no. 1(1990): 107–135.
Wilford, Rick. "Women, Ethnicity and Nationalism: Surveying the Ground." In *Women, Ethnicity and Nationalism: The Politics of Transition*, edited by Robert E. Miller and Rick Wilford, 1–20. London: Routledge, 1998.
Williams, Linda. "Film Bodies: Gender, Genre, and Excess." *Film Quarterly* 44, no. 4 (1991): 2–13.
Williams, Tony. "Song of the Exile: Border Crossing Melodrama." *Jump Cut* 42 (1998): 94–100.

Wilson, Sandra. "After the Trials: Class B and C Japanese War Criminals and the Post-war World." *Japanese Studies* 31, no. 2 (2011): 141–149.
Wilson, Sandra. "War, Soldier and Nation in 1950s Japan." *International Journal of Asian Studies* 5, no. 2 (2008): 187–218.
Winter, Jay. "The Generation of Memory: Reflections on the 'Memory Boom' in Contemporary Historical Studies." *Bulletin of the German Historical Institute* 27, no. 3 (2000): 363–397.
Winter, Jay. *Remembering War: The Great War between Memory and History in the Twentieth Century*. Ann Arbor, MI: Sheridan Books, 2006.
Winter, Jay. *Sites of Memory, Sites of Mourning: The Great War in European Cultural History*. Cambridge: Cambridge University Press, 1998.
Wu, Jia. "*The City of Life and Death* Premieres in Japan." China Radio International, August 23, 2011. Accessed June 15, 2014. http://english.cri.cn/7146/2011/08/23/2702s654767.htm.
Wu, Xu. *Chinese Cyber Nationalism: Evolution, Characteristics, and Implications*. Lanham, MD: Lexington Books, 2007.
Xu, Minghua. "Television Reform in the Era of Globalization: New Trends and Patterns in Post-WTO China." *Telematics and Informatics* 30, no. 4 (2012): 370–380.
Xu, Qiu. "Lu chuan, wo yong wo de fangshi jiyi." *Dianying* 6 (2009): 14–17.
Xu, Ruzhong. "Cong *Yi Pan Meiyou Xia Wan De Qi* xiangdao ying." *Dianying Yishu* 1 (1983): 10–11.
Yamamoto, Masahiro. "A Tale of Two Atrocities: Critical Appraisal of American Historiography." In *The Nanking Atrocity, 1937–38: Complicating the Picture*, edited by Bob Tadashi Wakabayashi, 285–303. New York: Berghahn Books, 2013.
Yan, Hao. "Cuowei de shijiao yu biandiao de qimeng: Lun *Nanjing! Nanjing!* de lishi xushi." *Lilun Yu Chuangzuo* 4 (2009): 31–35.
Yan, Min. "Xie jin xinzuo *Qingliangsi Zhongsheng* gongying hou weihe fanying lengqing?" *Dianying Pingjie* 4 (1992): 6.
Yang, Daqing. "Convergence or Divergence? Recent Historical Writings on the Rape of Nanjing." *American Historical Review* 104, no. 3 (1999): 842–865.
Yang, Daqing. "The Malleable and the Contested: The Nanjing Massacre in Postwar China and Japan." In *Perilous Memories: The Asia-Pacific War(s)*, edited by T. T. Fujitani, Geoffrey M. White, and Lisa Yoneyama, 50–86. Durham, NC: Duke University Press, 2001.
Yang, Daqing. "Reconciliation between Japan and China: Problems and Prospects." In *Reconciliation in the Asia-Pacific*, edited by Yōichi Funabashi, 61–90. Washington, DC: United States Institute of Peace Press, 2003.
Yang, Ziju. "Shenshi lishi shijian de hongda xushi: Qian yi dianying Dongjing Shenpan." *Dianying Pingjie* 23 (2006): 33–34.
Yau, Shuk-ting, Kinnia. "The Loyal 47 Rōnin Never Die." In *East Asian Cinema and Cultural Heritage: From China, Hong Kong, Taiwan to Japan and South Korea*, edited by Kinnia Yau, 125–150. London: Palgrave Macmillan, 2011.
Yau Shuk-ting, Kinnia. "Meanings of the Imagined Friends." In *Imagining Japan in Postwar East Asia: Identity Politics, Schooling and Popular Culture*, edited by Paul Morris, Shimazu Naoko, and Edward Vickers, 68–84. New York: Routledge, 2014.
Yeh, Emilie Yueh-yu. "Pitfalls of Cross-Cultural Analysis: Chinese *Wenyi* Film and Melodrama." *Asian Journal of Communication* 19, no. 4 (2009): 438–452.
Yin, Jindi. "Zhongguo duiwai hepai dianying qianjing kanhao." *Liaowang Zhoukan* 17 (1990): 33–34.

Yoneyama, Lisa. *Hiroshima Traces: Time, Space, and the Dialectics of Memory.* Berkeley: University of California Press, 1999.

Yoneyama, Lisa. "Traveling Memories, Contagious Justice: Americanization of Japanese War Crimes at the End of the Post–Cold War." *Journal of Asian American Studies* 6, no. 1 (2003): 57–93.

Yoshida, Takashi. "A Battle over History: The Nanjing Massacre in Japan." In *The Nanjing Massacre in History and Historiography*, edited by Joshua A. Fogel, 70–132. Berkeley: University of California Press, 2000.

Yoshida, Takashi. *The Making of the "Rape of Nanking": History and Memory in Japan, China, and the United States.* Oxford: Oxford University Press, 2006.

Yoshie, Akio. "*Daichi No Ko* to Chūgoku." *UP* 26, no. 8 (1997): 11–17.

Yoshiharu, Tezuka. *Japanese Cinema Goes Global: Filmworkers' Journeys.* Hong Kong: Hong Kong University Press, 2011.

Yoshimi, Shun'ya. "America as Desire and Violence: Americanization in Postwar Japan and Asia during the Cold War." Translated by David Buist. *Inter-Asia Cultural Studies* 4, no. 3 (2003): 433–450.

Yoshimi, Shun'ya. "'Made in Japan': The Cultural Politics of Home Electrification in Postwar Japan." *Media, Culture and Society* 21, no. 2 (1999): 149–171.

Yoshimi, Shun'ya. "Television and Nationalism: Historical Change in the National Domestic TV Formation of Postwar Japan." *European Journal of Cultural Studies* 6, no. 4 (2003): 459–487.

Yoshimi, Shun'ya. "Zasshi media to nashionarizumo no shōhi." In *Nashionaru hisutorii o koete*, edited by Komori Yoichi, 195–212. Tokyo: Tokyo Daigaku Shuppansha, 1998.

Yoshimoto, Mitsuhiro. "Melodrama, Postmodernism, and Japanese Cinema." In *Melodrama and Asian Cinema*, edited by Wimal Dissanayake, 101–126. Cambridge: Cambridge University Press, 1993.

Young, James. *The Texture of Memory: Holocaust Memorials and Meaning.* New Haven, CT: Yale University Press, 1993.

Young, James Edward. *Writing and Rewriting the Holocaust: Narrative and the Consequences of Interpretation.* Bloomington: Indiana University Press, 1990.

Young, Louise. *Japan's Total Empire: Manchuria and the Culture of Wartime Imperialism.* Berkeley: University of California Press, 1997.

Young, Marilyn Blatt. "In the Combat Zone." *Radical History Review* 85, no. 1 (2003): 253–264.

Yu, Qiang. "Cong *Yi Pan Meiyou Xia Wan De Qi* kan zuoteng fengge." *Dianying Yishu* 11 (1982): 26–32.

Yuval-Davis, Nira. *Gender and Nation.* London: SAGE, 1997.

Zalewski, Marysia, and Jane L. Parpart, eds. *The "Man" Question in International Relations.* Boulder, CO: Westview Press, 1998.

Zelizer, Barbie. *Covering the Body: The Kennedy Assassination, the Media, and the Shaping of Collective Memory.* Chicago: University of Chicago Press, 1992.

Zelizer, Barbie. *Remembering to Forget: Holocaust Memory through the Camera's Eye.* Chicago: University of Chicago Press, 1998.

Zhao, Guibo, and Qian Tan. "*Dongjing Shenpan* de aiguo zhuyi qinggan he sixiang jiaoyu." *Dianying Pingjie* 5 (2008): 42.

Zhao, Sheng. "Dongjing fating shang de Zhongguo faguan yu jiancha guanmen: Jian lun dongjing shenpan de yiliu wenti." *Daqing Shifan Xueyuan Xuebao* 29, no. 2 (2009): 139–143.

Zheng, Chenying. "Wei liao buneng wangque de jinian: Cong yingpian *Xin De Lei De Mingdan dao Nanjing 1937* you gan." *Zhongguo Fu Yun* 7 (1995): 44.

Zhong, Xueping. *Masculinity Besieged? Issues of Modernity and Male Subjectivity in Chinese Literature of the Late Twentieth Century.* Durham, NC: Duke University Press, 2000.

Zhong, Youxun. "'Chongsujinshen' de changshi: Ping *Qingliangsi Zhongsheng.*" *Dianying Yishu* 6 (1992): 70–72.

Zong, Daoyi, and Lu Chan. "Dianying *Dongjing Shenpan* de buzu he ying shang." *Xinwen Aihaozhe: Xia Banyue* 3 (2007): 4–7.

Index

Abe, Shinzō, 127
Aegis, 62–63
aggression
    American aggression, 65
    Japanese aggression, 1–3, 34, 47, 55, 61, 66, 89, 107, 116, 123
aiguozhuyi, 32, 37
Ainu, 64
AKB48, 116
Allies, 1, 12, 25–26, 29, 34–36, 64
Americanization, 29, 50, 78
Anderson, Benedict, 8, 11–12, 20
anniversaries
    of Sino-Japanese normalization, 54, 103, 108, 116, 125
    of the end of World War II, 1–2, 28, 51, 125
anti-Chinese, 118
anti-Japanese, 46, 82, 85, 108, 122–124
anti-war, 38, 43, 47, 66–67, 72, 87, 126
apologies, 27, 43, 74, 104–107, 122
army
    Eighth Route Army, 60
    Imperial Japanese Army, 20, 36, 39, 73–76, 84, 97
    Japanese Kwantung Army, 99
    Japanese Red Army, 94
Asahi Shinbun, 90
assault (*see* sexual violence)
assemblage, 21, 49, 118–119
Astuko, Maeda, 116 (*see also* idols)
Atarashii Kyōkasho wo Tsukuru-kai, 44
atomic bomb, 37, 44

atrocities
    American atrocities during the Vietnam War, 3
    Japanese atrocities during World War II, 38, 63, 116
    See also Nanjing Massacre; sexual violence
audiences
    Chinese audiences, 31–32, 36, 55, 57, 60–61, 71, 82, 85–87, 110, 121–125
    general, 8–9, 11, 14–15, 80, 101
    horizon of expectations, 8
    Japanese audiences, 46–47, 63, 66–67, 94–96, 125–126
    transnational/global audiences, 50, 128
    See also reception
authenticity, 5, 8–10, 123
Autumn Rain (2005 film), 100, 113, 117

Baidu, 16
bainian guochi (*see* One Hundred Years of Humiliation)
bases, 19
Bell of Purity Temple, The (1992 film), 103, 107
Bernard, Henri, 26
Best Wishes for Tomorrow, 28, 43–49, 67, 126
blockbusters, 32, 125
blossoms (*see* cherry blossoms)
bodies
    body genre, 101
    embodied memory (*see* memory)
    female bodies, 73–97 (*see also* sexual violence)
    and nations, 4, 18, 53, 69, 77, 119

bomb
  atomic bomb, 1, 37–38, 41–42, 44, 130
  indiscriminate or mass bombings, 26, 41, 43–45, 70
bonds
  China and Japan, 9, 23, 73, 81, 90, 98–119
  China and US, 36, 73, 96
  Japan and India, 44
  Japan and US, 4, 18, 22, 29, 31, 26, 42, 46–47, 49, 65, 102, 107
  male bonding, 57, 69, 105
  PRC and Taiwan, 34, 36, 123
Boxer Rebellion, 2
boys (*see* masculinities)
brides (see *hanayome*)
bridge (*see* reconciliation)
brotherhood, 57, 66, 69, 98
brutality (*see* atrocities)
Buddhism, 18, 45, 108–109, 112
Burmese Harp, The (1956 film), 72
bushidō, 46, 54, 70
Butterflies Bring Reunion (1980 film), 103

capitalism, 15, 24, 63, 40, 119
castration, 62
Caterpillar (2010 film), 93–95, 120
Caterpillar, 93–95, 120
Caucasian, 17, 19
CCP (*see* Chinese Communist Party)
CCTV, 57, 110, 113, 115
censorship
  Japanese wartime censorship, 66
  SARFT censorship, 15, 51, 85–86, 110, 123
  SCAP censorship, 29
  self-censorship, 49
Chang, Iris, 13, 43, 74–75, 82, 88–89, 92
Channel Sakura, 91–92
chastity, 86, 87, 96
Chen, Kaige, 102
cherry blossoms, 68–69
Children of Huang Shi, The (2008 film), 88–89
Chinese Communist Party (CCP)
  and film industry, 14
  and history, 12
  and national narratives, 3, 34–35, 55–62, 107, 123
Chineseness, 33, 111 (see also *Han* Chinese)
Chogukhaebangŭi nal (*Jogukhaebangŭi* nal), 1
chrysanthemum, 64

Chuan, Lu, 85–86, 123
Chūgoku zanryū Nihonjin
  zanryū fujin, 116–117
  zanryū koji, 3, 99, 103, 107–111, 112, 116
cinema
  diasporic cinema, 14
  scar cinema, 3, 6, 89
  third cinema, 13
  transnational cinema, 13–14, 121
citizenship, 78, 115, 117
City of Life and Death (2009 film), 83, 85–86
civilians
  China-Japan Civilian Meeting, 103
  Chinese civilians, 73, 75, 83, 107, 124
  general, 26
  Japanese civilians, 37
  male civilians, 48
Class-A war criminal (*see* war crimes)
Class-B/C criminal (*see* war crimes)
CNTV, 55, 113
Cold War, 3–4, 18, 29, 50, 73–74, 83, 107, 121
collaborator (see *Hanjian*)
colonialism
  and gender, 17–19, 30, 53, 75–79
  Japanese colonialism, 1, 3, 99, 105, 111, 116–117, 119
  and memory, 21
  and race, 44
  Western colonialism, 48, 53
combat films, 12, 23, 51–72
comedic war films, 56, 58, 122
comfort women (*see* sexual violence)
commemoration (*see* memory)
Communiqué of the Government of Japan and the Government of the People's Republic of China, 3
Confucianism, 14, 57, 106
Connell, R. W., 16, 17, 52
constitution, 12, 29, 30, 127
controversies
  textbook controversies, 2, 58, 74, 82, 90, 103
  See also Nanjing Massacre; Yasukuni Shrine
coproductions
  Australian-Chinese-German coproduction, 88
  China-Japan coproductions, 3, 98–119
  Hong Kong–PRC coproductions, 51, 59

Taiwan–Hong Kong–PRC coproductions, 84
transnational coproductions, 14
US-Japan coproductions, 31
counter-memory (*see* memory)
Cow (2009 film), 130
crimes (*see* war crimes)
cultural diplomacy, 110 (*see also* panda boom; reconciliation)
Cultural Revolution, 3, 60–61, 107–112, 115, 117
cultural trauma (*see* trauma)

Daitōa Kyōeiken (*see* Greater East Asia Co-Prosperity Sphere)
Deng, Xiaoping, 3
devil (see *Riben guizi*)
Devils on the Doorstep, 15, 22
Distant Bonds (2009 series), 100, 113–115, 117, 126
documentaries
 docudramas, 88, 92, 116–117
 documentaries on Japanese orphans, 103, 110–111
 general, 7, 75, 99
dongya bingfu, 19
Don't Cry, Nanking (1995 film), 83–85, 91
Douban, 36, 59–62, 87–88, 104, 113–114
Dower, John, 26, 28–29, 47, 62, 78
Drawing Sword (2005 series), 59–62, 125
drawing sword spirit, 23, 62
Dutch (*see* Netherlands)

eigateki girei, 68
emasculation, 18–19, 35, 53, 62–63, 79, 95, 121, 124
embodied memory (*see* memory)
Emperor (2012 film), 30–32
emperor (*see* Hirohito)
Emperor's Naked Army Marches On (1987 documentary), 22, 130
enshrinement, 2 (*see also* Yasukuni Shrine)
Eternal Zero, The (2013 film), 40, 125–126, 129
ethnicity, 16–17, 19–20, 33, 64, 77–78, 115
 (*see also* Han Chinese; Yamato)
ethnosymbolism, 16
executions, 38–39, 41–47, 73, 83–86, 93
 (*see also* International Military Tribunal for the Far East; war crimes)

fandom, 116, 118
Farewell My Concubine (1993 film), 102
fatherhood, 24, 66, 90, 105–118
fatherland, 1, 90
femininity, 17–19, 30, 53–54, 66, 77, 121
feminism, 76, 80, 88
feminist, 17, 19, 76, 90, 101
feminization, 17, 30, 35, 40, 53, 56, 62, 65, 66, 78–79, 116, 121, 125, 127 (*see also* masculinities)
fenqing, 124
filiality, 57, 108, 109
fireflies, 68
First Sino-Japanese War, 2
Flags of Our Fathers (2006 film), 9
flashbacks, 125–127
Flowers of War, The (2010 film), 87–89
flower vases (see *huaping*)
forgetting
 and memory, 2
 and World War II, 45, 63, 110, 116, 120, 124
forgiveness, 90, 105, 113
For Those We Love (2007 film), 67–70
Foucault, Michel, 129
foundational narrative, 4, 18, 22–25, 28, 36–38, 78, 93
Frühstück, Sabine, 54, 62, 65, 127
Fujioka, Nobukatsu, 90
furusato, 40, 43, 45

Gandhi (1982 film), 10
gaze
 cinematic gaze, 7, 10
 female gaze, 85, 94
 international gaze, 43
 male gaze, 88
 sentimental gaze, 118
 Western gaze, 17
generations and memory, 22, 24, 63, 99, 105, 110, 113, 119, 121–125
genocide (*see* Nanjing Massacre; sexual violence; war crimes)
genre, 8, 14, 16, 21–23, 31, 51, 60, 71, 98, 100–102, 122
Germany, 31, 75, 88
Gerow, Aaron, 63–64, 66–67, 126
globalization, 2, 4–6, 14–19, 37, 56, 74, 84, 128–129

global visibility, 4, 21, 81, 83, 96 (*see also* memory: memory loop)
globital memory (*see* memory)
gods
 god of war (see *gunshin*)
 living gods, 68
Go Masters, The (1982 film), 9, 81–83, 99–100, 103–108, 112, 118–119
gong'an, 33–34
Greater East Asia Co-Prosperity Sphere (Daitōa Kyōeiken), 44, 70, 79
grief, 61, 105–106
guizi (*see* devil)
gunshin, 78, 94
Gwangbokjeol (Kwangbokchŏl), 1

Hague, The, 27
hanayome, 116
Han Chinese, 12, 33–34, 52, 78
Hands Up! (2003 film), 56
Hands Up! 2 (2010 film), 56, 122
Hanjian, 23, 57–58, 114, 123
Hara, Kazuo, 130
Hashimoto, Tōru, 91
hegemonic masculinity (*see* masculinities)
hero
 Chinese heroes, 3, 23, 36, 52, 59
 marketized heroes, 60–62
 socialist heroes, 54–59
 heroine, 51
 Japanese heroes, 39, 43–44, 52, 62–72, 121
 hero-victims, 23, 39–40, 47
 negative hero, 47
 Western heroes, 29–30, 35–36
hikiagesha, 111 (see also *Chūgoku zanryū Nihonjin*)
hinomaru, 95
Hirohito, 4, 18, 26–27, 29, 31, 35–36, 41–42, 48, 64, 66, 70, 121
Hiroshima, 6, 38, 63, 70
Hirsch, Marianne, 9, 12, 123
history debate, 47, 50, 95
Hollywood, 10, 13, 17–18, 30–31, 36, 53, 65, 87, 92, 100, 122
Holocaust, 4, 6, 9, 12, 13, 76, 88, 100
homeland, 115
hometown (see *furusato*)
Honda, Katsuichi, 73–74, 90
Honda, Michael, 27–28, 74

honeymoon period, 3, 103–107
honor, 23, 41, 52–54, 67–69, 75–76, 93–97
Hoover Institute, 74, 88
Hora, Tomio, 73, 74, 90
Hotaru (2001 film), 69 (*see also* fireflies)
huaping, 59
huise, 86
hukou, 124
Human Condition, The (1959–1961 trilogy), 38–39, 72
humiliation (*see* One Hundred Years of Humiliation)
hypermasculinity (*see* masculinities)

idols, 40–43, 116
Ienaga, Saburō, 90
Igarashi, Yoshikuni, 4, 18, 68, 78, 78
imperialism
 Japanese imperialism, 19–20, 30, 43–46, 62, 65, 95, 104, 124, 126
 Imperial Japanese Army, 36, 39, 73–75
 Western imperialism, 17–20, 44, 70
India, 26, 32, 44
Indonesia, 44
International Military Tribunal for the Far East
 general, 25–50
 Tokyo Trial, 25–50
 Yokohama trials, 26, 39–42, 120
 See also *gong'an*; war crimes
internet, 4, 11, 13, 14, 16, 24, 57, 121, 122, 124
Ip Man (2007 film), 51, 59
Iraq, 53, 63
Ishihara, Shintarō, 67
Israel, 12
I Want to Be a Shellfish (1958, 1959, 1994, 2007, and 2008 films), 28, 39–43, 46–49, 65, 126

Japan-China Friendship Association, 1
Japanese imperialism (*see* imperialism)
Japaneseness, 45–46, 115, 117 (*see also* Yamato)
Japan Self-Defense Forces (JSDF), 62–63, 65
Jia, Zhangke, 6
jigyaku shikan (*see* masochistic history)
John Rabe (2009 film), 88
Joint Communique of the Government of Japan and the Government of the People's Republic of China, 3, 99

Index

judge (*see* International Military Tribunal for the Far East)

Kam, Louie, 56–57
kamikaze, 38, 67–69, 92, 126–127 (*see also* cherry blossoms; gods; Yasukuni Shrine)
Kangri ("resist Japan"), 56
karate, 23, 59
karayuki-san, 95
katana, 23, 58, 61
Kido, Hisae, 115
kikoku, 116 (see also *Chūgoku zanryū Nihonjin*; *hikiagesha*)
Kinema Junpō, 45, 94, 105
kinship, 20
Kobayashi, Masaki, 4, 38
Koizumi Jun'ichiro, 2, 63
Korea
  colonization, 26–27
  comfort woman discourse in Korea (*see* sexual violence)
  Korean War, 30
  Korean Wave, 115–116
  North Korea, 1, 118
  South Korea, 1, 5, 75, 90, 98–99
  See also *Zainichi* Korean
kungfu, 57, 61
Kuomintang (KMT), 34–36, 60, 123

labor, 17–18, 111
Landsberg, Alison, 7–9, 120
Lanzmann, Claude, 6
Last Kamikaze, The (1970 film), 66
Last Operations under the Orion (2009 film), 51
law
  film regulation, 14–15 (*see also* censorship)
  international law, 25–28, 44, 77 (*see also* International Military Tribunal for the Far East)
  lawsuits, 38, 107
left-behind (see *Chūgoku zanryū Nihonjin*)
left-wing, 22–23, 92–97, 129
Letters from Iwo Jima (2006 film), 9
Lévi-Strauss, Claude, 2
lieux de mémoire (*see* sites of memory under memory)
Little Soldier Zhang Ga (1963, 2004 series), 14, 54–56, 121

Lorelei: The Witch of the Pacific (2005 film), 51, 62–64
Lust, Caution (2007 film), 22

MacArthur (1977 film), 30
MacArthur, Douglas, 18, 25, 27–35, 38, 42, 48
machete, 23, 51, 58 (see also *Drawing Sword*)
Magee, John, 38, 88
mainstream melody (see *zhuxuanlü*)
Manchuria, 78, 99, 109, 116–117
manga, 92–93
manly states, 16–20, 53
Mao-era, 54–57, 82
Marchetti, Gina, 17, 20, 30
Marco Polo Bridge Incident, 1
marketization in China, 122
marketized heroes, 54, 60–62, 122
masculinities
  boys, 40, 43, 69, 127
  Chinese masculinities, 18–20, 23, 33–35, 53–57, 59, 61–62, 71, 83, 97, 106–107, 114, 118
  colonialism and masculinity, 16–19, 53–54
  American masculinities, 18, 28–32, 35, 38–39, 42, 48, 53, 62–63 (*see also* MacArthur)
  European masculinities, 18–19
  marginalized masculinities, 17, 53
  emasculation, 18–19, 23, 35, 53, 62–63, 66, 77, 79, 83, 95–95, 121, 124
  hegemonic masculinity, 17–18, 35, 52
  hypermasculinity, 18, 30, 57–60, 71–72
  Japanese masculinities, 18–20, 23, 30–33, 35, 45–46, 52–54, 59, 62–72, 75, 77, 85, 92, 94–97, 106, 114, 118
  nationalism and masculinities, 16–20, 52–54
  wen-wu, 56–57, 59, 71
  See also manly states; sexual violence
masochistic history, 37–38, 44, 92, 127–128
massacre (*see* Nanjing Massacre)
Massacre in Nanjing (1987 film), 82–84, 123
mediascape, 13, 49
Mei, Ru'ao, 32–37
melodrama, 9, 98–119 (see also *wenyi*)
Memorial Day for the End of the War, 1

memory
  commemoration, 1–2, 6, 14, 29, 70, 81, 88–89, 103–104
  cosmopolitan memory, 22, 129
  counter-memory, 10
  embodied memory
    female bodies and memory, 73–97 (see also bodies; sexual violence)
    general, 4, 9–10, 18–21
  film as memory, 11–16, 21–22
  global memory, 129
  globital memory, 21
  memory loop, 5, 20–25, 29, 37, 48–49, 71, 75, 96, 120–121, 128–130
  monumental history, 12
  postmemory, 9, 12, 123
  prosthetic memory, 5, 7–9, 12, 120–121
  sites of memory, 6, 11, 14, 21, 52, 120, 128
  vicarious memory, 127
Message, The (2009 film), 129
Michener, James, 30
minzoku, 16, 115 (see also Han Chinese; Yamato)
mise-en-scène, 21, 101
Mishima, Yukio, 91
Mizushima, Satoru, 91–93
Mongolia, 111–112
monuments, 74, 82 (see also memory)
Morris-Suzuki, Tessa, 7, 44, 70, 100, 120
Moscow Declaration, 25
motherhood (see women)
motherland, 20, 73, 78, 81, 85
Mukden Incident (9.18 Incident), 2
Murudeka 17805 (2001 film), 44
museums, 4, 6, 7, 10, 91
myth
  mythmaking, 11–12
  mythomoteur, 16
  myths and identity, 20, 39, 71, 76, 78, 87, 93, 96–97

Nakai, Masahiro, 40, 43, 127 (see also idols)
Nanjing Massacre
  in memory discourse, 4–5, 20–26, 73–97, 105–106
  Nanjing Safety Zone, 35, 75, 83–85, 88
  See also International Military Tribunal for the Far East; sexual violence; war crimes

Nanking (2007 documentary), 89, 91–92
national identity
  Chinese national identity, 3–5, 18–20, 23–24, 33, 52, 71, 100, 109, 111–113, 121–125, 128–129
  Japanese national identity, 3–5, 18–20, 23–24, 38, 46, 52, 64–65, 71–72, 109, 111–113, 115–118, 120–121, 128–129
  and masculinities, 16–20, 52–54
  neonationalism, 4, 47, 90, 127 (see also *fenqing*; right-wing)
  onscreen, 11–16
  and women, 20, 76–81
nativism, 18, 45, 49, 54, 70–71, 79
nature, 2, 8, 9, 15, 21, 23, 36, 38, 40, 63, 67, 72, 80, 81, 84, 84, 92, 94, 96, 103, 108, 127, 128
navy, 64 (see also Yamato)
Nazism, 44
neoliberalism, 101
Netflix, 48–49
Netherlands, 26, 48, 70, 130
netizens, 11, 85
Never Forget National Humiliation (see *One Hundred Years of Humiliation*)
NHK, 16, 36, 48–49, 109, 114–115
NHK-CCTV, 113
normalization
  military normalization in Japan, 23, 64, 71, 125, 128
  Sino-American, 73
  Sino-Japanese, 3, 81, 99, 103, 108, 116–117
nostalgia, 4, 45, 57, 64, 67, 69–71
Nuremberg Charter, 25
Nuremberg Trials, 25, 28

Oba: The Last Samurai (2011 film), 51
Occupation of Japan, 25, 29–31, 44, 62
Ōe, Kenzaborō, 127
Okinawa, 70
Olympics, 54, 87
One Hundred Years of Humiliation, 4–5, 19, 32, 35–37, 46, 53–58, 96, 107, 121–124
online discourse
  film availability, 16, 55, 71, 92
  neonationalism online, 127
  reception, 57, 85, 87, 104, 113
open-door policy, 3
opinion polls, 5, 13, 98
orphans (see *Chūgoku zanryū Nihonjin*)

Index

Pacchigi: Love & Peace (2007 film), 69
Pacific, The (2010 series), 9
pacifism, 38, 40, 49, 65, 67, 71
Pal, Radhabinod, 26, 32, 37, 45, 48
panda boom, 103
panpan, 78
paratext, 10–11, 14, 16, 21
pathos, 98, 101, 105, 118 (*see also* melodrama)
patriarch, 24, 45–47, 75, 105–106, 117 (*see also* fatherhood)
Patrick, William D., 48
patriotic education, 3–4, 32–33 (*see also* One Hundred Years of Humiliation)
Pearl Harbor, 5, 45
peasants, 55–57, 61, 99, 109, 130
Peck, Gregory, 30
"Peonies" (1955 short story), 91
perpetrator (*see* foundational narrative)
photographs, 1, 9, 12, 30–31, 34–35, 82–83
Pioneers, The (2012 series), 116, 125
politicians, 1, 29, 67, 90–93
postcolonial, 17, 76, 79
postmodernism, 1, 90, 102, 102
POW, 26, 28, 45, 73
Pride (1998 film), 43–45, 47, 49
propaganda, 74, 92
prostitute, 75, 78, 85–88, 93 (see also *Flowers of War, The*; *panpan*)
protests, 2, 43, 82, 91, 116, 127

Rabe, John, 88
race
 and gender, 16–19, 29, 71, 120, 128
 and purity, 78–79 (*see also* Yamato)
 racism at the postwar trials, 70
 and superiority, 19–20, 28, 44, 54, 78–79, 117
Railway Guerilas (series of films and shows), 56–59
Railway Guerrillas, 56–57, 61
Ranpo, Edogawa, 93
rape (*see* sexual violence)
reception
 by audiences, 36, 42–43, 46–47, 66–67, 82, 85, 87–88, 92, 94, 105, 113–114
 by critics, 38, 45–46, 104–105, 108
reconciliation, 98–119
Red Classic, 54–58, 122

redress movements, 89, 99, 124
remediation, 10–11, 21 (*see also* paratext)
Rentarō, Mikuni, 9, 104–105
reparations, 3
repatriation (see *Chūgoku zanryū Nihonjin*)
Return Home: The Forgotten Brides (2012 docudrama), 116–118
reviews (*see* reception)
revisionism (see *Atarashii Kyōkasho wo Tsukuru-kai*; controversies)
Riben guizi, 56
right-wing, 22–23, 46, 67, 71, 81, 90–94, 97 (*see also* national identity)
Röling, Bert, 26, 48
Russia, 26, 37
Russo-Japanese War, 2

SARFT (*see* censorship)
Saving Private Ryan (1997 film), 9
sayoku (*see* left-wing)
Scandal (1986 novel), 91
Schindler of Nanjing, 13, 88–89 (*see also* Rabe, John)
Schindler's List (1993 film), 9, 88
Seiron, 46, 91–92, 126
Self-Defense Forces (*see* Japan Self-Defense Forces)
semiotics, 10
Senkaku/Diaoyu Islands, 58, 103, 122, 124
sexual violence
 "comfort woman" discourse, 4, 20, 23, 27, 29, 38, 43, 70, 74–80, 90–91, 97
 Rape of Nanking, The (book), 13, 43, 74–75, 87–88
 redress movements, 90, 99, 124
 sexual assault, 51, 79, 81, 84, 94, 95, 97
 sexual slavery, 23, 27, 75, 77, 79
 watching rape onscreen, 80–81
shame, 79, 83–84, 86, 88, 91, 92, 97
shidōsha sekinin ron, 63, 65 (*see also* victimhood)
Shōdo Sakusen/Sanguang Zuozhan, 79
shōsha no sabaki (*see* victors' justice)
sick man of Asia (see *dongya bingfu*)
Silang Visiting His Mother, 113–114
Singapore, 26
SMAP, 40, 43 (*see also* idols)
socialist hero, 3, 54–57, 71, 107
Society for Liberal Views of History, 90

Soh, Sarah, 27, 38, 75–76, 79
soldiers
   American soldiers, 25, 28–33, 39, 41–48, 62, 65, 78
   Chinese soldiers
      in combat films, 54–62
      See also drawing sword spirit; hero: Chinese heroes
   Japanese soldiers
      in combat films, 62–71
      as comedic figures, 11, 56, 58
      and dignity, 23, 46–47, 54, 93–94
      kamikaze, 67–71
      at the postwar trials, 37–49
      and sexual violence, 89–96
      victim-soldier, 38–49, 125–127
   and sexual violence, 76–78
So Near Yet So Far (1980 film), 103
Song of the Exile (1992 film), 102
Son of the Good Earth (1995 series), 100, 109–112
Spielberg, Steven, 9
Stallone, Sylvester, 19, 53
statues, 55, 70, 74, 83
St. James Declaration, 25
Sugamo Prison, 40
suicide, 44, 60, 67, 70, 74, 85, 88, 88, 92, 94, 117
Supreme Commander for the Allied Forces SCAP, 28–32 (*see also* MacArthur, Douglas)
sword (*see* Drawing Sword; katana; machete)

Taiwan, 1, 23, 27, 32–34, 54, 58, 75, 84, 102, 123
Takakura, Ken, 19, 53
Tanaka, Yuki, 75, 77–79
tarento, 40 (*see also* idols)
tennō heika (*see* Hirohito)
textbook (*see* controversies)
Thick-Walled Room, The (1956 film), 39
Tiananmen, 32, 54, 99, 107, 113, 122, 124
tiexue wenxue, 60
Toba, Kōji, 39–40, 127
tokkōtai (*see* kamikaze)
Tokyo Trial
   1983 Japanese documentary, 4, 16, 38
   2006 Chinese film, 22, 32–37, 46, 50
   2017 Dutch-Canadian-Japanese miniseries, 48–49
   historical event (*see* International Military Tribunal for the Far East)
Tokyo Trial view of history, 37–38, 41–49
Torihama, Tome, 70
tragic hero, 39
traitor, 56, 86, 114, 123 (see also *Hanjian*)
translation
   of films, 13, 16, 23–24, 110
   at the postwar trials, 37–38, 42, 48, 128
transnational film
   and memory, 5, 13–15, 21–23, 48, 50, 54, 59, 121, 123, 128
   and Nanjing discourse, 75–76, 84, 86, 89, 96
   and reconciliation discourse, 102, 112, 119
transnational memory (*see under* memory)
trauma
   Chinese trauma, 124 (*see also* Nanjing Massacre)
   collective trauma, 34, 61–63
   cultural trauma, 2–4, 101
   and melodrama, 101–102, 105–109, 112, 118
   and postmemory, 9, 123
   vicarious trauma, 63
   and women, 73–97 (*see also* sexual violence; victimhood; women)
trial (*see* International Military Tribunal for the Far East)
truth (historical truth), 27, 35–36, 48, 82, 92–93, 122–123, 126
Truth of Nanking, The (2008–2009 manga), 92–93
Twitter, 65

Ueno, Chizuko, 25, 78–80, 90
Ueno Zoo, 103
Unit 731, 36
US-China relationship, 35–36
US-Japan relationship, 4, 18, 22, 29, 31, 36, 42, 46–49, 65, 102, 107
uyoku (*see* right-wing)

Vautrin, Minnie, 88
veteran, 9
vicarious trauma (*see* trauma)

Index

victimhood
  Chinese victimhood, 35, 55, 62, 123, 125
  female victimhood, 51, 70, 72, 80–83, 88–89, 94–96, 109, 116
  victim complex in Japan, 23, 38–44, 47–49, 63, 65, 67, 72, 121, 126–127
  victims of Japanese wartime violence, 42, 46
  victims of Western wartime violence, 44–45
  See also foundational narrative; sexual violence
victors' justice, 26–27, 37–38, 41–42, 45, 49, 97, 121
Victory Over Japan Day (V-J Day), 1
Vietnam War, 3, 12, 53, 89
visibility of historical narratives, 4, 21, 81, 83, 96, 121, 125

Wakamatsu, Kōji, 94–95, 120, 129
war crimes
  A-class, 2, 28, 43–49
  B/C-class, 26, 28, 39–43
  See also International Military Tribunal for the Far East
warrior (see *bushidō*)
weakness, 17, 19, 77, 95
Webb, William, 32, 34–35
wen-wu (see masculinities)
wenyi, 102 (see also melodrama)
Westerners and East Asian memory, 35–36, 83, 87–89
whiteness
  in film, 97
  and masculinities, 17, 65
  at the postwar trials, 29–30, 42, 44
  white knights, 20, 30
  white peril, 70
Wind Rises, The (2013 film), 13, 130
Winds of God (1995 film), 125
witness
  American and Western witnesses, 5, 36, 75–76, 83–84, 87–89, 93
  bearing witness, 38, 86, 106, 125
  Chinese witnesses, 48, 83–84
  Japanese witnesses, 33

Woman and War, A (2013 film), 95–96
womb, 19, 70, 85
women
  Chinese women, 75, 79, 89, 91–92, 85–96
  daughters/granddaughters and memory, 64, 85, 105–106, 115–117
  female bodies, 75, 76–81, 83 (*see also* sexual violence)
  Japanese women, 20, 85, 95, 116, 118–119
  mothers and memory, 20, 70, 73, 78, 84, 92, 95, 101, 108, 111–112, 115–117
  and national identity, 61, 76–81
  wives and memory, 45, 60, 84, 94, 105, 112, 125
  See also Nanjing Massacre; sexual violence
wushu, 23
wuxia, 58, 71, 122

xenophobia, 92
xunzhao nanzihan wenxue, 53

Yamasaki, Toyoko, 109
Yamato
  Yamato (2005 film), 63–67, 69–70
  Yamato (Japanese battleship), 64
  Yamato damashi, 64
  Yamato hero, 93
  Yamato minzoku, 16, 20, 64, 78, 115
  Yamato nadeshiko, 64
Yang, Daqing, 3, 73, 83, 98, 110, 124
Yasukuni Shrine, 2, 58, 69, 82, 103
Yen, Donnie, 59
yidebaoyuan, 110
yinsheng yangshuai, 53
Yoneyama, Lisa, 29, 63, 70, 79, 83
Yoshida, Takashi, 73–74, 82, 90
Yoshimi, Shun'ya, 4, 4, 15, 113, 128
Yu, Hua, 122
Yushukan, 70
Yuval-Davis, Nira, 20, 78

Zainichi Korean, 69–70
Zhang, Yimou, 87
zhuxuanlü, 15, 60